Communications
and History

Recent Titles in
Contributions to the Study of Mass Media and Communications

News of Crime: Courts and Press in Conflict
J. Edward Gerald

As Good As Any: Foreign Correspondence on American Radio, 1930-1940
David H. Hosley

Freedom for the College Student Press: Court Cases and Related Decisions
Defining the Campus Fourth Estate Boundaries
Louis E. Ingelhart

The Press and the Decline of Democracy: The Democratic Socialist Response in
Public Policy
Robert G. Picard

Innovators and Preachers: The Role of the Editor in Victorian England
Joel H. Wiener, editor

Press Law and Press Freedom for High School Publications: Court Cases and
Related Decisions Discussing Free Expression Guarantees and Limitations for
High School Students and Journalists
Louis E. Ingelhart

Free Flow of Information: A New Paradigm
Achal Mehra

Shared Vulnerability: The Media and American Perceptions of the Bhopal
Disaster
Lee Wilkins

COMMUNICATIONS AND HISTORY

Theories of Media, Knowledge, and Civilization

PAUL HEYER

Contributions to the Study of
Mass Media and Communications, Number 10

GREENWOOD PRESS
NEW YORK • WESTPORT, CONNECTICUT • LONDON

P
91
.H45
1988

Library of Congress Cataloging-in-Publication Data

Heyer, Paul, 1946-
  Communications and history : theories of media, knowledge, and
civilization / Paul Heyer.
    p. cm. — (Contributions to the study of mass media and
communications ISSN 0732-4456 : no. 10)
  Bibliography: p.
  Includes index.
  ISBN 0-313-26157-1 (lib. bdg. : alk. paper)
  1. Communication—History—18th century. 2. Communication—
—History—19th century. 3. Communication—History—20th century.
4. Civilization, Modern—History. I. Title. II. Series.
P91.H45 1988
001.51—dc19   87-29554

British Library Cataloguing in Publication Data is available.

Library of Congress Catalog Card Number: 87-29554
ISBN: 0-313-26157-1
ISSN: 0732-4456

First published in 1988

Greenwood Press, Inc.
88 Post Road West, Westport, Connecticut 06881

Printed in the United States of America

∞

The paper used in this book complies with the
Permanent Paper Standard issued by the National
Information Standards Organization (Z39.48-1984).

10 9 8 7 6 5 4 3 2 1

To Edmund Carpenter

One event is always the son of another
and we must never forget the parentage.
                                    —Bechuana proverb

Contents

Preface   ix

Introduction: Mapping an Unacknowledged Tradition   xiii

PART I.   THE EIGHTEENTH CENTURY   1

1. Enlightenment Foundations   3

2. Communications and Universal History   17

3. Jean-Jacques Rousseau on Language and Writing   39

PART II.   THE NINETEENTH CENTURY   49

4. The Establishment of Linguistics and the History of Writing   51

5. Social Evolution and Social Theory   63

6. Edward Tylor, Anthropology, Culture-History, and Communications   75

PART III.   THE TWENTIETH CENTURY   91

7. Archaeology, Technology, and Civilization   93

8. The Canadian Connection I: Harold Innis   111

85283

9. The Canadian Connection II: Marshall McLuhan   125

10. History and Discourse: Michel Foucault   141

Conclusion: Current Directions   157

Notes   171

Bibliography   181

Index   191

Preface

The pages that follow selectively assess three centuries of inquiry into the role of communications in the history of civilization. Today this is an area of growing interest. Numerous researchers have made important contributions to various aspects of it, but until now no overall assessment of past discussions has been attempted. Perhaps the reader can better appreciate the present one if I begin by highlighting some of the relevant circumstances from which it emerged.

In 1951 an important event in interdisciplinary scholarship occurred: *The Bias of Communication*, written by Canadian scholar Harold Innis, was published. It constitutes a major exploration of what many still hold to be a new field, the social history of communications. However, the book was unheralded in its own time. For good or for ill, rediscovery of the Innis communication legacy was due in part to the phenomenon of Marshall McLuhan during the sixties. He championed these researches when few others did and argued that his own work was in the same tradition. Ultimately McLuhan inspired many people to give serious attention to the communications/history question, including this writer in 1967, although that inspiration was rarely accompanied by complete agreement with his perspective.

During the late seventies I began to pursue my teaching and research interests in the Department of Communication at Simon Fraser University, after initially being trained in geography, sociology, and anthropology. It was gratifying to see that some fundamental issues raised by Innis and McLuhan were being further elaborated, sometimes as a homage to their efforts, sometimes not, by a new generation of innovative, interdisciplinary writers (including Jack Goody, Walter Ong, Elizabeth Eisenstein, Eric Havelock, and Neil Postman, to name a few of the most prominent). All are concerned with some aspect of the role that communication (as a process) and communications (as information technology) have played in historical change. The former area has also been of concern to recent members of the French philosophical tradition. Michel Foucault and Jacques Derrida have looked at discourse in history as a powerful mode of social communication, and I have not been the first to draw connections between their work and the Innis-McLuhan project.

Today, both within and outside the field of communication studies there is increased recognition that to understand the nature of the information age we live in we must have some sense of how it came to be. The present has to be seen as part of a long sequence of developments that cannot be regarded as mere historical curiosities. Those who fail to understand the past will be ill-equipped to comprehend a contemporary world where major cultural-technological shifts often occur in less than a generation. Also, few modern technological innovations have no precedent in some past development. For example, several researchers now studying the impact of computers are beginning to look at the early years of moveable type printing for parallels, which although they do not explain, can certainly inform our current situation.

For many people this historical interest in communications is a new concern, dating from the work of Innis, McLuhan, and some of the previously cited writers. Acknowledging that communications has a history is not tantamount to conceding that the history of communications as a subject area also has one. Nevertheless, I argue that it does and this book will endeavor to outline several major aspects of that history. It is an attempt to merge my long-term interest in social thought and intellectual history with some important developments in media related research.

At this point the reader might logically want to ask, "What is communication(s)?" To give a proper answer would require another book! In this book, communications includes the social interactional role of language and speech, various systems of writing, and any subsequent technology used to organize information and impart knowledge. This usage is fairly concrete and close to what we mean today when we refer to "communications media," provided we include relevant aspects of the spoken word under this heading. To talk about communication in a more general sense, as synonymous with the social process, is certainly valid but would not be useful for my purposes—every social theorist would thereby become a communications theorist—nevertheless there are times when such a notion must be utilized in order to clarify a particular medium related discussion.

Using a medium oriented concept of communication has enabled me to be conceptually specific. In other words, it provides a focus on those times and places where particular media were seen as integral aspects of social communication, and became the subject of direct philosophical and historical assessment. There is also a certain shock value intended in my approach, directed toward those who assume that communication as a consequence of its medium is a view that is unique to the twentieth-century world of omnipresent technology. This allows me to assess, with special emphasis, some relevant observations made in previous centuries, for example, Rousseau's perspective on the psychological and cultural contrast between an oral and a literate tradition, and Condorcet's examination of the differences between the manuscript and print tradition in defining and disseminating knowledge.

Although I will endeavor to assess the past and the present, as much as possible on their own terms, it is not my intention to produce an archival exercise, but one that might enhance our understanding of contemporary research and suggest directions for further study. Throughout, my motivation is a belief that I regard as fundamental to contemporary inquiry in the human sciences: what has been learned is a necessary prelude to what can be learned.

Many people have played a role in the odyssey that led to this book. Although I was inspired initially by the writings of McLuhan during the sixties, it was the work of his occasional collaborator, Edmund Carpenter, that convinced me to pursue further, and eventually establish a career in anthropology and communication studies. By happenstance and good fortune, Ted became my teacher when we were both at the New School for Social Research during 1970-1971. This personal contact made me understand why so many who study the history of communications venerate exchange through the oral tradition.

During my stay at Simon Fraser, support for my somewhat unorthodox teaching and research interests has been constant and enthusiastic. I could thank almost everyone I have been in contact with there over the past decade. Realistically I wish to mention those who directly, by way of encouragement and sometimes constructive criticism, responded to the ideas presented here. They include Amparo Cadavid, Cheryl Dahl, Jane Dickson, Angela Dunbar, Anne Francis, Madeline Hardin, Lynne Hissey, Laurie Jones, Martin Laba, Firoozeh Riahi, Phil Savage, Suzanne Scheuneman, Ron Trepanier, Frans Vandendries, Phil Wagner, Tony Wilden, and Bohdan Zajcew.

Outside of Simon Fraser, I owe a debt to Alison Beale, Pierre Belanger, Shelly Cox, David Crowley, Robert Davidson, Bill Ewing, Marike Finlay, Bill Gilsdorf, Mike Haslam, Sut Jhally, Derrick de Kerckhove, Ed McLuskie, Vanneau Neesham, G. J. Robinson, Don Theall, Heather Trexler-Remoff, Robert Walker, and Ania Zofia.

For typing the manuscript during its various stages, the assistance of Karen Gardner and Lucie Menkveld has been indispensible.

Introduction: Mapping an Unacknowledged Tradition

No conception can be understood
except through its history.

                          —Auguste Comte

The history of communications as an aspect of the general history of civilization is not a new concern. Although Harold Innis was perhaps the first to see the field as distinct and give it disciplinary or subdisciplinary status, communications/history inquiry has been part of Western European thought since at least the eighteenth century. During those nearly three hundred years it has been distributed among several diverse scholarly and national traditions. In this sense it is not unlike theories of social organization, law, or religion, which have all had their histories mapped on numerous occasions. But communications, being more a study of forms than of specific content, is a topic less easily visible and therefore often overlooked by researchers in intellectual history and the history of social thought. What follows is an attempt to redress this unintentional oversight.

The task of bringing together the kind of material that will be assessed in subsequent chapters has few if any precedents. This is both a curse and a blessing. Unfortunately there are no well-defined role models to follow. The closest is perhaps the history of linguistics, but it is relatively young, has a sparse literature, and is characterized by some vociferous debates as to how things should be done. The project is blessed insofar as it can naively arrange and relate a body of literature in ways, though not intended as definitive, that may perhaps be perceived that way due to the scarcity of prior studies along similar lines. Nevertheless, the gaps and omissions should be obvious. It is impossible to say all things about all relevant discussions of the question. My familiarity and bias is with English and French thought. I touch on German and Italian contributions insofar as they are available in translation or sufficiently appraised in secondary accounts. Yet research I have already done tells me that there is much relevant literature in those languages, especially German, which awaits assessment. If these omissions can prompt someone to the task it will be worth whatever criticisms are directed at my limited scholarship.

Because of the diverse nature of the perspectives to be scrutinized, and the fact that some of the names will be unfamiliar even to many learned academic minds—general readers take heart—I have followed a rather pedestrian plan for the overall organization. Parts 1, 2, and 3 accommodate the eighteenth, nineteenth, and twentieth centuries, respectively. In addition there is variability in the way each century is approached. It would be impossible for me to feign uniformity when dealing with theories that in some instances are resurrected from dusty shelves three centuries old, while in other cases they constitute hot contemporary property and are discussed in the pages of popular journals.

My general rule of thumb in this regard is that the earlier the theoretical situation being assessed, the more general background material will be brought to that assessment. For example, before dealing with formulations from the eighteenth-century Enlightenment, a general outline of the dominant social and intellectual climate of the era will be given, including the state of communications, insofar as it has a bearing on the communications/history question. The complexity of attempting this with more recent formulations should be obvious. Therefore, emphasis will be directed toward the formulations per se and their specific contexts, with the hope that readers will bring with them enough familiarity with some of the general issues of the day to appreciate the examples used and positions taken. Dealing with theory that is more contemporary will also entail a critique of its shortcomings and the suggestion of supplemental, or in some cases alternative strategies. To try to effect a posture of detached neutrality would be hypocritical in a study that is part of the very milieu it attempts to assess.

There is at least one major recurring theme in this work that should be mentioned at the outset because it links contemporary media studies with their ancestral forerunners dating back over a quarter of a millennium. Loosely stated it refers to the belief that the transformation of basic information into knowledge is not a disembodied process. It is powerfully influenced by the manner of its material expression. In other words, the medium is never neutral. How we organize and transmit our perceptions and knowledge about the world strongly affects the nature of those perceptions and the way we come to know the world. In the first half of the twentieth century a variant of this notion came to the fore in linguistic circles with what became known as the Sapir-Whorf hypothesis (discussed in chapter 9). In the field of media studies, the theme was given a more technological and historical framing by Innis and McLuhan. And while historians of linguistics have at times acknowledged that the roots of this important concept can be traced at least to the Romantic period, if not the Enlightenment, many involved in media history and theory have usually assumed it to be the result of an awareness inspired by the great proliferation of communications technology in the twentieth century.

Part 1 will attempt to explain how the eighteenth-century Enlightenment elaborated on this and related "modern" themes. It deals with the establishment of a science of man and relates aspects of it to the newly formed notion that the sign, the way we represent the world, be it through word or thing, is an arbitrary human construct. This contrasts with previous inquiry, which held that there was a divinely ordained, natural connection between the word and world. After considering the work of John Locke, who definitively grounded this new perspective, the notion of the linguistic sign as an arbitrary human construct will be traced through its influence on the field of universal history. It was here that parallels were drawn between the making of meaning through signs and the assumed progress of technology, a consideration which accommodated a variety of modes of communication.

Part 1 will conclude with an assessment of Jean-Jacques Rousseau. Few eighteenth-century thinkers were as critical as he was of the unbridled optimism of the age and belief in the emancipatory power of reason and science. And few used its tenets with such devastating insight to further their own arguments. Commenting on Rousseau invites discussion of the paradoxes that abound in his thought, and this responsibility will not be shirked. However, most of what I have to say about his thought will be directed toward his remarks on the implications of living in a literate versus an oral tradition. This is a concern that resounds in the work of many contemporary communications scholars, though few cite Rousseau.

In Part 2, the nineteenth century is approached on two fronts. The first is a subset of part of the history of linguistics and deals with the emergence of historical comparative philology and the concepts of communication it employed. This field was initially shaped by numerous assumptions of the romantic rebellion, which challenged several Enlightenment beliefs. In the second half of the century, philology began to reconsider and appropriate aspects of the Enlightenment legacy. It also inspired a variety of studies on the history of writing and some of the more representative contributions will be assessed.

The second area where communications/history inquiry flourished in the nineteenth century was in the field of social evolution. This was a direct descendant of the universal history of the Enlightenment and rejuvenated that inquiry with a rapidly accumulating body of new information on non-Western and archaic societies. As will be shown, not all the social evolutionists dealt with communications. However, those who did opened up new vistas in our understanding of the development of civilization. One in particular, Edward Tylor, has done this with such thoroughness and acuity that an entire chapter will be devoted to him. Within anthropology Tylor is regarded as a founding father; outside that field his work is barely known. Yet, not only did he define the modern anthropological concept of culture, he elaborated it into a comparative historical perspective that accommodated communications as a central feature.

In dealing with the twentieth century in Part 3, I was faced with perhaps the most difficult choice regarding what to include. Innis and McLuhan constitute the logical centerpiece and will garner appropriate consideration. But what other theorists have both historical breadth and have given us significant observations on communication processes and technology? Interestingly enough, Innis and McLuhan provided me with an answer. Innis's citation of Australian archaeologist Gordon Childe, coupled with Childe's review of Innis's *Empire and Communications*, and the latter's gracious response, led me to an examination of Childe's work. I found that in addition to having been the foremost synthesizer of world archaeology, as many have acknowledged, he had a pronounced interest in the role of technological innovations in the history of civilization, which concedes communications a prominent role. McLuhan in turn led me to Lewis Mumford. This resulted from his citation of the latter, and the debate between them that emerged out of the eventual dissatisfaction Mumford was to feel toward McLuhan's work, part of it based on Mumford's belief that he anticipated McLuhan in a number of areas.

Perhaps the most unusual figure to be assessed in Part 3 is French philosopher-historian Michel Foucault. There are a number of reasons for his inclusion. He has provided a historical legacy that, despite beginning from premises unlike those of the other twentieth-century theorists who are considered, arrives at some similar conclusions. Although Foucault is not concerned with communications (media) per se, he is interested in communication. This is evidenced in his historical examination of discourse, a concept he frequently uses and never satisfactorily defines. We can generally assume that it refers to the largely unconscious textual strategies employed in given disciplines and their associated writings. Foucault's analysis of shifts in discourse and their dominant characteristics parallels what has been observed by Innis and McLuhan and attributed to more technological factors. Foucault's later work also evidences a concern with the relationship between power and knowledge, and it will be worthwhile to compare his notions in this area with those of Childe, Mumford, Innis, and McLuhan.

In the conclusion I will try to highlight the contemporary status of the communications/history question. This will entail assessing the work of several writers who can be seen as heirs to this "unacknowledged tradition." It will also include tentative observations as to how relevant material can be related to the communications/history field and suggest areas for future research.

Finally, in order that the reader not be misled, it should be noted that the central concern of the following chapters is how discussions of communications media have been an important aspect of the history of social thought. Although a more general examination of social thought, which may not discuss communications directly but be otherwise applicable to contemporary communication studies, would be a worthy project, it is not mine. Instead, precedence will be given to the central subject matter, communications, sometimes at the expense of the generally accepted importance of the theorist in question. For example, although Marx and Marx-influenced perspectives are a vital aspect of contemporary communication studies, what Marx actually said about communications comprises only a small aspect of his work. It will receive judicious but brief treatment. In contrast, Tylor assessed almost every type of communications technology, and as noted, his contribution merits an entire chapter. Perhaps this strategy can reduce somewhat the inevitable injection of a contemporary research bias into the assessment of earlier periods, and clarify further the original context of particular discussions as well as highlight their continuing relevance.

Part I

The Eighteenth Century

1 Enlightenment Foundations

When men no longer believe in us,
we are dead.
                    —One deity advising another in a Maori myth

Along with numerous other aspects of human science inquiry, concerted examination of the communications/history question began in the eighteenth century.
This is the age referred to by subsequent historians, sometimes in almost reveren-
tial tones, as the Enlightenment. Although no precise dates can frame the period,
frequently used criteria place its onset in 1690, the year John Locke's *Essay on
Human Understanding* was published, and bring it to a close in 1789, following
the outbreak of the French Revolution. Sometimes 1713, the year of the Peace
of Utrecht, is held to indicate Enlightenment beginnings. Occasionally this cultural-historical transformation is called the Age of Reason and is said to have
been born in the mid-seventeenth century. No matter how it is demarcated there
is no shortage of portraits of the era; most depict it as a major break with what
went before. For the first time in an extensive way, the elements of human nature, society, and history became subject to an examination informed by science
and guided by reason. This vision constantly endeavored to separate itself from
the theological and abstract metaphysical systems of previous centuries, often
daring to question traditional systems of authority in the process.

Much was explored during the Enlightenment that relates to what we refer to
today as the social or human sciences. Although modern disciplines such as sociology, anthropology, political science, economics, and communication studies,
did not come into being during this time, their central subject matter and several
key premises are visible in fields such as moral philosophy and universal history.

To understand the significance of eighteenth-century inquiry dealing with links between the development of civilization and media such as writing, printing, and language, speech, and discourse as social communication, we of course must have a sense of the general social and intellectual character of the age. With the Enlightenment this is doubly important because the foundations on which it arose have, to the present day, provided ongoing underpinnings for considerable research in the social sciences and humanities. True, the early nineteenth century reacted negatively to many Enlightenment revelations, but the social evolutionists of the second half of that century built on and extended the universal history of their eighteenth-century forebears by using an enriched data base on non-Western societies. In the twentieth century few social scientists may read David Hume (1711-1776) or other eighteenth-century philosophers, yet these earlier writers provided considerable raison d'être for empiricist assumptions about the way the world works. Historians have been more respectful, as is their wont. Today Edward Gibbon's (1737-1794) monumental study the *Decline and Fall of the Roman Empire* is read and re-read—and not just to learn about Rome.

The study of the influence of communications media on cultural change, although a burgeoning concern today, was only a minor segment of Enlightenment inquiry when compared to the period's grand historical schemes and powerful examinations of the psychology of human nature. However, it is a major-minor segment, a recurring motif with far-reaching implications that were continually glimpsed, if not always extensively elaborated—not because the problem was deemed unimportant, but because other concerns had priority. Yet several writers did much more than note that the area was of significance. Their work anticipates and provides foundations for more recent communications/history research. Innis's historical conceptions are an outgrowth of what was made possible in the universal history of the Enlightenment; McLuhan's sometimes obsessive concern with the role of the senses in understanding the implication of communications was pioneered by Condillac; and Goody's insistence on studying the implications of the oral versus the written tradition was also stressed by Rousseau.

CHARACTERISTICS OF THE NEW AGE

No historical period has ever produced a uniform theoretical world view divorced from antecedent thought. Nevertheless, the Enlightenment has frequently been viewed with such a leaning, and not without just cause. When Gay uses the term *family of philosophes*, he is not oblivious to strong disagreements within that family, but like many historians he recognizes that even writers in most severe disagreement with one another underwrote their studies with similar conceptual tools. A pronounced example of this occurs in the work of Rousseau. Although one of the severest critics of Enlightenment developments, he used many of those very developments to further his own arguments. Also, Rousseau, along with the philosophes—those eighteenth-century thinkers who applied reason and knowledge

gleaned from the sciences to understanding human nature, society, and history—
were explicitly aware of the newness and distinctiveness of the age they were
helping to define, despite their varied evaluations of it.

This is not to suggest that the original and definitive nature of the Enlightenment has not been challenged. For example, Becker has argued that the philosophes were far closer to the medieval vision they rejected, and sometimes ridi-
culed, than either they, or later historians, have suspected.[1] The philosophes, he
notes, may have denounced the idea of a six-day creation and the garden of Eden,
but they substituted a beautifully articulated machine structured according to a
rational plan, as well as the notion of a state of uncorruption and innocence in
ancient civilizations and savage society; this was paralleled by a faith in reason
and science that substituted for faith in the Bible. Citing Voltaire's dictum that
"history is a trick we play on the dead," Becker accuses the philosophes of doing
it in their own quest for peace of mind. In other words, the principles they discovered are those they started with, or in more modern social science parlance
we might say they selected their examples (data) to fit preconceived theories.
Despite the fact that Voltaire's criticism was directed at bad history, not all history, Becker's skepticism (itself perhaps an Enlightenment legacy) nonetheless
performs an important service by causing us to pause and weigh whatever an epoch
says about itself against how it appears in a wider angle, historical lens. However,
his overall thesis has received as much challenge as support.[2] Although no historical perspective can deliver the objectivity it promises, what came out of the Enlightenment were several principles that demonstrated greater inclusiveness, will-
ingness to examine divergent examples, and awareness of origins, than any that
were elaborated previously.

What, then, united thinkers of such diverse political orientation as Hume the
conservative and Condorcet the radical democrat? Despite acrimonious infighting
and major ego battles among the Enlightenment sages—not unreminiscent of the
contemporary academic scene—they nonetheless could present a solid front when
threatened from the outside by censure, imprisonment, and book burning.[3]

At a fundamental level there arose a conception of human nature, not just different in kind from what went before, but a whole new subject of legitimate inquiry capable of being informed by the scientific revelations that previous orthodoxy was just beginning to accept regarding the physical world. Theoretical
inspection of the human animal as a natural species whose habitat is society led to
the belief that theologically inspired notions of innate depravity were misguided.
It fostered an affirmation of life on earth as good and the desire to realign op-
pressive social institutions toward more human and humane ends. Notions regarding the way this should be done varied widely, but there was near unanimity in
rejecting the view of this life as a way station en route to divine life after death.
Ignorance and superstition were to be condemned, and traditional religion was
not exempt. On this, as in other matters, opinion among the philosophes ranged
widely, but in most instances orthodoxy was questioned. For example, both

Montesquieu (1689-1755) and Turgot (1727-1781) were uncomfortable with a number of church practices but nevertheless defended Christianity, believing that ultimately its virtues outweighed its inequities. However, these attitudes were little solace to an institution unwilling to bend with the times and they ultimately became a source for the harsher criticisms to follow, none more vitriolic than the writings of Baron d'Holbach (1723-1789). His tirade against religion has all the fervor and religious zeal a born-again atheist can muster. It makes the more well-known critiques of Voltaire and Hume pale in comparison.

The Enlightenment was a time characterized not merely by the emergence of many individual learned minds, but by the rise of an entire learned class who took an active role in interacting with their society.[4] It was a pan-European phenomenon, with centers in Scotland, England, Germany, and Italy, but the major source for the most representative notions of the age was France, birthplace of the philosophes. It was the largest and one of the most prosperous nation states, and because of Paris one of the most urbanized. French became the lingua franca of the educated throughout Europe.

A major coalescence for the new spirit of inquiry was the French *Encyclopedia* edited by Denis Diderot (1713-1784) and Jean d'Alembert (1717-1783). It symbolized the age more than any other writing project. Subject to censure and secretly edited at times, the *Encyclopedia* often identified its contributors, thus giving us a sense of their degree of commitment as well as range of interests. It was also unparalleled as a feat in the pure technology of publishing. At that time paper was relatively expensive and would remain so until the beginning of the next century, but changes in the technology of printing, especially typesetting, made books more affordable. This was accompanied by the rise of a new bourgeoise who linked the growth of their prosperity and power to reason. These factors contributed to an overall increase in the rate of literacy and created audiences who could now be provided with abundant copies of major texts. When works were deemed too controversial to be replicated and distributed through normal channels, they would often be published abroad and smuggled back into their home country.

It has been estimated that the literate reading public in France went from four in ten in 1680 to seven in ten in 1780, and that during the same period a ratio of two out of three books in Latin versus French shifted to one in twenty.[5] The wider reading public was also sustained through the advent of lending libraries, often affiliated with universities and academies. Learned journals multiplied, largely as a result of increasing scientific activity and the formation of scientific associations. To be sure, the new thought was still a domain of the privileged, but the number of those so privileged continually increased. In Scotland, particularly at the Universities of Glasgow and Edinburgh, attendance increased as the cost of tuition decreased. Also, a more diverse student body was perhaps attracted to the universities by the lively philosophical exchanges that took place in the cosmopolitan arena of salons and taverns, often involving some of the most notable thinkers of the day—a kind of eighteenth-century version of adult continuing education. Shortly after the appointment of Francis Hutcheson (1694-1746), a founding father of the Scottish Enlightenment, to the chair of moral philosophy at the University of Glasgow in 1730, the language of instruction shifted from Latin to English. This change was over half a century away from occurring at Oxford and Cambridge.

The philosophes, whose goal was to reform not revolutionize society, argued for a human nature that was basically good, insisted on the equality of all citizens before the law, and advocated free speech and a free press. They were critical of war, especially the kind waged by dominant imperialist powers trying to extend influence, an all too familiar activity in our own time. Scientific and technological progress was acknowledged and said to be a good thing, for it would help bring about the more enlightened and emancipated future many of them envisioned with such optimism. The period was not without streaks of pessimism, however, notably in Rousseau, but by and large most of the major figures regarded the world in which they lived, despite evil and injustice, as the best of all possible worlds and a marked improvement over the immature circumstances of previous epochs.

In almost all these attitudes, the philosophes were guided, or believed that they were guided, through direct application of the tenets of reason.

REASON AND SCIENCE

What did reason mean to eighteenth-century thinkers? The view of the great philosopher of the German Enlightenment, Immanuel Kant (1724-1804)—that reason is an active force in the world—was typical of the way this concept was used by the philosophes. They regarded it not just as an inevitable historical agent, but also one that should be consciously appropriated by high-minded administrators and directed toward the conflict between traditional beliefs and practices and the emerging secular order.

Reason and the closely allied notion of order in science and nature, although taking a distinct turn in the eighteenth century, were not born during that time. Earlier thinkers such as Descartes (1596-1650), Spinoza (1632-1677), and Leibniz (1646-1716) saw reason as a realm of eternal verities, truths held in common by both the human and divine minds, which give access to the intelligible world. According to Cassirer, in the eighteenth century a change occurs; reason becomes "a concept of agency not of being."[6] No longer the sum of a priori innate mental activities revealing the essence of things, reason becomes an acquisition rather than a natural endowment, an intellectual force born of the interaction between human nature and society. Reason is revealed through its functional operation rather than by reflective contemplation. Even writers such as Hume and Rousseau, who challenged the power of reason both as a motive for human activity and as a goal toward which our actions should aspire—Hume's intriguing position is that we reason because it gives us pleasure—themselves used reason's analytical strictures to argue the priority of the senses and emotions.

In a sense the methodology of reason is analysis, France the birthplace, and Descartes the patron saint. However, in the Enlightenment, analysis was no longer confined to reflection about conceptual essences purely abstract in nature. It begins with facts relating to sensory experience and societal interaction, the condition of the world as apprehended rather than comprehended. For example, taking a topic close to the concerns of this study, language, we find that in the Enlightenment it is almost synonymous with active social communication. In earlier inquiry, especially in the Renaissance, language was regarded as something divinely ordained, "the gift of God," and held to be as natural as the physical and organic world. This Adamic view, as it is known, linked the origin of words to the naming of things rather than to human exchange, and assumed that there are congruencies—*similitude* and *resemblance* are the terms Foucault uses—between the essence of a word and the nature of the thing it signifies. The attempt to discover these connections, the quest for the original or Adamic language, was an exercise that fused theology and mysticism with some of the newer tenets of scientific discovery. Lest we mock this research strategy, as the Enlightenment sometimes did, it should be noted that some useful comparative linguistic work was done as a result of it.[7] By the eighteenth century, however, language was no longer regarded as a natural phenomenon having an underlying conceptual congruence with the world. It was held to be a humanly created phenomenon, an arbitrary system of representation through which we come to know the world: a creative, historically derived expression of the necessity for increased social communication; not the residue of a rational mind but the tool that makes reasoned inquiry possible.

The growth of reason as an active force in Enlightenment theory and practice was intimately tied to science—not just a science capable of discovering immutable laws of nature, but one that could also help explain and guide human nature and historical development. The success of science in dealing with events in the physical world gave it enormous legitimacy in the eyes of Enlightenment thinkers. Copernicus (1473-1534), Galileo (1564-1642), and Kepler (1571-1630) had already heralded a new way of knowing and provided a model of understanding having an application that was regarded as nearly limitless. Truth was no longer to be found in God's word but in his work.[8] To partake of nature through science was to give man new power and control. A key figure in this transformation, both through his research and writings, was Francis Bacon (1561-1626), whose multifaceted influence has been revealingly traced by William Leiss.[9] In the eighteenth century the Baconian temper moved from physical nature to human nature and society. The inductive method of trying to discern general principles from marshalling empirical facts, especially regarding human behavior, infected many thinkers, none more than the Scottish moral philosophers, most notably Hume, Adam Smith (1723-1790), Thomas Reid (1710-1796), Dugald Stewart (1753-1828), and Adam Ferguson (1723-1816).

Science was not merely a source of inspiration for the eighteenth-century philosophes, it was something many of them actually did. Rousseau wrote on botany and chemistry, Montesquieu dabbled in physiology, and Voltaire was competent enough in physics to participate in several debates. Perhaps the last generation of the so-called "Renaissance man" lived several centuries after that period.

When applied to human understanding in the eighteenth century, science was significantly influenced by aspects of the Cartesian method. This entailed breaking down a phenomenon into its irreducible components. Descartes's usual subject was ideas. With the substitution of sense impressions for ideas, part of the Cartesian method made a successful transition from seventeenth-century rationalism to eighteenth-century empiricism. However, Descartes's abstract metaphysics and infamous mind/body dualism, whereby the human essence was separated from the rest of creation, were not readily transposed to the Enlightenment. In fact several of the philosophes, a subgroup known as the physiocrats, which included d'Holbach and Lamettrie (1709-1751), accused Descartes of not being Cartesian enough. In other words, he did not take his premises regarding the explanatory power of science and mathematics to their logical limits. He avoided dealing with human nature in this way despite potential applications. This gave rise to the accusation that in the human domain Descartes secretly believed one thing but wrote another.

Of all the scientific influences on Enlightenment thought the most historically immediate was Isaac Newton (1642-1727). He was regarded with reverence by almost all the philosophes, who freely adapted his cosmic revelations to earthly pursuits. It is ironic that the thought of someone so conservative and devoutly Christian could contribute to undermining those self-same values. No one lauded and defended Newton more vociferously than Voltaire. Newton's famous world-machine and the scientific and mathematical laws he deduced to explain it, were regarded by Voltaire as paragons of certainty. In commenting on Newton, Voltaire wrote that although there may be conflicting sects in religion, there "are no sects in geometry."[10] When Kant, after reading Rousseau's *Social Contract*, referred to him as the Newton of the moral world, he was conceding not only the former's brilliance, but also the widespread application of the models and methods of scientific theory to social understanding, which had become a mainstay of eighteenth-century intellectual life.

MIND AND SIGN: LOCKE

The basis of almost all Enlightenment and social theory was a concept of human nature, more specifically of mind, which denied innate ideas. It presupposed that the bulk of our understanding consists of a gradual acquisition of varied sense impressions drawn from both the physical and social environments and acted upon by reflection. No one contributed more toward establishing this perspective than Locke (1632-1704), whose *Essay on Human Understanding* (1690) became as indispensable to the philosophes as a desk dictionary.

In the eyes of many eighteenth-century thinkers, especially the encyclopedists, Locke was to philosophical investigation and epistemology what Newton was to science. Voltaire did not equivocate on this: "Locke has set forth human reason just as an excellent anatomist explains the parts of the body."[11] But in the next century Locke was often misinterpreted and treated negatively. Even today he is the subject of controversy and reassessment. It has been shown that his attack on innate knowledge, often thought to be directed at Descartes, was in fact aimed at others less subtle than the great French rationalist.[12] Recently, Aarsleff has argued convincingly that the differences between Locke and Descartes are far less pronounced than early interpretations have indicated, and that Locke, in rejecting innate ideas, was also rejecting what Descartes rejected; both subscribed instead to variations on a concept of innate operations of mind.[13]

For the philosophes Locke's denial of innate knowledge was accompanied by a thorough and profound game plan to explain how knowledge is acquired. This plan presupposes that the mind at birth is a tabula rasa. Not only ideas, but categories and moral principles are acquired through sense experience acted on by a capacity for reflection that brings memory, comparison, and imagination to the world of the senses:

> I see no reason therefore to believe that the *Soul thinks before the senses have furnished it with ideas* to think on; and as those are increased and returned; so it comes by Exercise to improve its faculty of thinking in the several parts of it, as well as afterwards, by compounding those ideas and reflecting on its own operations, it increases its stock as well as facility, in remembering, imagining, reasoning and other modes of thinking.[14]

This view did not go unchallenged during Locke's lifetime. It was respectfully contested by Leibniz, who attempted to demonstrate that rather than being a tabula rasa, the mind, a priori, is an irreducible source for various notions and doctrines that Locke attributed to experience.[15]

To some of the philosophes, debates regarding whether or not innate knowledge could be demonstrated were linked to proof or disproof of the existence of God. Locke was not of this view, for on several occasions he affirmed "demonstrative knowledge" of the existence of God. Nevertheless, his researches lent themselves to some of the extreme antireligious attitudes of the later Enlightenment. This was no doubt aided by the radical stance he took on several issues. Locke challenged the divine right of kings and the authority of the Bible, and argued for a liberalism that advocated free thought and speech. As a result, he has a reputation as a political theorist that parallels his acceptance as a founding father of the empiricist tradition in philosophy and psychology.

Although Locke cannot be called a philosopher of language, there are foundations for a philosophy of language and of communication in his writings. This aspect of Locke either directly, or through its interpretation by Condillac, influenced almost every eighteenth-century theorist who discussed the communication/history question. The question itself owes a debt to the third possibility in Locke's tripartite division of knowledge, which appears at the close of the *Essay*. The first is natural philosophy, a study of the nature of things, mind, body, the material world, and so on; the second entails the application of our powers and activities toward the good and the useful, and is thus related to ethics; the third is the way in which understanding gleaned from the previous two is communicated. Locke used the term *semeīotike'* to indicate this third category, the nature of signs the mind uses to comprehend the world and convey knowledge of it to others. Thus he saw the need for semiotics, the study of signs, a field that has had significant development and influence in this century partly following from the work of Ferdinand de Saussure (1857-1913).[16]

For Locke, language is the dominant sign system we employ to represent and exchange our views about the world. Aarsleff rightly notes that "Locke's view of language is entirely functional."[17] It can also be seen as communicational, particularly when Locke himself notes that words are not like natural species, but are abstractions of the mind "for convenience of communication."[18] This applies to the origins of language as well as to its use. Locke rejected the Adamic notion of language as a divine, natural phenomenon sharing an essence with the things to which it makes reference. Rather, he held it to be a humanly created, arbitrary system of representation, born of conventions elaborated by social beings experiencing, reflecting, and sharing views on a world of sensations.[19] This concept of origins, it should be noted, is philosophical rather than historical, and would remain so until Condillac, Rousseau, and others would conjecture on the more specific circumstances that rendered the making of conventional signs a dominant, species-wide activity.

MIND AND SIGN: CONDILLAC

Etienne Bonnot de Condillac (1715-1780) was the key link between the new Lockean inspired philosophy of the senses and many theoretical elaborations of the philosophes from the mid-eighteenth century onward. His *Essai sur l'origine des connaissances humaines* (*Essay on the Origins of Human Knowledge*) was published in 1746 and gained a ready audience. The English edition (1756) was subtitled, "A Supplement to Mr. Locke's Essay on the Human Understanding," indicating Condillac's relationship to his renowned predecessor. In fact, it is frequently said that Condillac was more Lockean than Locke in affirming the primacy of the senses and endeavoring to study them in as rational and scientific a manner as possible. He also developed a significant aspect of Locke further by arguing that knowledge is not something innate or a priori, but a direct result of the nature and operation of the signs we use in communication. Condillac's *Essai* attempts to give this view the temporal perspective present, but not developed, in Locke.[20] In doing this he provided the later Enlightenment with important foundations for psychology, linguistics, aesthetics, economics, and history.[21]

The man himself is fascinating and worth at least passing mention. He was a homely youngster and thought to be a dullard. Partly as a result of this his family encouraged him toward the priesthood, not an uncommon practice at the time. Although he wore clerical garb throughout his life he never practiced that calling, or perhaps he celebrated mass just once, depending on which account you read. At a young age he was inspired by some of Voltaire's early essays on English thought. This led to a fascination with Newton and Locke and the pursuit of a secular and rational mode of explaining how we come to know the world. Eventually he met with and was appreciated by Voltaire, Diderot, and Rousseau. Rousseau, in his autobiography, claims to have discovered Condillac. He was certainly influenced by him and may have been a factor in getting the *Essai* published; in addition he was also a tutor to the two sons of Condillac's elder brother. Condillac also appears in *Emile*, where Rousseau berates Condillac's family for equating their son's shy demeanor and unattractive appearance with lack of intelligence.

Despite his secular philosophical studies, which fueled an antireligious sentiment, Condillac remained a believer in both God and in a material and spiritual domain. A friend to the philosophes and a tutor to royalty, he somehow avoided the wrath of the church. He died in 1780 of a fever, which he suspected resulted from a cup of bad chocolate he had at the home of Condorcet, one of the few philosophes he disliked.[22] Ironically, Condorcet was as indebted to him as were those philosophes whose company and writings Condillac found more congenial.

Condillac's *Essai* deals with a variety of philosophical and social science subjects; however, it begins with a general discussion of epistemology and the psychology of human nature. This was a common eighteenth-century practice and is an aspect of more purely historical treatises such as Rousseau's *Discourse on Inequality* (1755) and Monboddo's *Of the Origin and Progress of Language* (1773-1779). Later in Condillac's career, the discussion at the beginning of his *Essai* would be amplified in his *Traité des sensations* (*Treatise of the Sensations*, 1754) where in a famous philosophical exercise he creates his speechless statue-man who, through gradual acquisition of each of the senses in turn, acquires a human level of awareness.

Correctly identifying Condillac's philosophical position is difficult. Several nineteenth-century commentators and twentieth-century historians of psychology have viewed him as a blatant materialist and a mechanist. Recently Aarsleff, in his excellent work on the history of linguistics, has argued for a less simplistic assessment. In emphasizing the importance of Condillac he suggests that the "single principle" to which Condillac claimed human knowledge can be reduced, is not a pure mechanism of the senses, as other writers have concluded, but *la liaison des idées* (the connection of ideas). This principle is grounded in reflection, which is as natural and innate in Condillac as in Locke; for both thinkers it supports a theory of linguistic acquisition that is active and creative rather than passive.[23] But there are times when Condillac appears to be saying the opposite. Isabel Knight is sensitive to this when she notes how his work contains both radical sensationalist as well as rationalist assumptions, and refers to him as a "great equivocator."[24] Regardless of where we try to situate him there can be little doubt about the significance of the areas he explored and his influence.

The *Essai* begins with an attack on metaphysics, which Condillac argues fails to live up to its high promises because it presents illusory speculation rather than solid foundations to further our understanding of human knowledge. Descartes is respectfully criticized (Condillac, however, like many of the philosophes, was undoubtably influenced by his method) and Locke zealously lauded. It is clear from the beginning of the *Essai* that Condillac is concerned with understanding human knowledge more through its mode of operation than via the question of its ultimate nature. As a result, one of his primary tasks was to understand how we came to make and use signs: "ideas are connected with the signs, and it is only by this means, as I shall prove, that they are connected with each other."[25]

The importance of signs for Condillac led him to group them into a threefold typology: (1) accidental signs, whereby there exists an object and a perception of it that cannot be controlled; (2) natural signs, the cries of nature, such as joy, fear, and so on; and (3) instituted signs, those that are arbitrarily chosen. The first two preclude memory and we share them with the brutes. He makes an interesting distinction here between memory and imagination; brutes express the latter in their recall of past perceptions without conscious reflection when in the presence of a familiar object. However, memory and reflection are a solely human legacy, the result of an arbitrarily chosen repertoire of signs with a range of ideas affixed to them. These signs are not only essential to communication, they form the basis for thought itself: "if a person wanted to calculate for himself he would be equally obliged to invent signs, as if he wanted to communicate his calculation."[26] Instituted signs enable us to analyze and separate essential qualities from objects under consideration, and to think of the qualities they share, rather than those that emphasize differences.

Thus, in Condillac's scheme, from perceptions there develops a capacity to have ideas about those perceptions. Ultimately we are creatures of reason—not in the sense that it is something sacrosanct or innate, but because of abilities that emerge from the concerted outcome of all the reflective judgments associated with remembering and processing sensory experience. This is a more extreme empiricist position than that taken by Locke, as Condillac himself notes when he insists that we must have adequate sensory input before any operations of mind are possible.[27] It might also be fair to state that for Locke the linguistic sign represents knowledge; it is ultimately a tool.[28] For Condillac it is coterminous with the very nature of knowledge.

THE ORIGIN AND PROGRESS OF WORD AND SIGN

The rest of Condillac's *Essai* is devoted to the question of language origins and progressive development of the multiplicity of ways human beings communicate. The very possibility of such a discussion set a precedent, and was an ongoing influence for the more historical attempts in this direction that continued until the end of the century. It is no coincidence that Lord Monboddo titled his own great work, *Of the Origin and Progress of Language*, the same title used for part 2 of

Condillac's *Essai*, even though he was forced to disagree with Condillac on several points.

In dealing with language origins Condillac assumed that there was once an omnipresent soul, and that language was the gift of God. However, after the deluge the soul retained only its immortal aspect and language was lost. From then on all life activity was governed, and can only be explained by, the senses. Thus without challenging scriptural authority he cleared the way for his admittedly hypothetical reconstruction of human development.

For Condillac, the dawn of history breaks over postdiluvian survivors communicating their needs and perceptions through the cries of passion. Objects and actions were referenced through manual gestures. Gradually these gestures were accompanied by deliberate vocalizations. When this occurred with greater frequency, memory improved and reflection began to replace instinct. Through repetition and recall vocalizations accompanying objects became the names of those objects. (He also assumes that the first animal names were probably imitative cries, thus partly subscribing to what nineteenth-century linguist Max Muller immortalized as the "bow-wow" theory of language origins.) Early languages, therefore, placed a heavy emphasis on gesture, especially dance, and several pages of the *Essai* are devoted to this mode of communication. Only in more recent history—no specific chronology is given—has the admixture of gesture and speech given way to the predominance of the latter. It should be noted that a number of these ideas were not original to Condillac but borrowed from and credited to Warburton's *The Divine Legation of Moses* (1737), a widely known work that tried to infuse theological doctrine with aspects of conjectural secular history.

Early speech, according to Condillac, was permeated with musicality. He cites evidence to indicate that this was the case for Greek and Latin; Chinese, with its intonations, is said to be a holdover from this stage. But there is no veneration of the ancients here, as we will later find in Rousseau and Monboddo, because Condillac assumed that the invention of more numerous and complex words at the expense of tonality was an improvement and the foundation for future progress, a view that was readily incorporated into the historical schemes of Turgot and Condorcet. Musicality in speech was held to be congruous with the type of communication necessary in ancient civilization. Condillac claims that when messages have to be imparted over a wide area through oration, as in ancient times, modern languages, with their minimum tonal coloration, would be less advantageous than prosodic discourse. The fact that gesture accompanied such discourse is noted by citing evidence of it in drama, poetry, painting, and architecture.

Condillac's discussion of writing is especially interesting. He notes how various laws and transactions in ancient society multiplied to such a degree that the memory became overtaxed. In order to instruct people of these changes writing was invented. It constituted a new series of signs created to extend the knowledge traditionally handed down through speech and gesture. Not only did writing enable such knowledge to be communicated over a wide area, it gave it more temporal durability as well. The first examples he cites are pictograms, out of which grew painting. He notes that the most "civilized" notions of the Americas never advanced beyond this stage, an observation probably more indicative of the paucity of eighteenth-century knowledge of meso-American civilization, than an oversight by Condillac.

Egyptian hieroglyphics fascinated Condillac as they did other eighteenth-century theorists dealing with language and communications. It should be noted that it was not until after the discovery of the Rosetta stone in 1799, with its three different scripts (one being hieroglyphics) replicating the same text, that the complex nature of Egyptian writing began to be known. Nevertheless, Condillac discerned at least part of its meaning. He noted how hieroglyphics were an advance over pictograms in that they could deal with ideas as well as objects. For example, a shield and a bow might signify a battle, a serpent the universe, and so on. What he failed to note was that a number of Egyptian signs were also phonograms; in other words, a given image may represent not an object or a symbolic referent, but the sound uttered when what is indicated is spoken—and a given text might combine all of these features. What he did point out is that Egyptian writing was developed to record events, laws, and policies relating to civil matters; that it evolved from simple to complex, thus taking on a character of mystery that lent itself to control by a privileged group, the priests; and that even after the alphabet was known, Egyptian priests had such a considerable investment in the earlier mode that change was impeded.

Despite consideration of the emergence of the alphabet as a stage in the evolution of human knowledge, Condillac did not give much thought to its full ramifications.[29] But he does note how writing changed poetry and music. These communicative modes were once crucial to the transference of essential social information. With the rise of writing they became consigned to entertainment and amusement. Once integrally bound together, poetry and music became more distinct and autonomous as the written word exerted its dominance. Condillac is a somewhat dispassionate observer when chronicling these changes. It would remain for Rousseau to give them full critical assessment.

Finally, although Condillac's research is a major contribution to the great body of eighteenth-century literature on language origins and history, the breadth of his conception aligns it with the more expansive field known today as the history of communications. Condillac himself conceived the historical study of language as including "gesture, dancing, speech, declamation, arbitrary marks for words or things, pantomimes, music, poetry, eloquence, writing, and the different characters of language."[30] In linking these activities to the "progression of mental operations," he founded a tradition of psychological interpretation in communications/history inquiry. Although considerably influential to subsequent eighteenth-century thinkers, this vision has been somewhat discontinuous through post-Enlightenment generations, until it independently resurfaced in the writings of Tylor in the nineteenth and McLuhan in the twentieth centuries.

2 Communications and Universal History

And in what large-scale chronological table may distinct series of events be determined?

—Michel Foucault

The Enlightenment was frequently denounced as unhistorical by the Romantic movement that succeeded it. This appears surprising, because from our present vantage point we can clearly perceive several continuities between the two epochs, such as their high regard for the importance of non-Western societies in understanding humankind. It seems that the romantics simply rejected as history the universal history of the Enlightenment—known also as theoretical history, conjectural history, or philosophical historiography. Practitioners of universal history, true to the spirit of their age and somewhat alien to the spirit of the next, sought to bring reason and science to bear on the stages of human development. They hoped to discern the laws that govern it in order to align the institutions of their day more consonantly with this assumed progressive transformation. The immediate heirs to this vision were the social evolutionists of the second half of the nineteenth century, and Karl Marx and his followers.

History as a discipline did not begin in the Enlightenment, but it took a distinctly theoretical turn during that age. Eighteenth-century historians attempted to embrace all known people and cultures. A conscious effort was made to transcend personalities, battles, and heroes, to get away from what Marx would later call "the high sounding drama of princes and states."[1] There arose a concern with history as a study of the progress of the human mind as evidenced by the stages of civilization and their requisite criteria. From the scientific and philosophical influences we have already considered there emerged a model of historical understanding based on the belief that human nature is constant, and it is custom, which we might today refer to as culture, that varies. This view was just as important for Hume's historical study of England as it was for Condorcet's grandiose outline of the entire history of the human race.

Before its distinctive character waned, the Enlightenment passed through several phases, and as a result the historiography it produced also underwent change. Gay has divided the period into three generations: the first, pre-1750, saw Montesquieu become a dominant figure, with the writings of Locke and Newton still fresh and controversial; the second, the mature mid-century period, witnessed Condillac, Diderot, Rousseau, and Hume transform the anticlericism and scientific speculations of the earlier generation into a new vision of the world; and finally, near the close of the Enlightenment, Turgot, d'Holbach, and Jefferson moved toward materialist metaphysics, political economy, and reform politics.[2] It is in this final phase, particularly in the writings of Turgot and Condorcet, that historical schemes acquired their most inclusive tendencies. Science and technology became diagnostic of the character of a particular epoch and communications became a vital element in the configuration. This partly resulted from the fact that significant changes in these fields were occurring within the century in which the philosophes lived.

THE ESTABLISHMENT OF SECULAR HISTORY

Although our major concern will be with the emergence of communications as a key facet of the historical schemes of the later Enlightenment, it is important to note some of the essential developments and personalities that prefaced this possibility. The historiography that we take to be so characteristic of the Enlightenment did not emerge fully formed from a completely antithetical background. There were positive influences consciously built upon, and negative influences important because they served as a backdrop against which the philosophes could react and more fully elaborate their positions. The most notable of these negative influences was Bishop Jacques Bossuet (1627-1704), whose *Discours sur l'histoire universelle* (*Discourse on Universal History*), a work that was never completed, provided a ready target for later secular theorists.

Bossuet couched the interpretation of history in religious assumptions. The authority he attributed to historical facts derived from his belief in the authority of the Bible, which in turn rested on tradition.[3] He was appointed tutor to the dauphin, Louis XIV's son, in 1670 and the degree to which this position was compatible with his outlook is reflected in his arguments affirming the divine right of kings and the authority of the church. Bossuet's history was not just a selection of events informed by biblical chronology and interpretation; it was tinged with moralistic explanations as to why things happened as they did. For example, the fate of empires was held to be governed by divine decree. Strong emphasis was placed on the necessity for obedience and discipline, and social equality and freedom were viewed as disruptive and dangerous. His historical overview begins with the creation, and is dominated by a periodization based on religious events. Along with other authors of this time Bossuet argued that Egypt was the first true civilization, and that many of the later contributions of Greece and Rome— pagan societies about which surprisingly little is said—derived from Egypt.[4]

Needless to say, Voltaire, whose historical studies are a centerpiece of Enlightenment thought, found Bossuet a ready subject for criticism. He challenged the *Discours*, sometimes with materials unavailable to his predecessor. This is an indication of at least one area where Enlightenment thinkers showed intolerance: at times they were too quick to denigrate past efforts without fully considering the circumstances and data available to earlier writers. One of Bossuet's omissions is humorously referenced in an essay in Voltaire's *Dictionnaire philosophique* (*Philosophical Dictionary*, 1764). A story is told of a Chinese man of letters and merchant who is given Bossuet's *Universal History* and assumes it is as inclusive as the title suggests. Curious to see what the learned European would say about the great Chinese empire and its history, he is aghast to find it completely omitted. Voltaire almost revels in using this scenario to demonstrate the magnitude and significance of Chinese civilization at the expense of the circumstances of the Jews and Egyptians, whom Bossuet found so crucial to understanding world history.

In a major work, *Essai sur les moeurs et l'esprit des nations* (*Essay on the Customs and Spirit of Nations*, 1769), Voltaire responded indirectly to Bossuet by starting where the latter left off, the time of Charlemagne. A few years before, Voltaire had published this programmatic and controversial *La philosophie de l'histoire* (*The Philosophy of History*, 1765). This work deals with primitive society and ancient non-Western civilizations such as India and China. In it Voltaire also expressed the conviction, directly aimed at the kind of historiography championed by Bossuet, that the Hebrew religion was based on superstition, prejudice, and fanaticism, and that this legacy passed directly into Christianity. He believed that mankind has an innate moral sense, an instinct for right and wrong, which exists prior to the religious precepts that often distort it. Here he diverged from one of his major influences, Locke, who argued that our moral sense derives exclusively from education and environment. Voltaire was perhaps the most well-known eighteenth-century thinker advocating that the study of history should be a secular pursuit subject to rational methods. However, this direction was already taken in the writings of two earlier figures, Pierre Bayle (1647-1706) and Bernard Fontenelle (1657-1757), who exerted considerable influence, not only on Voltaire, but on his successors as well.

Bayle was a late seventeenth-century skeptic whose *Dictionnaire historique et critique* (*Historical and Critical Dictionary*) appeared in two volumes, the first in 1695, the second in 1697. It contained biographies of little-known thinkers, extensive digressions on numerous philosophical problems, and well-thought-out criticisms employing careful data analysis of many orthodox positions. Bayle argued for toleration and defended the moral behavior of atheists, often showing how the moral practice of believers was disgraceful in comparison, a view not destined to win favor from the ecclesiastical powers at the time. He started out as a Calvinist, underwent conversion to Catholicism, then returned to Calvinism, though many accused him of being an atheist. His father and brothers died as a result of religious persecution and he was forced to flee to Geneva and finally Rotterdam. Nevertheless, his work became widely known. His ardent admirers included Voltaire, Hume, Gibbon, and Diderot. In addition, he exerted significant influence on Ludwig Feuerbach (1804-1872) who in turn influenced Marx. All were doubtless impressed by his insistence that the study of history be separated, not only from theological concerns, but from political and national biases as well, and that the historian approach his craft as a world citizen. No recent commentator has been more lauditory toward him than Cassirer, who notes that he did "scarcely less for history than Galileo did for natural science," and that he directly anticipated the "idea of a general history with a cosmological design."[5] In a sense the spirit of Bayle's two-volume dictionary, when collectively realized, became the great French *Encyclopedia*.

Fontenelle, like Bayle, was a skeptic when it came to traditional values. He began his career as an unsuccessful poet and dramatist, but later achieved success as an essayist and popularizer of science. Among the several influential works he wrote were: *Entretiens sur la pluralité des mondes* (*Conversations on the Plurality of Worlds*, 1686), a lucid general account of the Copernican system; *De l'origine des fables* (*The Origin of Fables*, 1727), a study of the basis of religion, not excluding Christianity, in supernatural belief and ignorance of natural phenomena—this daring contribution to the study of comparative religion was written around 1680 but controversy delayed its publication; and *Digressions sur les anciens et les modernes* (*Digressions on the Ancients and Moderns*, 1686), which concluded that science gives superiority to the moderns. The French Academy admitted him in 1691 despite delays resulting from his unorthodox thought. As a key influence on the philosophe's attempt to bridge scientific theory with humanistic studies, Fontenelle also figured significantly in the historiography of Voltaire and eventually Turgot and Condorcet. He insisted that the past be studied less from the point of view of political and military events and more from a perspective that accommodated science, technology, and commerce—the foundations on which the stages of civilization and progress of the human mind arise.

VICO'S NEW SCIENCE

One last figure should be added to the pantheon of groundbreaking thinkers who pioneered secular modes of historical theorizing: Giambattista Vico (1668-1744). He was an Italian philosopher and jurist whose *Scienza nuova* (*The New Science*) appeared in three editions (1728; 1730; 1744). This work has gained increasing admiration and respect in recent years. It is not difficult to see links between what Vico did at the onset of the Italian Enlightenment and the developments we have been looking at in the rest of Europe. However, whether owing to his isolation in Italy from the mainstream of Enlightenment thought, difficult style, points of theoretical incompatibility with the philosophes, or a combination of all these factors, his influence on the central intellectual currents of the Enlightenment was nil. It was not until the German historian Johann Herder (1744-1803), whose own work paralleled Vico's in interesting ways, read him in 1797 that Vico began to be regarded by a wider European audience.

The New Science is an obscure and challenging book. In it Vico argues for a science of history by seeking to do for that discipline what Galileo and Newton did for the physical sciences. He was also an admirer of Bacon, though he disliked and reacted to Descartes. In a free-ranging and aphoristic style Vico seems to be saying that although history should draw inspiration from the natural sciences, it is ultimately a separate domain. Science deals with truths external to man, not of his making, while history is a product of the human mind and hand. Yet historical truths can be grasped if the historian forgoes laws of human nature or the social contract and instead concentrates on the unique and different ways of understanding the world developed in past epochs, what we might today call culture, ethos, or world view. In this quest Vico is credited by Isaiah Berlin with virtually inventing the concept of *understanding*, which would later be known as *verstehen* following from Wilhelm Dilthey (1833-1911), a notion that has been extremely influential on twentieth-century humanistic social science; he also argues that Vico may have come close to implying "that our historical consciousness, even in our most sophisticated, self-conscious civilized condition, may be no more than the vision which belongs to the particular stage we have reached."[6]

Vico stressed that each stage of history developed a corresponding set of laws, government, religion, language, and belief system. And he held that in the grand scheme of things, cyclical tendencies such as growth and decay, rise and fall, are omnipresent, thus anticipating a view elaborated extensively in this century by Oswald Spengler and Arnold Toynbee in history, and Alfred Kroeber in anthropology. Surprisingly, Vico was a devout Catholic and believed divine providence played a role in history, a view certainly out of synch with what was happening in France. But this may have been his way of dealing with what Hegel, Marx, and Engels would later confront and try to resolve in a somewhat different manner: the notion that the overall movement of history is on a separate plane from the totality of individual wills that make it up.

Communications—in the form of language, gesture, and systems of visual representation—figure significantly in Vico's scheme. They are the clues to understanding past ages, as well as our own. He notes how various poetic, mythical, and metaphoric associations that appear as engaging allusions in contemporary communication may have been integral and valid ways of coming to terms with the world in past "poetical" ages, a precursor of the concept of "survivals" that Edward Tylor would develop in the second half of the nineteenth century. In dealing with history in terms of a movement from a poetical understanding of the world to one that is more abstract and analytic, in assuming that language provides a basis for the way we experience the world as well as think about it, and for bequeathing validity to the way earlier peoples and different cultures communicate, Vico paralleled Rousseau in the eighteenth century and foreshadowed the tradition of cultural-linguistic relativity that developed in twentieth-century anthropology. Ultimately, like Tylor and Innis, Vico's importance does not rest on his achievements as a historian or his discovery of original materials, but on the way in which he regrouped what was known into a new configuration, which provided a revealing strategy for future research.

TURGOT'S "TREASURE HOUSE OF SIGNS"

With the writings of Anne Robert Jacques Turgot (1727-1781) we get, for the first time, a well-developed consideration of the role of economics, technology, and communications in historical interpretation. The span of his interests and involvement is truly impressive, even in an age when such breadth was not unknown.

Turgot began as a student of theology and always retained the belief that Christianity is essential to progress, though he held that the laws of history operate independently of theological influence. In 1753 he started a long and often frustrating career as a government administrator, which culminated in 1774 when he was appointed comptroller general of finance. Valiant attempts to moderate extreme tendencies in the ancien regime through various tax and trade reforms, and his views in favor of toleration, brought opposition from several quarters and Turgot was forced to resign from this prestigious but vulnerable post after only twenty months. During his career as an administrator he studied a wide variety of subjects and was capable enough to contribute entries to the *Encyclopedia* in history, linguistics, and economics. In 1766 we wrote his *Reflexions sur la formation et la distribution des richesses (Reflections on the Formation and Distribution of Riches)*. This treatise on economics, along with his other studies in the field and his administrative career, gave him rare distinction as a person who sought to contribute to both theory and practice by constantly being aware of the links between the two realms.

Many of Turgot's writings, especially those dealing with history, were not published in their entirety during his lifetime—his collected works were unavailable until 1811. Nevertheless entries appeared in the form of contributions to the *Encyclopedia*, anonymous statements in periodicals, and articles available to selected recipients. His influence was definitely felt, especially by Condorcet who would continue to develop the concept of a secular universal history. Turgot outlined the basis of his historical vision in *Tableau philosophique des progres successifs de l'esprit humain (Philosophical Panorama of the Progress of the Mind)* written about 1750, and *Plan de deux discours sur l'histoire universelle (Plan of the Two Discourses on Universal History)* written about 1750 or 1751. Like Voltaire he was partly responding to Bossuet. Although Turgot rejected the providential view of history contained in the latter's writings, the title of his work bears more than coincidental resemblance to the label Bossuet employed for his own magnum opus. It is also possible to see parallels between Bossuet's view of history as a succession of religious epochs and Turgot's interpretation based on socioeconomic stages.[7]

History for Turgot is the story of the progress of the human mind as evidenced in scientific and technological achievements. He believed that unlike the realm of nature, which is governed by recurring cyles (following Newton), history is ever-changing, because human beings possess perfectability—which in the eighteenth century referred to a capacity for improvement or development rather than to movement toward some divine, harmonious state. Arguing that progress is the inevitable result of history, Turgot did not, like some of the other philosophes, denigrate earlier times. He emphasized continuity with the past. Every event that has occurred, all chance happenings, and trial and error experiments are related to the laws of progressive development. Owing to circumstances, change may occur at different rates at different times, but the general tendency is unyielding.

What role do individuals play in this scheme? According to Turgot they are the starting points for change. Ideas based on sensations, realized first through individual minds, lead to progress. As Frank Manuel has shown, this view indicates that "Turgot's man, though created by God, is bound by the laws of the Locke-Condillac epistemology."[8] We can add that Turgot's notion of individual vari-ability is also similar to Condillac's. Turgot notes that the human mind every-where contains the potential for progress; however, there is a degree of difference: certain minds have more potential than others. Thus he avoids the radical envir-onmentalism of writers such as Helvetius, whose appropriation of the Locke-Condillac tradition led him to assume that all individuals are equally endowed and it is circumstance that determines achievement. However, he still leaves un-answered the question of why endowed individuals exist more frequently at certain times than at others. Actually this never became an issue for Turgot be-cause he assumed that talented individuals are produced in all societies, including the most primitive, and that in the latter case the crude level of economic and technological development inhibits the expression of exceptional ability; we only seem to have a higher percentage of these individuals because our circumstances allow for, rather than determine, their capacities. And the main factor contribut-ing to these more enlightened circumstances, and human progress as a whole, is improved communications, especially writing, which "rescues from the power of death the memory of great men and models of virtue, unites places and times, arrests fugitive thoughts, and guarantees them a lasting existence, by means of which the creations, opinions, experiences, and discoveries of all ages are accu-mulated. . . ."[9]

Turgot's view that history is cumulative and progressive and that it is charac-terized by the constant accumulation of information and ideas, which in turn become stages in the development of human knowledge, reflects the influence of

Condillac's view of language and mind, especially when Turgot notes that "the arbitrary signs of speech and writing, by providing men with the means of securing the possession of their ideas and communicating them to others have made all the individual stores of knowledge a common treasure house. . . ."[10] The major difference is that Condillac approached the historical dimension of his subject with generalities, while Turgot tried to be more specific by citing numerous social and technological achievements that arise from new developments in knowledge. He also sought to elaborate more fully the concept of progress, a topic that has foundations in Condillac but no systematic development.

The *Discourse on Universal History* is the plan for a book-length project that Turgot never completed. It is sketchy and disjointed in some places and highly suggestive in others. Turgot argues that the basis of human development is the "treasure house of signs," which can be multiplied almost infinitely. In dealing with the successive advances of humanity, he includes the earliest beginnings surrounding the origins of language, the emergence of government, manners, morals, the arts, sciences, and the foundation of nations. He directly confronts the Bible and argues, as Condillac did, for its utility in outlining the earliest events in human history. However, after the deluge, when the human race was reduced to its most basic resources, a new development based on secular progress took over. This entailed the acquisition of language and associated mental operations and Turgot's discussion of this follows Condillac's quite closely. Eventually scattered groups of hunters and gatherers learned to domesticate animals for greater subsistence efficiency. These new societies merged into nations, often in open conflict with one another. Out of these struggles empires rose and fell as imperfect laws were subject to challenge by the emergence of reason, a view that is reminiscent of the later philosophy of history elaborated by Hegel (1770-1831). But unlike Hegel and more along the lines of Rousseau, Turgot notes how smaller societies can be less subject to despotism and closer to the consent of the people, while many great empires have been corrupt and exploitative, guided by greedy monarchs and evil administrators.

Later history is seen as strongly influenced by developments in the arts and sciences. Everything from music, dance, and poetry, to astronomy and navigation is considered. In addition the importance of inventions such as the compass, gunpowder, clocks, mills, and glass is evaluated. Great minds are given their due. Turgot mentions Newton, Kepler, Galileo, Locke, and appropriately, Condillac. He also exhibits a tendency to emphasize the role of genius at the expense of historical inevitability. For example, Turgot argues that if Columbus and Newton had died before they made their contributions, progress would have been delayed by two centuries—an overreliance on the "great man" view that would be less extreme in the work of his successor, Condorcet. Yet, ultimately it is communications that enables important discoveries to disseminate and have powerful effect. In the modern era the printing press spread not only the knowledge of books, but also that of the modern arts, and it has greatly perfected them. Before its invention, a host of admirable techniques, which tradition alone passed on from one craftsman to another, excited no curiosity at all among the philosophers. When printing had facilitated their communication, men began to describe them for the use of the craftsmen. Through this men of letters became aware of thousands of ingenious operations of which they had been ignorant, and they found themselves led toward an infinity of notions that were full of interest for physics. It was like a new world, in which everything pricked their curiosity. Thus was born a taste for experimental physics, in which great progress could never have been made without the help of inventions and technical processes. . . .[11]

Although this interesting line of thought is incomplete, it is another aspect of Turgot's thought developed further by Condorcet.

Out of Turgot's analysis emerged a model for the stages of history based on socioeconomic criteria, which with modification has survived to the present in various quarters: hunting, pastoralism, agriculture, and commerce.[12] Although these stages are founded on economic activity, we must remember that it is the degree to which the "treasure house of signs" enables human beings to exchange ideas about their social and natural environments that makes widespread activity of any kind possible. Turgot felt this way about his own studies and in later years, consistent with his view of history, looked into the possibility of cheaper processes for reproducing written communications, believing that this would help spread important ideas and foster new ones.[13] Toward the end of his life he became less certain that progress is inevitable and sought refuge in mathematics, perhaps as a premonition of the revolutionary turmoil to come.

CONDORCET'S TEN-STAGE *SKETCH*

One of the youngest of the philosophes who contributed to the *Encyclopedia*, Marie-Jean-Antoine-Nicolas de Condorcet (1743-1794), was also one of the few of that circle to take an active role in the French Revolution, a costly involvement that led to his death. His *Esquisse d'un tableau historique des progres de l'esprit humain* (*Sketch for a Historical Picture of the Progress of the Human Mind*, 1795), which was written while he was in hiding shortly before he died in Robespierre's prison, can be considered a quintessential expression and concluding summation of many of the ideals of the Enlightenment. Like the *Discourse on Universal History* written by his friend and onetime administrative colleague, Turgot, Condorcet's *Sketch* is both unfinished and the abstract for a longer work that was never completed. It played a role in the attempt to establish a science of society that preoccupied Claude Saint-Simon (1760-1825) and Auguste Comte (1798-1857), out of which emerged the discipline of sociology.

In addition to being a disciple of Turgot, Condorcet was also a friend and pro-tégé of d'Alembert from whom he further inherited the notion that history can be seen as stages in the advance of science. Condorcet rose to prominence as a mathematician, historian of science, and social reformer. Much of his mathema-tical work was devoted to bringing social issues under the methodological purview of the physical sciences, especially through the use of probability theory. From his own research as well as the teachings of Voltaire, Condorcet derived the belief that science held the key to challenge tyranny, prejudice, and ignorance, and this led him to put the final touches on the Enlightenment concept of progress before it passed over into the nineteenth-century tradition of social thought. An op-ponent of slavery, he frequently advocated egalitarian social reform and tolera-tion. For some of the revolutionaries a bit too much of the latter quality was in evidence when he voted against the death penalty for Louis XVI. Further prob-lems arose when the constitution he drafted for the new republic was opposed by the Jacobins. Condorcet went into hiding and wrote his *Sketch*. Eventually caught, he died during his first night in prison, some say by his own hand.

The sweep of Condorcet's *Sketch* is all-encompassing. History is divided into ten stages, each characterized by a configuration of social, economic, and tech-nological factors. Historical development of these factors depends on man's ability to bestow meaningful signs on sensations through "communication with other beings like himself; . . . through artificial methods . . . ."[14] The result is the progress of the human mind on a grand scale, which is subject to the same laws of development as the acquisition of understanding on the part of the indi-vidual. This analogy, also used by Condillac and Monboddo, was widespread in the Enlightenment. It is perhaps an eighteenth-century precursor of the concept of ontogeny (history of the individual) recapitulating phylogeny (history of the species) that figured in the Darwinian debates of the next century. It should also be noted that as in the case of Turgot, Condorcet's epistemology of mind and sign, which comes at the beginning of the *Sketch*, is heavily influenced by Condillac.

Human beings, unlike animals, possess perfectability. This capacity, when ramified through scientific and technological achievement, yields inexorable pro-gress. However, Condorcet notes, the rate of progress varies—it is faster during some epochs than in others. A major accelerator of progress is writing, which was not merely a good idea that occurred, but one which resulted from specific needs. As society increased in scope and complexity, it became necessary to have a method "of communicating with those who were absent, of perpetuating the memory of an event with greater precision than that afforded by oral tradi-tion. . . ."[15]

According to Condorcet the first writing systems were directly representa-tional: the sign looked like the object indicated. Out of this emerged conventional representation, preserving certain characteristics of the object; eventually these signs could stand for moral ideas as well. Writing became the art of attaching conventional signs to every idea and word. This tendency ultimately led to the alphabet when men observed how words are but combinations of a limited range of sounds and devised visible signs corresponding to the elements of words, rather than to the ideas they represented. With the alphabet "a small number of signs sufficed to unite everything, just as a small number of sounds sufficed to say everything. The written language was the same as the spoken language."[16]

From our present vantage point we can see the error in Condorcet's assumption that the number of sounds in spoken language is so minimal that it corresponds closely to the number of signs in the alphabet. Anyone who has ever tried to copy the utterances of a foreign language using their own alphabet, even when the foreign language employs the same alphabet, or mispronounced a new word read but never heard, knows otherwise. Although it may be ungracious to point out such an oversight in Condorcet, it is fair in this instance because the trap into which he fell on this issue was avoided by Rousseau, who wrote on the subject forty years before. Rousseau knew that the richness of oral discourse far exceeds the ability of any writing system to give it accurate representation, and that while the alphabet accentuates developments in certain areas, science and technology for example, its reductive, analytic character sacrifices the fuller communicative range of oral discourse. As a result, progress founded on it is never complete.

The early historical stages delineated by Condorcet are based on scanty data, as little empirical research had been done in the areas of archaeology and ancient history at the time he wrote. The criteria and sequences he employed resulted from a commonsense view of the way early societies were organized and how they might have changed, a view based on a kind of ad hoc socio-logic informed by the available traveller and missionary accounts of non-Western and primitive societies. His scheme utilizes a forerunner of the comparative method: the assumption that certain non-Western and primitive societies correspond to stages in the early history of civilization. The pitfalls of this approach have been more obvious to twentieth-century anthropologists than to their eighteenth- and nineteenth-century predecessors. Nevertheless, as a provisional grouping of societies on the basis of social, economic, and/or technological criteria it has been employed as a useful strategy from the Enlightenment, through the nineteenth-century social evolutionists including Marx, to contemporary archaeology.

The first stage in Condorcet's grand scheme begins with small-scale tribal societies based on family organization subsisting through hunting, fishing, and gathering. Language, moral ideas, and common laws of conduct were established at a basic level. The beginnings of scientific inquiry were found in superstitious practices when people began to divide into two groups, teachers and believers. Emphasis was on individual skills necessary for survival rather than handing down a legacy to posterity. The limited leisure time inhibited extensive combinations of ideas.[17] Eventually plant and animal domestication was adopted to reduce the chanciness of communal hunting. As a result property—in the form of weapons, utensils, cattle, and land—increased. A less hazardous and more leisurely life came into being and was characterized by specialization of labor, trading of surplus, and increased population growth: "acquired ideas were communicated more quickly and perpetuated more surely in a society that had become more sedentary, more accessible and more intimate."[18]

The second stage is characterized by pastoralism, whereby animals captured during hunting were domesticated. The sedentary trend continued and favored increased mental development. It was noted how some plants were better for the herds than others, and as a result people studied the differences; extensive agriculture began when cereals, fruits, and roots that could sustain increased numbers of people were developed, again a product of increased leisure. Language became richer without becoming less figurative and people became gentler, but there also came into being differences in wealth, occasional slaves, political inequality, and the priesthood. Although greed and corruption were clearly present, Condorcet notes how these traits are also aspects of later civilization, where they would be magnified to degrees unknown in early societies. Thus, his wide-eyed optimism regarding historical progress becomes momentarily tempered, and he adds: "the progress of the mind has not always resulted in the progress of society toward happiness and virtue."[19] This bit of critical reflection, plus his general description of early society, indicates the influence of Rousseau's *Discourse on Inequality*. But Condorcet takes a less extreme overall assessment than Rousseau by noting that crises in progress do not result from the growth of knowledge, but from its decline, and that gains in knowledge are always positive. Rousseau's position is that scientific and technological knowledge always result in a tradeoff: we lose happiness and virtue but we are given the illusion that we possess it in abundance. However, an inescapable anxiety remains that is unknown in primitive society.

The third stage gave rise to a more extensive division of labor and trade. Onto the earlier class structure of owners, servants, and slaves were added workers of every kind and merchants. This led to various federations of nations having a common language and customs—the beginnings of feudalism and despotism. Progress was slow because the dominant communications hieroglyphics—a term Condorcet uses to cover any ancient representational writing system—is secretly guarded by a priestly class. This disdain for priests as agents who retard knowledge is a consistent theme throughout Condorcet's work, an Enlightenment attitude where his kinship to Voltaire is most obvious. As the priests lost control toward the end of the third stage, writing moved away from complex representational schemes and toward conventional signs and the invention of the alphabet.

The fourth stage encompasses Greece to the time of Alexander. Unlike the earlier stages, which are never located in precise historical time or geographic space, specific details of Greek history are given. Condorcet notes how knowledge once restricted under the priests became more widespread owing in large measure to the alphabet. The alphabet also yielded a true history for the first time, Condorcet admits the uncertainty of knowing the earlier stages with accuracy. An important trend was initiated in the fourth stage, one that would play a key role in Condorcet's own century: science as an organized body of knowledge became not only a tool of technological innovation but a challenge to the control over society exerted by superstition.

The fifth stage extends from Greek science and Aristotle, to Rome, the rise of Christianity, and the displacement of science and philosophy by the latter. The attenuation of knowledge that took place in early Christendom is traced directly to communications. Condorcet notes that manuscripts were few in number and difficult to procure. Books kept the light of knowledge alive and it was easy for them to vanish during this time. The state of the sciences was intimately linked to the fate of books and religion conspired against both. "So it is not be be wondered at, that Christianity which after the invention of printing was not powerful enough to prevent their dazzling renaissance was at this time powerful enough to consummate their ruin."[20] This trend continued into the sixth stage, which extends to the Crusades and is another period not to his liking.

The seventh stage reaches from the revival of science following the Crusades to the advent of print. In an interesting observation Condorcet notes that during this period—he does not use the term *renaissance* in its modern historical sense—much of human knowledge and conduct derived from the authoritative study of traditional texts rather than from systematic inquiry into nature:

> There was no question of examining a principle in its own right: it was always a matter of interpreting... one set of quotations by appeal to another. A proposition was accepted not because it was true, but because it was written in such-and-such a book and had been recognized in such-and-such a country since such-and-such a date. . . . In this way the authority of men was everywhere substituted for the authority of reason. Books were studied much more than nature. . . ."[21]

This intriguing observation is somewhat paralleled two centuries later in Foucault's analysis of written discourse during the Renaissance.[22] He notes how the authority of written texts began to take primacy over unwritten traditions. Even in theology, it was believed that in the beginning was the written word and it is in texts that the embodiment of truth is to be sought. In the secular domain few distinctions existed between what was seen and what was read, and this was reflected in schemes classifying the natural world, Aldrovandi's for example. Such schemes presented an inextricable mixture of description, reported quotes, fables, myths, and medical and magical uses for the various species discussed. The role of knowledge was not in seeing or demonstrating—using reason in Condorcet's sense—but in interpreting; and the written word and natural world were regarded as continuous. The great eighteenth-century naturalist Buffon (1707-1788) was critical of such textual reflections substituting for careful observation, and his work, well known among the philosophes, may have influenced Condorcet's attitude toward this earlier period.

The eighth stage is characterized by the spread of printed books, which enabled science and philosophy to finally break with tradition. For Condorcet the invention of the printing press created an unparalleled revolution. The quality and diversity of books increased while the cost decreased, and a wider public could gain access to knowledge, which "became the subject of a brisk and universal trade."[23] Traditional authority was challenged by public opinion as reason and justice gained rapid ascendancy and education became increasingly separated from religious and political considerations. Owing to the wide distribution of many copies of a given text, mistakes could be noted and rectified in subsequent editions, an almost impossible task during the manuscript period. Into extensive circulation came

> elementary books, dictionaries, works of reference containing a host of facts, observations . . . experiments in which all proofs are developed . . . all doubts discussed; valuable compilations containing all that has been observed, written or thought about one particular branch of the sciences, or setting out the work of all the scientists of one country . . . tables and diagrams of all kinds, some that show us conclusions that our minds would otherwise have grasped after a long struggle. . . .[24]

He also notes that at the same time as print was in its early ascendancy the Turks took Constantinople and numerous Greek men of letters sought refuge in Italy. They brought to Europe various classic works in science and philosophy, which contributed to the questioning of traditional authority. Modern sciences too, particularly the discoveries of Copernicus, Galileo, Kepler, and Bacon, became known to more than just a select few.

The ninth stage ranges from Descartes to the foundation of the French Republic. Printing was still a major factor in the spread of ideas. Locke and Rousseau are given a prominent role in revealing truths essential to the realization of freedom. Newton is mentioned, but surprisingly not given as much prominence as he is in the work of Voltaire. The ideals elaborated in this stage, which encompasses the cultural present of Condorcet's own time, are projected into the future in the tenth stage, where increased scientific, technological, and artistic progress would, he believed, give them full expression. He made some interesting predictions regarding future developments in science and technology, and although several came to pass, their consequences are not what he would have expected. In the area of communications he saw the possibility of a universal written language based on mental universals. Perhaps this was conceived as one last hopeful counter to the intolerance which closed in on him during his final days.

MONBODDO'S UNORTHODOX SYSTEM

Without doubt James Burnet, Lord Monboddo (1714-1799), is one of the most bizarre and idiosyncratic figures, not only of the Scottish Enlightenment, but of any of the other national traditions as well. He was regarded as one of the most learned men of his time and place, no small honor when we remember that the Scottish school included such luminaries as David Hume and Adam Smith. However, he was also derided by many, perhaps most notably by Samuel Johnson (1709-1784). Monboddo's uncritical use of traveller's tales leading to his beliefs in races of men with tails, his extensive reflections on the orangutan, which he though to be of the human species, and recurring attempts to see beaver social organization as analogous to early human society, were the subjects of considerable snickering. Our century has been somewhat kinder. Arthur Lovejoy has given him serious consideration for grappling with some major eighteenth-century problems in natural history.[25] Ever since, Monboddo has at least received respectful mention in almost all comprehensive histories of the concept of evolution, usually regarding the degree to which he is, or is not, a legitimate forerunner of Darwin.

But it is Monboddo's work as a philosophical historian that compels our interest. This is a significant aspect of his two major works, *Of the Origin and Progress of Language*, published in six volumes from 1773-1779, and *Antient Metaphysics*, also in six volumes, released from 1779-1799. In these texts we find one of the most comprehensive discussions of Western thought on the nature, origin, and history of language, and an appraisal of the philosophy of classical antiquity with few eighteenth-century parallels, in breadth if not in accuracy. This legacy, coupled with the frequent discussions of Monboddo's work in his own time, and his acknowledged niche in the history of biological thought pertinent to evolution, make omission of an entry on him in the recent eight-volume *Encyclopedia of Philosophy* a major oversight.[26]

Like Rousseau, to whom he is occasionally compared, especially on primitivism and the orangutan—but the analogy should not be pushed too far—Monboddo is a figure both of his time and out of phase with it. Even his appearance was unusual. He was diminuitive and elfin-like, with a quick mind and tongue. His family line, which went back many generations and was said to have once included giants, had dwindled considerably in all respects, a factor that contributed to his view that civilized men had diminished rather than progressed in physical and mental vigor from the Greek ideal. Monboddo had a fondness for the Greek language and culture, which intensified while he was studying law at Edinburgh, after having been an undistinguished graduate of King's College, Aberdeen. His thesis dealt with Roman law, thus adding to his knowledge and appreciation of antiquity. Eventually he took his place as a judge of the session, and even in this capacity he was known for some unconventional views. An interesting rivalry of sorts developed with another Scottish judge, Henry Home, Lord Kames (1692-1782). Occasionally writing about related topics they were in frequent disagreement and it was said that the only thing they had in common was their longevity.[27]

Monboddo venerated ancient philosophy and saw himself as its reviver, one who would restore Aristotelean metaphysics to a prominent place in the face of the empiricism and skepticism of his day.[28] This was to counter the many aspects of civilization that have declined since Greek and Roman times. Inasmuch as this can be seen as a critical stance challenging inevitable progress, Monboddo can be seen as political. But unlike his antiprogressivist predecessor, Rousseau, and the French philosophes, Monboddo avoided contemporary political critique in his writings and in his capacity as judge.[29]

Involvement with the works of Plato, Aristotle, and the Neoplatonists, led Monboddo to be critical of two of the most dominant Enlightenment figures, Locke and Hume; the former, for his alleged view that mind operates only via the senses, and the latter for his skepticism and supposed failure to understand the difference between sense impressions and ideas. Condillac does not receive consideration in this context despite the fact that the title of part 2 of his *Essai* is exactly the same as one of Monboddo's books, *Of the Origin and Progress of Language*; although their perspectives differ there is considerable overlap of subject matter. *Antient Metaphysics* demonstrates a further attempt to challenge the scientific ideals of the day when it takes on Newton and Galileo, who are seen as representatives of the idea of mechanical causality that has richly fueled atheism. Monboddo's arguments are based on the notion of a supreme mind constantly in operation. They were not impressive, either to other members of the Scottish school or religious orthodoxy. No doubt theologians must have also had trouble with his contention that the story of Adam and Eve is an allegory, like the parables of the New Testament, and his secular explanation of language origins and history. Indeed, he is a philosopher of many paradoxes.

The writing style Monboddo employs can be downright exasperating to the contemporary reader. It is wordy, rambling, and repetitive; after a time it is possible to predict what will be said when a given topic is broached and the examples to be used. The claim to a plain style at the outset of *Antient Metaphysics* seems strange at second glance, but it probably refers to the absence of esoteric philosophical terminology and discussions. Because of the overlap and the fact that despite contradictions there are no significant changes of position, it will be useful to consider Monboddo's works as a unified corpus. In addition, it should be noted that the listed division of subjects runs approximately as follows: in *Origin and Progress*, volume 1 deals with epistemology and the origin and nature of language and society; 2, with the elements of language, especially words and tenses, with an emphasis on Indo-European; 3, with style via reference to Plato and Aristotle; 4 compares various languages with Greek; 5 is a history of Rome based on Latin and Greek sources; 6 covers rhetoric; and in *Antient Metaphysics*, volumes 1, 2, 3, and 6 deal with epistemology, along with critiques of science and philosophy; and 4 and 5 cover the history of man and civilization.

Within this sweeping philosophical vision are numerous observations pertinent to the communications/history question. And despite Monboddo's preference for the ancients over the moderns, the assumptions he held in many areas fit quite consonantly into the Enlightenment tradition. For example, his discussion of human nature presupposed natural faculties and acquired faculties. The latter predominate leading him to comment that habit and custom are "second nature," and in an observation closer to Hume than he might have wanted to admit, he observed that "we are much more creatures of custom and habit than of nature."[30] Nevertheless, he did believe in a priori capacities and powers, which the mind brings to sense experience, such as thinking, believing, and doubting. These attributes do not equate to intellect, which is held to be a learned rather than a natural trait, but their existence enables us to acquire faculties we are not born with to a greater degree than any other species. Although Monboddo's belief in various innate propensities was a bit extreme for the Locke-Hume tradition, it does share points of compatibility with the concept of human nature that was being developed by his Scottish contemporaries, Thomas Reid, Dugald Stewart, and Adam Ferguson.

For Monboddo the most important factor in the human species achieving the intelligence and dominion that it has, is language: "It is only by that communication among men that language bestows upon them, that any art worth mentioning, or any science can be invented or cultivated."[31] Yet his view presupposes that even though language is a human creation, it is such a complex phenomenon that human society must have been in existence for a long time before language (spoken language) came into being. This is an acknowledged point of disagreement with Rousseau's argument that language and society are reciprocal because they came into being together. Monboddo astutely points out that numerous animal species have elaborate social groupings, though they lack language. Of particular interest to him, and cited at length, are the creative accomplishments and social life of orangutans and beavers. Some of his observations about their behavior are quite poignant and mesh well with the contemporary studies, while others are silly and outrageous by the standards of any age. The whole area is certainly worth further study by researchers interested in the history of thought pertaining to animal behavior and communication.

If human societies once existed for a considerable period of time prior to language, what brought them into being and what held them together?

The first question is answered with much equivocation. Monboddo refuses to come down on either side of the divide as to whether our original nature is social or solitary. He wants it both ways. We are creatures, like the orangutan and beaver, who by natural inclination can partake of both. The list of ill-documented cases he cites of human beings living in a solitary state is far less impressive than the one conjured to demonstrate animal social organization. To commit himself completely to the position of original human nature as solitary would perhaps align him too strongly with the position of Thomas Hobbes (1588-1679), whose notion of a self-seeking human nature having origins in a solitary brutish state was out of phase with the Enlightenment concept of original goodness, and a position strongly opposed by other Scottish philosophers, notably Dugald Stewart and Adam Ferguson, who argued that man is by nature social and cooperative.

Since the contention that man is naturally social has foundations in one of Monboddo's favorite thinkers, Aristotle—who is also cited by Marx and Darwin in the next century in support of similar views—it is puzzling that he sidesteps allegiance to this position. Instead he argues that we began developing from the partly social, partly solitary state of our original nature, in which we were peaceful vegetarians—a deliberate counter to Hobbes's warlike state—then shifted to hunting, pastoralism, and agriculture largely as a response to multiplying beyond the numbers capable of being sustained by available resources. This is a position similar to the one taken by Rousseau in his *Discourse on Inequality*.

All of this, and the acquisition of language as well, are hypothesized to have occurred after the flood, which itself is regarded as a hypothesis. Monboddo questions the literalness of the Old Testament in volume 1 of *Origin and Progress*, and although he does not attempt to refute it, he postulates that even if it is true it has no bearing on his scheme because even after the dispersal, when language and society as the gift of God were lost, they could have been reacquired in the manner outlined.

The question of what held societies together through their prelinguistic transformations is answered by citing the importance of other communicational modes. In the long period of human social development prior to language, extensive use was made of inarticulate cries, gestures and facial expressions, imitative sounds, and painting (by which Monboddo means visual representation in general). The first two we partly share with the brutes; the last two are uniquely human. Gesture (he includes dance in this category) is deemed to be of particular importance. Monboddo argues that among the ancients the use of gesture through pantomime could allow an orator to express almost any sentiment or idea that could be presented in words, and therefore it must have had a highly significant role to play in prelinguistic social communication; visual representations such as paintings are seen as gestures rendered into permanent images. This line of thinking represents a contribution to what has become known as the gestural origin theory of language, a tradition that extends from the eighteenth century to the present day, where it has undergone a revival from the disfavor into which it had fallen, a revival that has resulted from several implications of the recent sign language experiments among captive great apes.[32] Although these experiments have surprised, confused, and led to debates among scientists for over two decades, one can imagine Monboddo, and perhaps Rousseau, saying "of course, it is as I have said," especially since one of the most communicatively revealing species has been the orangutan.

Eventually spoken language gained preeminence. One of the first areas where Monboddo contends it was employed was in coordinating joint labor, a view Marx would independently reelaborate over a half century later. Like Rousseau, Monboddo argues that men sang before they could speak, the first languages being musical, perhaps birdlike, a conclusion also reached by Darwin. Egypt is held to be the birthplace not only of language but of writing and civilization as well.

Monboddo believed that the degree to which language is developed in a given society reflects the state of mind of its inhabitants. In this respect history exhibits movement toward and away from the pinnacle of perfection exemplified by the Greek language and culture. Considerable discussion in both his major works is given over to language stages antecedent to the Indo-European ideal based on Greek, particularly in his attempt to hierarchically arrange various non-Western languages on the basis of their sound features and grammatical components. What results is not a list of stages based on the languages per se, but one that grades the accounts of those languages and assumes the two are coterminous: the better studied tribes with more complete documentation of their languages rate more highly than the converse, regardless of other factors such as social complexity.

The degree to which he lauds the Egyptians and Greeks for their monumental contributions to developing not only language but also writing is strangely countered by his pronounced depreciation of the Chinese legacy. The Chinese language is held to be imperfect, awkward, and difficult for a stranger to learn. It is more musical than Greek and than "any language ought to be."[33] Monboddo argues that the "hieroglyphic" state of Chinese writing indicates an undeveloped speech, one sufficient for carrying on everyday activities but inadequate to "communicating matters of art and science."[34] According to Monboddo the Chinese derived their writing from the Egyptians (this is not accepted today), but being a dull, uncreative people they remained the same while the Egyptians progressed to the alphabet. The Chinese therefore retained two languages—one spoken, the other written—and did not have the foresight to link them. Monboddo's attitude is indeed puzzling. He dismisses Marco Polo as a source and cites earlier Islamic accounts much less favorable to the Chinese. Voltaire is not referred to at all, and Warburton's *Divine Legation of Moses* is cited with reference to the Chinese being the least inventive people on earth, an observation that seems astounding when we consider who invented paper, printing, gunpowder, and the compass.

Citing ancient sources such as Herodotus, Monboddo elaborates on how the alphabet was invented by the Egyptians, who discovered that abbreviated characters could be made to stand for elemental sounds, a discovery eventually perfected by the Greeks. The Phoenicians are mentioned but said to have derived their alphabet from the Egyptians. Not only is Egypt held to be the cradle of civilization, laws, government, the arts, architecture, language, and the alphabet, but the first representational writing systems, which led to hieroglyphics, are also said to have been created there. The argument he puts forth for the myraid cultural traits having one origin, Egypt in this case, from whence they spread to the rest of the world, is now known as diffusionism. Its converse is independent invention which holds that when traits or inventions appear in widely separate contexts having no evidence of contact, it is plausible to surmise that they resulted from parallel responses of the people in question to similar needs and conditions. For example, we are now certain that numerous representational and conventional writing systems developed separately throughout different parts of the world at various times.

However, with respect to the alphabetic script, the diffusionist argument carries more weight as evidence indicates Phoenician origins as the source for all known alphabets, either directly or in terms of providing the idea for this kind of writing. The whole issue of the respective merits of diffusion versus independent invention would be taken up in earnest by Tylor in the latter nineteenth century and given a judicious treatment.

Although Monboddo argues that the Greek alphabet is the fullest and most perfect known, he admits that there are sounds in other languages which cannot be captured by it. Our alphabet is even more deficient because a single letter can sometimes refer to several sounds. This is another example of his talent for being blind to the obvious, for which he was well known in his own time. Since knowledge of how ancient Greek was spoken can only be derived from its alphabet, we must work with an assumed congruency that may not necessarily have been the case in the original context.

Despite the insight evident in perfecting the alphabet and the advantages it has for communicating with absent persons, preserving facts and dates, and its use as a scientific tool, alphabetic writing for Monboddo does not invariably equate with progress. He notes that the art of writing is not an art of memory but of reminiscence (the very terms Plato uses when he discusses writing in the *Phaedrus*), and that it weakens memory, which is often more developed in nonliterate societies. The North American Indians are favorably cited. Even the ancients, who possessed writing, preferred oral exchange for the transfer of numerous forms of knowledge. In contrast to the unbridled praise of writing found in Turgot and Condorcet, Monboddo is more cautious and insists on the necessity of retaining a proper oral tradition, a view that is independently restated in the twentieth century by communications historian Harold Innis. Monboddo observes:

> I have likewise said, that I doubted whether the use of letters had contributed to the improvement of knowledge; and if it be true that it weakens memory, as knowledge depends so much on memory, it must be likewise true that it retards our progress in knowledge. Besides as nothing improves knowledge as much as mutual intercourse and communication of our thoughts to one another, such intercourse is better carried on by conversation, than by writing; and therefore if the frequent use of writing was the effect of making conversation upon subjects of science less frequent, which I doubt is the case among us, instead of advancing learning it will be a hindrance to it.[35]

A work briefly cited by Monboddo, and doubtless a contribution to his understanding of the spoken word, is *An Essay on the Original Genius and Writings of Homer* (1775) by the English diplomat and archaeologist Robert Wood (1717-1771). In addition to being clearly written and well focussed—in contrast to Enlightenment writers such as Monboddo who were verbose and wide ranging—Wood is extraordinarily insightful, especially regarding what he referred to as the oral tradition. One of his main theses is that Homer could neither read nor write and did not know the alphabet, though he may have been aware of some form of picture writing. In arguing this position Wood notes that the musical and poetic character of the epics facilitates memorization, and that they are not unlike traditional oral histories in more recent nonliterate (pre-alphabet) societies. In addition, Wood provides a host of useful observations on the different concepts of time and history that exist between nonliterate and literate societies.

Unfortunately we cannot consider other interesting facets of Monboddo—for example, his detailed analysis of particular languages and their development; attempts at historical demography; and his critique of the growth of trade and commerce. However, several aspects of his work will forever remain oddities, including his belief in mermaids (and mermen); early races of giants; and the superiority of health and longevity of the ancients. The last volume of *Antient Metaphysics* was written as he neared death and sought to affirm proof for the existence of God, often by trying to undermine concepts of science central to Enlightenment thinking. We include him here because he dealt with human communication on a vast scale, and also, because like Rousseau and unlike many of the philosophes, he realized that improving the technology of communications does not necessarily improve human communication.

For any discipline in search of ancestral figures an inevitable problem arises regarding what to do when someone like Monboddo turns up who yields insights centuries ahead of his time, yet commits blunders that throw doubt on his basic common sense. Should he be exalted as a seer or dismissed as a buffoon? We are not yet ready to pass judgment. Therefore we must preserve the legacy.

3   *Jean-Jacques Rousseau on Language and Writing*

The spoken word involves all the senses dramatically. . . .
—Marshall McLuhan

One of the most controversial figures of his age, Jean-Jacques Rousseau's (1712-1778) influence has continued almost unabated to the present. The magnitude of his contribution can be seen, both in the works of those who have accepted and sought to develop his key ideas, and with respect to numerous critics who have tried to disavow his legacy with such vehemence one would think that Rousseau was the Antichrist. The details of his life are well documented and much interpreted: born in Geneva; his mother died as a result of his birth; abandoned by his father who was a watchmaker; the wandering waif existence that brought him under the protection and tutelage of several older women; the illegitimate children he sired and consigned to a foundling home; the personal and intellectual conflicts that underscored his diverse and controversial writings, the persecution he faced, both real and imagined; and his quiet death and eventual noisy resurrection by the revolutionaries. No one has done a better job studying this odyssey of a life than Jean Guehenno, whose biography of Rousseau is written with thoroughness, imagination, and a passionate conviction so appropriate to his subject.[1]

Rousseau's major works in the area of social and political thought include the *Discours sur les sciences et les arts* (*Discourse on the Sciences and Arts*, 1750); the *Discours sur l'origine d'inegalite* (*Discourse on the Origin of Inequality*, 1755); the *Contrat social* (*Social Contract*, 1762); and *Emile* (1762). It is the *Discourse on Inequality* that will be our main concern. This treatise constitutes Rousseau's program for a general history dealing with the emergence of humanity from a primeval state of nature and its progress through various social and technological developments up to and including the political corruption of his own time. The critique of eighteenth-century society in the *Discourse* is implied rather than overtly stated, but implied with such force that it is little wonder the work was received with such hostility; even Voltaire thought it was extreme. Although later assessments often treat the *Discourse* as an allegorical work, while recognizing its considerable insights, the value it has as a historical outline has rarely been considered. Marx and Engels are notable exceptions. Not only is Marx's concept of alienation anticipated in the *Discourse*, but Rousseau's historical sequence, as Engels has noted, corresponds to the one Marx used right down to "a whole series of the same dialectical developments."[2]

In dealing with the communications/history question the *Discourse* is complemented by another work, albeit one unpublished during Rousseau's lifetime (though excerpts were published in the *Encyclopedia*): the *Essay on the Origin of Languages.* This study was written during and shortly before the period in which the *Discourse* was conceived. Taken together they provide a legacy that is of its time, and yet disconsonant with both orthodoxy and other radical critiques.

In the area of communications Rousseau came to a fundamental conclusion that differed from the position reached by the philosophes. He did not accept the view that history represented inevitable progress, nor did he hold knowledge to be strictly cumulative. For the philosophes, mankind moved from ignorance to enlightenment as improved communications, such as writing and printing, enabled us to add and make more accessible greater amounts of knowledge about the world. In other words, media were seen as augmentative but basically neutral. Knowledge changes because it is added to. Rousseau's position is more reminiscent of, but not as extreme as McLuhan's adage "the medium is the message." For Rousseau, the way in which dominant communication occurs, be it through different languages or various forms of written script, profoundly affects the way we come to know and experience the world and ultimately other human beings. For example, a medium such as alphabetic writing differs from spoken language. It does not merely preserve and increase what exists, but transforms it into a new version of reality and truth without those involved being aware of what has happened.

PLAN OF THE *DISCOURSE ON INEQUALITY*

The *Discourse* begins with an obsequious dedication to the republic of Geneva that even the most naive must have been able to see through. It did not win for Rousseau the favor he had hoped for, nor did it soften reaction to the heresies that come later in the text. The work itself was written in response to a contest proposed by the Academy of Dijon. The question asked was, "What is the origin of inequality among men; and is it authorized by natural law?" The earlier *Discourse on the Sciences and Arts* was also written in response to a proposal from the Academy. In attacking modernism it appealed to the judges and won the prize.

The *Discourse on Inequality*, in attacking almost every institution since creation, did not win and led to a scandal that contributed to the persecution already confronting Rousseau.

The preface of the second *Discourse* is an important statement of methodology. Rousseau, the critic of modernism, in order to further challenge its many tenets, uses some of those self-same tenets for the task. For example, morality and values are not to be accepted blindly. Their legitimacy must be examined using reasoned inquiry informed by scientific hypotheses such as those he regarded as being useful to physicists.[3] Is this the path to be followed by one of the most outspoken critics of reason and science produced in the eighteenth or any subsequent century? Needless to say, Rousseau abounds in paradoxes (he recognized many of them himself), which have been easily pointed out by later critics. Yet the more thoroughly we study him, as a growing group of contemporary Rousseau scholars such as Roger Masters has revealed, the more we find a consistent overall plan and logic uniting his work.[4]

The baseline of human history for Rousseau is the natural man, the human species at the dawn of history living an isolated, autonomous existence, governed by presocial survival instincts. This is, as Emile Durkheim (1858-1917), a Rousseau-influenced founder of modern sociology has emphasized, more important as an inner psychological portrait of mankind than as a supposed prehistoric stage of development.[5] The kinship with Hobbes's version of natural man and with natural (individual) man in eighteenth-century political economy is obvious. Rousseau was aware of this and it is interesting to note that although he was indebted to Hobbes's methodology, the theory of human nature that emerged in each writer is quite different. Rousseau has an explanation for this not directed specifically at Hobbes, but the implications are clear. He notes how earlier writers "carried over to the state of nature ideas acquired in society. . . ."[6] Thus, earlier portraits of human nature as unsavory and self-seeking merely reflected attitudes of the era in which the inquirer lived. He, Rousseau, would avoid doing this, a view that recalls his immediate predecessor, Montesquieu, who noted at the outset of *De l'Esprit des lois* (*Spirit of the Laws*, 1748), "I have not drawn my principles from prejudices, but from the nature of things."[7] The issue crops up a century later in Marx, who in a critique of bourgeois political economy that reads like an early example of the sociology of knowledge notes that "as every society has its own peculiar nature, so does it engender its own peculiar natural man."[8] For Marx the archetype of natural man for the eighteenth-century political economists is Robinson Crusoe.[9] Returning to Rousseau, we can see that despite his contention to be unbiased, he carries into his theory of the state of nature one of the dominant values of his age, individualism. He clearly reveals this in *Emile* when he recommends that the first book a child should read, preferably several times, is *Robinson Crusoe*.

Rousseau's state of nature is bountiful, capable of satisfying man's need without the necessity of social liaisons. But it is no Eden. There are difficulties that have to be overcome by developing physical capacities, such as fleetness of foot to escape predators and climbing ability to get at additional food. Rousseau explains these developments with reference to what he calls the "law of Sparta," which preserves the robust and eliminates the weak, an anticipation of the concept of natural selection Darwin would elaborate one hundred years later. Actually, Rousseau comes even closer to an evolutionary perspective when he speculates on the possibility that early humans may have possessed fur and moved on all fours, but he rejects this view on the basis of lack of solid evidence and concludes that early man had the basic body design and movement patterns of his contemporary descendants. Nevertheless, like Condillac, who greatly influenced his formulations in several ways, Rousseau does not disavow biblical accounts regarding origins, but sees the process he describes as taking place in the great void following the flood and dispersal. Although the biblical story of the fall is sometimes said to be the direct inspiration for Rousseau's more secular account in the *Discourse*, the analogy cannot be pushed too far. Unlike the paradise of Eden, the state of nature is seasonably variable, and contains hazards as well as occasional conflicts between its early human inhabitants.[10]

In the state of nature any technique acquired through chance or experiment would be easily lost as social communication was virtually nonexistent. Eventually social groupings emerged because "men had multiplied so greatly that the natural productions no longer sufficed to nourish them. . . ."[11] Thus, using a materialist hypothesis, Rousseau postulates that population pressure on available resources led to cultivation of the land and the manufacture of appropriate implements. This economic explanation is restated in his *Essay on the Origins of Languages*: "When one investigates the origin of the arts and considers primitive customs, one sees that everything corresponds in its origins to the means of providing subsistence."[12] From these exigencies there arose various forms of communication based on sacrifice, which eventually resulted in subjugation and exploitation, as property emerged along with new technologies, rules of justice, and the establishment of small kingdoms that eventually merged into nations. The last part of the *Discourse* is devoted to describing the consequences of this transformation and appears to contain plausible speculation on early state formation.

THE EMERGENCE OF LANGUAGE

In the *Discourse* observations on the role of language in human communication are confined primarily to early developments resulting from abandonment of the state of nature, while the *Essay on the Origin of Languages* deals with some later historical ramifications.

Like Condillac before him, and Monboddo after, Rousseau regarded language as an invention, not something natural. This position was contested by Herder in his own *Essay on the Origin of Language* (1772). Herder, who is sometimes seen as Rousseau's rival for the title, "father of romanticism," argued that language, rather than being the gift of God or a human invention, is natural only to the human species. One of his arguments is that spoken language cannot be perfectly reduced to written characters, which *are* seen as a human invention. Therefore it must have a deeper organic basis. He criticizes the notion of language being an invention as having led Condillac to turn animals into men, and Rousseau to turn men into animals.[13] However, it must be pointed out that Rousseau subscribed to the notion of language as an invention with full awareness of the inherent difficulties, and not without some degree of reservation.[14]

For Rousseau, language was not necessary in the state of nature because encounters were fleeting. As exchanges became more regular, with increased populations and dwindling resources, natural cries along with manual gestures served to convey basic information. The cries were useful as warnings, the gestures indicated objects. As ideas increased beyond a rudimentary level, the inflections of voice diversified and were joined to existing gestures. Using Condillac's terminology, Rousseau notes that eventually the articulation of voice alone was best suited to the ideas of "instituted signs." Naming was first done in a very specific manner whereby, for example, each tree of a given species was labelled differently. No doubt this connected to the individualist epistemology that created the solitary natural man as the essence of humanity. But given our capacity for perfectability, as words increased it became possible to form the generalizations that led to the variety of spoken languages we know today.

FROM WORD TO SCRIPT

The *Essay* expands on several points raised in the *Discourse* regarding language and communication in general. The style of the *Essay* is along the lines of what McLuhan would later refer to in a description of his own *Gutenberg Galaxy* as the "mosaic approach." Its exploratory and traditional lineal sequence is not followed. Arguments arise and disappear only to return again, and chapters range from one paragraph to a dozen pages.

According to Rousseau, need prompted communication through gestures, which depend less on convention than words and can convey more in less time. Passion and sentiment led to the first words. When human beings recognized others as being like themselves there arose a desire to communicate, which exists independently of whatever form that communication might take:

> The invention of the art of communicating our ideas depends less on the organs we use in such communication than it does upon the power proper to man according to which he uses his organs in this way and which if he lacked these, would lead him to use others to the same end.[15]

Language, therefore, is not natural. It is but one mode we utilize for expressing our feelings and ideas. However, it could be argued that Rousseau regards desire to communicate as an almost natural and inevitable aspect of human association.

Although gesture can convey ideas, by speaking to the eye rather than the ear it cannot convey the full emotional range of any message that extends beyond basic needs. Language, by contrast, can stir the passions, because it is love, hate, pity, and other emotions that led to the first words. Since feelings spoke before reason, the first languages were figurative, poetic, and musical. These are qualities that would also figure significantly in Darwin's view of language origins. Music is a recurring aspect in Rousseau's thought. It not only enters into his formulations on language, but he also wrote excerpts for the *Encyclopedia* on the subject in addition to devising a new system of music notation and doing a bit of composing on the side. His preference was for melody, which he likened to drawing. It speaks directly to the emotions. Harmony, by contrast, is conventional and requires a practiced ear. Rousseau argued for a parallel evolution between language and music. As language moved from its rich figurative beginnings to a colder, duller, and more analytic state, so music shifted from melodic dominance to an increasing concern with harmonics.

Rousseau did not believe that language developed fortuitously, but as a result of changing circumstances. In an observation already made by Condillac, and reiterated later by Monboddo, he notes that early oral languages had to be persuasive and eloquent to get people to do what was needed, especially when used to address assembled masses. In modern times persuasion is by force. Therefore languages have lost the powerful rhetorical quality they once had. Writing has been one of the main factors behind this shift.

In the *Essay*, a major chapter titled "On Script" is given over to the subject of writing. For Rousseau, writing does not merely preserve language, it is the fundamental agent involved in its alteration. Writing changes the spirit of words by substituting exactitude for expressiveness. In written form words must be used according to their conventional meaning, whereas in speaking one can vary meaning through tone of voice. According to Rousseau one of the reasons writing caused language to lose its vitality was through the suppression of dialects: "The more a people learn to read, the more are its dialects obliterated. . . ."[16] Specific discussion is given over to Homer, who Rousseau contends did not know the written alphabet and whose work is therefore richly composed of various dialects.

In Rousseau's scheme, writing of any kind offers a clue to the development of language. The older the written script the more ancient the language. The earliest writing systems indicated objects by direct representation; he cites the example of Mexico. Later, written images took on an allegorical function, such as was the case in Egypt. The next stage incorporates conventional characters and necessitates a fully formed language and people united by common laws. Chinese is the example mentioned and said to be a script that appeals to the eye rather than the ear. Finally, script is broken down into elementary parts which are held to constitute the words and syllables of a given language. This technique, which led to our alphabet, is held to have been invented by a commercial people, who in their travels and exchanges needed a way of having permanent records of several different languages. This may seem like another one of Rousseau's infamous contradictions, given that elsewhere in the text he notes how traders can carry on a transaction using gestures without speech, and how inadequate alphabetic writing is in accurately reproducing the language of its users, let alone a foreign language. However, he is careful to point out, with respect to the invention of the alphabet, that its purpose was not to represent speech but to analyze it. In other words, the original function of what he called "that dangerous supplement" was auxillary, but centuries later its abstract reductionist qualities would become a dominant arbiter of language.[17]

From our contemporary perspective this makes sense if we consider how new technologies, especially in communications, are usually developed as supplements or adjuncts to earlier modes, rather than as discrete, separate systems. For example, the first printed books complemented earlier manuscripts, as the content and form were similar. It was only after several generations that the unique aspects of the new system came to modify the organization of knowledge by changing the structure of its presentation to coincide more effectively with the limits of the new technology.

Yet there are other points in the text where there appears to be no way around Rousseau's inconsistencies. He notes how the three ways of writing described correspond to three stages of social development: (1) the depiction of objects, the savage state; (2) conventional signs, barbarism; and (3) the alphabet, civilization. If we assume that he adheres to the eighteenth-century interpretation of savagery as characterized by hunting and fishing, barbarism by pastoralism, and civilization by the alphabet (these correlations were extensively developed by the nineteenth-century social evolutionists), which seems to be the case in the *Discourse*, then the typology is confusing because he later refers to the Egyptians and Mexicans as civilized while discussing difficulties in their pre-alphabetic writing systems.

All alphabets are held to be related in Rousseau's scheme and he speculates that the Phoenician may have been their prototype. As the myth of King Cadmus suggests, Rousseau assumes the alphabet was brought to Greece from Phoenicia, although the languages are not related. The Greeks adopted the Phoenician characters to their own language, though they never achieved perfect correspondence, and changed the progression of characters from right to left, to an alternate right-left, left-right script known as *boustrophedon*, which refers to turning as oxen do in pulling a plow (Rousseau does not use this term), to the left-right convention later adopted by most Indo-European scripts. In an intriguing observation he notes that the alternating script, writing "in furrow fashion," is the easiest to read, though it is difficult to write, and he expresses surprise that it did not return with printing. Today these are apt areas for research in the psychology of literacy and communications design.

DERRIDA ON ROUSSEAU ON WRITING

In concluding this chapter on Rousseau it might be pertinent to draw brief attention to the work of a contemporary scholar, Jacques Derrida, who has undertaken an extensive analysis of Rousseau's observations on writing. Derrida is a figure whose stature in the world of poststructuralist, semiotically inspired textual criticism is rapidly growing. Much of his work, sometimes known as deconstructionism, is devoted to identifying unsuspected biases imposed on our thought by the Western philosophical tradition. In doing this he has dealt with a wide range of figures from Plato to the contemporary French anthropologist Levi-Strauss.

In his *Of Grammatology*, Derrida devotes almost two-thirds of his commentary to Rousseau, and by also critiquing related themes in the work of Levi-Strauss, endeavors to contrast language (spoken) with writing. One of Derrida's central theses is that in most studies of language speech has been favored over writing. In various linguistic traditions, especially in the work of Saussure, writing is held to be a secondary or derivative system that need not be taken into account when studying language. Derrida, informed by Rousseau, tries to deal with aspects of language that strongly affect our thought, not by dealing with speech in the traditional linguistic way, but by recognizing the enormous influence on the spoken word that emanates from the written one. Although his approach differs from the one taken here, in that the main focus is on literary and philosophical texts rather than on general historical-technological assessments, there are, nonetheless, important connections.

To draw out relevant insights from Derrida's writing is no easy task and requires a degree of patience. He is a difficult and idiosyncratic writer, continually using familiar concepts in new ways and developing an original terminology. Interpreting him can be, as Jonathan Culler, one of the few contemporary critics who has managed to gain perspective on Derrida notes, a "combination of exasperation and insight"; part of the reason for this is that Derrida consciously avoids letting any of his writings yield the "central concepts of a new theory or system."[18] Nevertheless, the fact that his thought is rendered into a written text precludes full achievement of the privileged position he appears to be seeking.

In *Of Grammatology*, the term *grammatology* refers to the study of writing. Derrida notes that to understand writing it is necessary to comprehend the differences between it and speech. We should also take into account how previous linguistic inquiry, in privileging speech over writing, failed to indicate the way the written word has come to alter spoken discourse. His observation that there was no linguistic sign before writing can be bolstered with reference to recent anthropological studies which show that in many nonliterate societies there does not exist a word for *word*.[19]

Rousseau is regarded by Derrida as "undoubtedly the only one or the first one to make a theme or system of the reduction of writing profoundly implied by the entire age," a problem that neither Descartes nor Hegel were able to grasp.[20] More recently Levi-Strauss, in his autobiographical ethnographic narrative *Tristes Tropiques*, has discussed not only writing but his debt to Rousseau as well, a connection Derrida assesses in his critique of Levi-Strauss. When dealing with Rousseau, Derrida puts strong emphasis on the *Essay* as a statement about some of the dangers that inhere in writing: *"The Essay on the Origins of Language* opposes speech to writing as presence to absence and liberty to servitude."[21] The presence/absence dichotomy refers to the situation whereby writing gives uncertain access to the thought of the writer, who is not present to explain it. Therefore misconceptions and misunderstandings can result. This is a view that harks back to criticisms in Plato of writing as a representation of a representation. Yet Derrida is fully cognizant of the fact that Rousseau was well aware of the abuses that could arise in spoken language. In addition to the *Essay*, Derrida uses fragments from other Rousseau texts, particularly *Emile* and the autobiographical *Confessions*. He also employs psychoanalytic techniques to examine aspects of Rousseau's life that relate to his attitudes about writing. In cultivating this strategy Derrida's analysis is far from unique, as Rousseau perhaps more than any other major philosopher has had his personal life and idiosyncracies connected to his theoretical positions.

According to Derrida, Rousseau never published a finished theory of writing, often spoke negatively of it—for example, in *Emile* he refers to "the nonsense of writing"—, and yet presents an unyielding effort toward theory that uses writing and succumbs to it, with rare effectiveness. Near the end of *Of Grammatology*, he notes how "Rousseau condemns the evil of writing and looks for a haven within the writing."[22] This in itself indicates the very situation of writing within the history of Western metaphysics, where it is "a debased, lateralized, repressed, displaced theme, yet exercising a permanent and obsessive pressure from the place where it remains held in check."[23]

For Rousseau, and later for Marx with regard to technology, the progress of writing is seen as a natural evolution tied to increased social necessity. Yet in the case of Rousseau, as Derrida points out, this natural progress is a dangerous one, tied as it is to the unquestioned dominance of reason. Derrida insists that for Rousseau "progress as regression is the growth of reason in writing."[24] This view is certainly consistent with the major thrust of the *Essay*. If Derrida errs it is not on the issue of the directions he charts in Rousseau, but in the factors selected for emphasis. If writing is as important to the growth of reason and modernism in Rousseau as he suggests, why is it scarcely mentioned in the *Discourse on Inequality*, certainly the foundational work for Rousseau's critique of civilization? The answer perhaps is that Derrida might be overrating the role of writing in Rousseau's thought. However, in contrast to other Rousseau interpreters who have given it little or no consideration this is understandable and necessary. Writing is one element in a vaster configuration of social and technological factors that Rousseau saw as contributing to the establishment of civilization. Doubtless it is an important element. But it is also one that Rousseau himself was so intimately involved in doing, as well as understanding, that reflections on it recur in scattered fashion throughout several texts rather than there being one concerted effort at exorcism.

Many of the psychological, social, and political aspects of writing explored by Rousseau are utilized by Derrida in his own formulations, hence his extensive homage to the eighteenth-century master. Derrida performs a welcome service by examining further what Ong calls the "chirographic [writing] and typographic bias," which is "in the same territory that Marshall McLuhan swept through with his famous dictum 'The medium is the message'."[25] However, Derrida's major shortcoming is his failure to consider the nature of communication in oral societies, a necessary aspect of any comprehensive account of the effect of writing on Western thought. Yet Rousseau provides an opening for this undertaking as well by bequeathing an anthropological legacy that has been frequently cited by Levi-Strauss.[26]

Rousseau's writings on writing, as well as other subjects, are highly compelling, if not always plausible. One reason for their impact is the fact that he is one of the great prose stylists in the French language, and more than occasional glimpses of his energy survive translation. When reading Rousseau one feels his presence. He encourages the reader at one moment and admonishes him the next. In few other writers do personal feeling and inclination transform so directly into theoretical statement. Perhaps part of the sense of immediacy and intimacy in his work results from his understanding of the power of words as used in the oral tradition he favors. This may in fact account for some of his inconsistencies, since oral discourse contains numerous ambiguities and contradictions that become more apparent when it is replicated in written form.[27]

In emphasizing deep qualitative differences between various communicational modes, such as orality and literacy, Rousseau was far ahead of his time, so much so that it took nearly two hundred years for concerted examination of this problem to occur again.

Part II

The Nineteenth Century

4   *The Establishment of Linguistics and the History of Writing*

Here discussion will follow the major lines of extant scholarship, although some attention will be given at relevant points, to scripts other than the alphabet and to cultures other than just those of the West.
—Walter Ong

The nineteenth century is more difficult to characterize than the eighteenth. Its first several decades, as well as the latter part of the previous century, are sometimes referred to as the romantic rebellion. However, the conscious break with the past championed by the romantics was not as total as they, or subsequent interpreters believed. Several diagnostic traits of the romantic vision—love of the exotic, pantheism, individualism, idealism, emphasis on the emotions, and the critique of reason—grew out of Enlightenment sources such as the work of Vico, Rousseau, and Diderot; and as Jacques Barzun has noted, none of these traits can be found uniformly distributed among the romantics.[1] Even major figures in the history of social thought whose careers partly fit within the chronology of romanticism—Saint Simon, Comte, and Marx, for example—nevertheless were more influenced by the Enlightenment. Many of the problems they dealt with would come to dominate the inquiry about man and society from mid-century onward. The latter half of the nineteenth century was also accompanied by a reaffirmation of the Enlightenment belief that language is the expression of human activity, especially communication, and that the linguistic sign is arbitrary, a position developed out of disaffection with the belief held by some of the romantics that language has an independent natural existence.[2]

Although the romantics inherited the discipline of history from the Enlightenment, they rejected several of its central tenets, such as laws of inevitable progress and stages of socioeconomic development. Romantic historiography did not draw from, or aspire to science. It emphasized what we might today refer to as the cultural history of particular peoples, and opted for a meticulous research strategy that yielded impressive results.[3] Nevertheless, during the first half of the nineteenth century, the eighteenth-century concern with society, culture (writ large), and technology, did not vanish. It became a preoccupation of the rapidly burgeoning social evolutionary studies—precursors of the modern disciplines of sociology and anthropology—of Saint-Simon, Comte, and Marx at first, then ultimately Henry Maine (1822-1888), Lewis Morgan (1818-1881), Herbert Spencer (1820-1903), and Edward Tylor (1832-1917).

The nineteenth century also saw the rise of more specialized human science disciplines. As a result, the communications/history question, which during the Enlightenment was virtually predicated on a perspective that crosscut several fields of inquiry, became fragmented and distributed among at least three newly formed domains.

The first was comparative and historical philology, direct ancestor of the modern discipline of linguistics. It dealt with the nature of language, albeit in diverse ways, and considered the degree to which the ultimate purpose of language is either to foster thought or facilitate communication. Philology also touched on the characteristics and implications of various forms of written script. In fact the bulk of its analysis derived from written (often literary) texts, but since the goal was to understand the language behind the text, the unique properties of the text as medium were not often considered.

The second area was the study of writing as a field unto itself. Today this inquiry has been called "grammatology," following Gelb and later Derrida, and "alphabetology" by Diringer. In the nineteenth century no such label existed. The discipline emerged primarily in the second half of the century as an offshoot of philology, ancient history, archaeology, and anthropology. It was partly an attempt to make sense of a growing body of data on non-Western civilizations—especially in response to the numerous archaic scripts being unearthed and decoded, and partly the result of Darwinism, which gave new intellectual impetus to studying the origins of the most sacrosanct and seemingly eternal of civilized institutions.

A third broad area where discussions of the link between communications and history appeared was in Anglo-American social evolutionary thought and the German tradition of historically informed social theory. The examination of communications in the German tradition eventually helped give rise to the modern sociological study of mass communications, losing many of its original historical concerns in the transition. The legacy of social evolution, particularly through the work of Morgan and Tylor, provided foundations for a good deal of twentieth-century anthropology, either through direct influence, or because of the need to challenge and displace some fundamental social evolutionary assumptions.

ASPECTS OF LANGUAGE STUDY IN THE NINETEENTH CENTURY

Linguistics is a field where extraordinary theoretical efforts have been put forth, yet until recently serious study of the history of the discipline has been largely neglected. Over the past several decades journal articles and a separate journal devoted to the subject have appeared.[4] In addition, attempts to historically ground contemporary linguistic theory have been put forth by several linguists, perhaps the most eminent of them being Noam Chomsky, whose *Cartesian Linguistics* has spurred interest within linguistics in historical problems.[5] Chomsky's efforts, however, are not without controversy. They have been forcefully challenged by Aarsleff who offers some radically different interpretations.[6]

A number of linguists have put the date of the emergence of modern linguistics as 1786.[7] This is the year that Sir William Jones of the East India Company delivered a renowned paper to the Royal Asiatic Society in Calcutta in which he established kinship between Sanskrit—the classical language that once dominated the Indian subcontinent—and the Indo-European family of languages. This pronouncement had appeared in the work of earlier writers, just as prior to Darwin evolutionary hypotheses had been put forth. However Jones's work was based on more extensive research and solid interpretation than the claims of his predecessors. In addition these years represent the beginnings of romanticism and the accompanying interest on the part of European scholars in Indian and Near Eastern studies, no doubt as an adjunct of the imperialist quest for exotica along with basic resources such as cotton. Several decades later Napoleon would become a major supporter of Near Eastern archaeological research.

The extensive studies of Sanskrit by Europeans defined the first stage in the emergence of comparative and historical philology as a distinct field, and marked the emergence of a tradition in Indian linguistics that has continued to the present.[8] The main emphasis of these early studies was on comparative grammar as a key to historical connectedness. Comparative grammar—the study of the internal structure of language—later figured significantly in the work of three of the most renowned linguistic scholars of the first half of the nineteenth century: Wilhelm von Humboldt (1767-1835), whose younger brother Alexander achieved notoriety as an explorer and geographer; Jacob Grimm (1785-1863); and Franz Bopp (1791-1867). Their research often countered the Enlightenment tendency to regard language as primarily a vehicle of communication, by viewing its role as one preeminently responsible for thought. Language was held to be a naturally empowered organ synonymous with the thinking process, and whatever characteristics it possessed as an agent for the exchange of knowledge were seen as secondary to this primary purpose. As a result, their historical studies challenged Enlightenment historiography, and rejected the view of universal stages where linguistic features could be viewed in the same light as social or technological phenomena. Instead, emphasis was placed on the particular history and character of a group or culture, and the growth and structure of its language was seen as the foundation of its thought or world view.

During the second half of the century the study of comparative and historical philology, the increase in anthropological accounts of non-Western linguistic communities, and the work of Darwin as well as other discoveries in biology and archaeology, compelled reassessment of the place of language study among the pantheon of sciences. In the English speaking world the two figures most exemplifying this tendency were Max Muller (1823-1900) in England, and William Dwight Whitney (1827-1894) in the United States. Both engaged in a reexamination of basic eighteenth-century notions regarding the nature of language, communication, and history, and both were German trained, although this was no assurance that they would arrive at parallel views.

MAX MULLER

Although Muller built on the tradition of comparative and historical philology that developed in the first half of the nineteenth century, he wanted that field, and his work within it, to be more than just an adjunct of classical scholarship. He claimed a place for language study among the physical sciences and sought to establish the parameters and assumptions that should define it as a discipline. In the *Science of Language* (1863), a work that established him as a leading authority on the subject and provided a basis for his subsequent writings, he argues that language is not a work of human artifice such as "painting, or building, or writing, or printing . . ."[9] He notes that if this were the case then language study would have to be grouped with the historical and moral rather than physical sciences. Although he does concede that language exhibits development through time, this is not held to be a historical change akin to what takes place in the arts and sciences, but an organic growth in which linguistic change cannot be consciously produced, prevented, or altered. In this respect he shares the romantic vision of language as part of the generic endowment of the human species. This is in opposition to the Enlightenment attitude whereby it was held to be the most preeminent of human inventions—though not necessarily one that the inventors were completely conscious of producing.

As might be expected, Muller felt compelled to address certain Enlightenment presuppositions in order to establish his view. He criticizes the eighteenth-century position regarding language as an arbitrary agreement that certain sounds would become words after the limits of gesture and expression were reached. Not only does he argue that language is generic to mankind and essential to reasoning, he contends that it is the Rubicon between human beings and animals. Following Locke he observes that the brutes cannot form abstract ideas and therefore do not have reason, though they do possess sensation, will, memory, and intellect.[10] Monboddo is also cited. Though Muller regards much of his Scottish precursor's linguistic work as shallow speculation, he does credit him with recognizing the importance of Sanskrit, and he cites Monboddo's observations on the beaver in support of his own view that no other animal has language. This is a somewhat dubious citation since Monboddo's beavers, although they do not speak, have rudimentary reasoning and nonverbal communication modes similar to the scenario of early human society, a situation which he regarded as a direct precursor of what would later become conventional spoken language.

Muller also notes that instinct and intellect are not mutually exclusive in either man or other animals. This would seem to bring him close to Darwin. Yet he insists that language is uniquely human in a qualitative sense and incapable of arising through natural selection operating on the "cries of beasts and songs of birds."[11] Muller argues that if he can establish that language is uniquely human then Darwin ought to accept the conclusion that man cannot have descended from any other animal: "Language is a property of man of which no trace has ever been found in any other animal."[12] Darwin also regarded language as uniquely human and he discusses it in his *Descent of Man* (1871), but the uniqueness is viewed in terms of degree in that human language is said to have precursors in the gestural and expressive communication systems of other animals. Interestingly, rather than engaging in a debate with Muller, Darwin used some of the former's linguistic ideas for his own ends, such as Muller's observation that a struggle for existence goes on among the grammatical forms and words in each language as better forms and pronunciations eventually gain prominence.[13] In any case, Muller mistakenly believed that natural selection implied a purposeful agent, and he declined to express any opinion on the origin of things by citing the Buddhist prohibition against such speculations. The seemingly evolutionary notons that can be found in his work in historical linguistics do not derive from Darwin, but rather from Kant, Herder, and Goethe.

Throughout his writings Muller's position is predicated on the belief that language and thought are inseparable and that the former was/is the necessary precondition of the latter: "Thinking is nothing but speaking *minus* words."[14] For Muller we do not begin with thinking and then proceed to speaking. We begin with naming, and through various auxilliary processes arrive at what we call thought. He attempts to substantiate his position by noting how writing is impossible without speech, shorthand without writing, and our alphabet is unthinkable without its hieroglyphic precursors. In contrast to the Enlightenment view of Condillac, for example, which regards thought as born out of the interplay of the senses and the development of rudimentary prelinguistic signs, Muller sees language and thought as an irreducible organic whole, a position that represents one aspect of the romantic reaction to the analytical vision of the eighteenth century.

In the *Science of Thought* (1887), Muller again cites Locke, along with Hume and Condillac—this time for purposes of criticism. Although he praises the Lockean notion that language may be the route to understanding the nature of thought, and that words are not the signs of things but of concepts, he notes how Locke's stance derives from an attitude whereby words can be chosen to represent ideas, which admits of the possibility of thought without language. As a result Muller disagrees with the Enlightenment notion that language was invented for social intercourse: "The formation of thought is the first and natural purpose of language, while its communication is accidental."[15] This position is bolstered by referencing Hobbes's observation that language came into being for ourselves first and only secondarily for others. Words, Muller contends, are never arbitrarily agreed-on conventions but "reasonable" and "intelligible" signs for concepts. However, he does not go into an examination of how this situation came about.

Although the bulk of Muller's work is devoted to a classificatory scheme for languages, comparative grammar, verb forms, roots, and families, he does not discount completely the communicative function of language and its extensions. There was, he argues, literature before letters. In early societies an oral tradition served to hand down religious, legal, and poetic documents. This became augmented through the emergence of various mnemonic devices such as wampum shells and tally sticks. A considerable mnemonically assisted oral literature existed in, for example, India before writing. The narratives possessed a metrical structure that facilitated memorization. The transition to writing, both in India and elsewhere, was a dramatic occurrence that effected wholesale changes in the societies in question. Muller observes that nowhere when this occurred, even in Greece, was suitable wonderment and reflection expressed over this transition. He compares the development of writing to printing, and while the latter is deemed to have major repercussions, the former remains the more historically impressive achievement:

> The invention of printing is after all, a purely mechanical improvement, which any woodcarver might have made without much effort or ingenuity. Its effects, however were colossal, and such words as printing, imprinting, publishing, edition & c., soon found their way into the dictionaries of every language. The invention of the alphabet and its application to the preserving and spreading of literary compositions, required a much greater expenditure of ingenuity, and must have caused an immense revolution in the intellectual constitution of the trading nations of the world, and yet we meet almost nowhere any expression of "wonderment and admiration."[16]

According to Muller the importance of the development of early writing did not hinge on its use for literary purposes, but rather resulted from its application to political and commercial transactions. In this view, as well as in giving the edge to writing over print as the historical-technological innovation with greater ramifications, he anticipates a position taken by Innis in the middle of this century. But Muller remained a linguist and his forays into history were brief. Nevertheless, despite the fact that he took a stance whereby the foundations of language were regarded as grounded in thought, not communication—as for example, Chomsky has done in our time—he did give us several perceptive observations on its communicative role.

WILLIAM DWIGHT WHITNEY

An interesting contrast to the work of Muller can be found in the writings of William Dwight Whitney, who had an eminence in the field of language study in the United States which paralleled that of Muller in Europe. Like Muller, Whitney was compelled to address aspects of the Enlightenment view of language that predated the German tradition of comparative and historical philology to which he was an heir.[17] However, unlike Muller, Whitney was in positive accord with several dominant Enlightenment assumptions and was part of the favorable reassessment of Enlightenment views that took place in several human science disciplines during the second half of the nineteenth century.

In his classic work, *Language and the Study of Language* (1867), Whitney notes that "words are not exact models of ideas; they are merely the signs for ideas..."[18]; and "language is made up of signs for thought...."[19] Although he is in accord with Muller in regarding language as "instinctive" and "natural," an organized body that no one has planned, there are parts of it that are "conscious" and "intentional." This results from the fact that, in contrast to the view of Muller and the romantic tradition, for Whitney language "is brought forth for the practical end of convenient communication."[20] However, this view is not totally absent from either the first half of the nineteenth century or German thought. It was forcefully championed by Marx and Engels in their *German Ideology* (1845-1846).

Whitney was more cautious than Muller when connecting stages of social-historical development with linguistic features. He critiqued the latter's effort to correlate patriarchal or family society with monosyllabic languages, nomadic tribes having an unsettled life with agglutinative languages, and political or state societies having a regulated and constant tradition with inflective languages. This ingenious scheme, he argues, does not conform to linguistic history. For example, to argue that the Chinese empire, with its monosyllabic speech, is an exaggerated family is an overstatement.[21] However, Whitney apparently failed to perceive the significance of such typological efforts for the history of communications. Even if the posited correlations can be challenged, this does not preclude more rigorous study yielding improved results.

Unlike Muller, Whitney does not dismiss the question of language origins. But he does qualify its use as a research tool. The first utterances, he contends, are not apt subjects for historical study, which can at best only yield the roots of words. The issue of origins therefore falls not within the historical science of language study, but is more appropriate as an aspect of linguistic philosophy as it relates to anthropology. Nevertheless he ventures several observations on the subject.

Like Condillac, his illustrious Enlightenment precursor, Whitney holds that although creation may have been divine, language came about through human instrumentality, as "a body of conventional signs, deriving their understanding from the mutual understanding of one man with another. . . ."[22] Man is regarded as coming into the world with the organic equipment for speech and the potential to use it, but what happened historically was a result of communal activity. Speech developed out of the need to communicate as an adjunct of social needs and instincts. Words are not mental acts innately grounded, but acoustic conventions. Ultimately speech is "arbitrary" and "conventional" because thought "is anterior to language and independent of it. . . ."[23] This eighteenth-century notion was picked up by others around the turn of the century, most notably Saussure (who cites Whitney) and it is partly through his linguistic and semiological work that eighteenth-century views regarding the nature of word and sign have entered twentieth-century linguistic and structuralist studies.

Given Whitney's belief in the arbitrary nature of the linguistic sign, and his position regarding the priority of thought over word, it is not surprising that he views writing as a natural counterpart and extension of speech, growing out of man's capacity and wants as a social and "indefinitely perfectable being."[24] Again, in the tradition of Enlightenment writers such as Condillac, writing is seen by Whitney as a slow, laborious development resulting from the desire to communicate at a distance, and through time, with future generations. Its beginnings are located in the objects brought by heralds to symbolize what was transpiring, an observation that is also made by Rousseau in his *Essay on the Origin of Languages.* Whitney considers the greatest prewriting elaboration of this mode of communication to be the quipus, the knotted cords of different lengths, colors, and thickness that the Incas used to organize information necessary for the maintenance of their state.[25] He also discusses picture writing, which is held to be analogous to onomatopeia in language, and he considers its development in both Egypt and Mexico. The origins of the Greek alphabet are also assessed. However, around the third quarter of the nineteenth century the growing mass of archaeological and historical data necessitated a more comprehensive coverage of the history of writing than was possible within the linguistic purview of writers such as Whitney and Muller. A separate field of study became necessary.

WRITING THE HISTORY OF WRITING

Several scholars devoted themselves to this new field of study. In England, Isaac Taylor (1829-1901) was probably the most significant and influential among them. His book, the *Alphabet* (1883; 2 vols.), remains a landmark compilation. In France studies such as M. Philippe Berger's (1848-1912) *Histoire de l'écriture dans l'antiquité* (*History of Writing in Antiquity*, 1891) laid the foundations for later work on the subject in that country. But Berger, and almost all later contributors, nonetheless owed a debt to Taylor that most of them willingly acknowledged.

Studies of the history of writing such as Taylor's grew out of two traditions that established themselves in the first half of the nineteenth century, and expanded and diversified in the second half. The first is comparative and historical philology, which led to various branches of linguistic inquiry; the second is the archaeological tradition that emerged out of classical scholarship. These two situations were in turn influenced by the widespread interest in origins and development that Darwinism bequeathed to the latter nineteenth century. The research that resulted helped establish the sequential stages of, and cultural links between, various civilizations. This included their modes of communication. However, explaining the complex interplay between communications and the historical development of knowledge—a subject of concern to more recent scholars—became subordinate to mapping chronologies of development based on as much data about writing systems as could suitably be gathered, arranged, and interpreted. This tradition of rigorous empirical chronicling in the history of written scripts has continued into the twentieth century, right up to the present day. Writers such as Edward Clodd, William Mason, Ignace Gelb, Hans Jensen, and David Diringer, to name only the most prominent, have added considerably to our knowledge of the details, connections between, and history of the scripts of the world.

Taylor's work, as the title of his book suggests, deals primarily with the alphabet. He does not seem to have the high regard for nonalphabetic scripts that would typify later writers. His lack of interest, for example, in the writing systems of Central America, which he regarded as being too obscure and little known to be more than literary curiosities, unsuitable for serious reconstruction of the early stages in the development of writing, was pointedly critiqued by Clodd.[26]

The genealogy of the alphabet is traced by Taylor through Egyptian, Semitic, and Greek traditions. Written scripts are divided into two broad categories, ideograms and phonograms. Ideograms include pictures of objects (which we would today designate as pictograms), pictoral symbols suggesting ideas, and conventional signs representing concepts. Phonograms include verbal signs for words, syllabic signs, and alphabetic letters. Techniques involved in the production of all these signs are discussed, and although Edward Tylor's work is cited, there is no attempt, such as we find in Tylor, to link specific forms of written script to the character of knowledge in a given epoch.

Although influenced by classical scholarship, Taylor diverged from one of its tenets by refusing to regard the problem of origins as insoluble. Unlike, for example, Muller, Taylor subscribed to the Darwinian theory and Leibniz's famous dictum *natura non facit saltum* (nature makes no leaps). Slow differentiation through minute variations was held to be a law of nature, and one governing the history of writing, particularly the alphabet. Taylor also refers to what he calls the "law of correlated variation," whereby any change within a system brings about other changes.[27] This is remarkably similar to Darwin's law of the "correlation of growth," but Darwin is not cited in this instance, nor is Edward Tylor, whose view that writing systems evolve according to general laws must have also influenced Taylor—though some of Tylor's examples are mentioned in other parts of the text. Taylor goes on to show how the development of the alphabet was influenced by trade routes, colonization, and religion, without saying much about the reciprocal effects, which have been of interest to more recent historians of the subject. In a brief and suggestive passage he does mention that writing and its impact were influenced by what we might today refer to as media elements, such as aspects of parchment, paper, the quality of ink, and the nature of writing implements. But this line of inquiry is not developed as Taylor remains content to chronicle rather than theorize.

During the time when various studies of the history of writing such as Taylor's were being undertaken, numerous studies of the history of printing were compiled. Few were done in English and most are detailed compilations of events and discoveries, often biased toward the nation of the researcher. At least one comprehensive account worth discussing appeared. In 1867 H. Noel Humphreys (1810-1879) published *A History of the Art of Printing*, which considered the history of printing within a broad communications context that also included the nature of the oral tradition, or "the tradition of memory" as he refers to it, and the development of the alphabet and its precursors.

Humphreys argues that the first written inscriptions were carved on durable materials such as stone, but as knowledge of writing became more widespread it became necessary to develop more portable written documents—an anticipation of Innis's hypothesis that light, space-biased media emerged in response to the need for administration over distance. Papyrus came into use in Egypt and was widely employed in the Roman Empire. He goes on to show how in China not only paper, but block printing was developed. The latter, brought to Europe by Marco Polo (a view that contemporary historians might contest), did not gain wide use until the early fifteenth century, and Humphreys offers several interesting observations on the survival of block books after the advent of print.

Moveable type printing is held by Humphreys to be the most important of all human inventions, a prejudice resulting no doubt from his choice of subject matter. In contrast, at the turn of the century when Clodd wrote about the history of writing, he cited Carlyle, who remarked that printing was a "simple and comparatively insignificant corollary" of writing, the true bringer of miracles.[28]

The printing press is regarded by Humphreys as being the result of gradual development coupled with sudden innovation. It is seen as an inevitable consequence of the progress of civilization and knowledge, rather than the work of singular genius. He thus carried the Enlightenment vision of Turgot and Condorcet into the nineteenth-century realm of increasing concern with data and detail. Koster, rather than Gutenberg, is held to be the inventor of printing, but circumstances and a concise history of the time take precedence over personalities. The sequence of the establishment of printing in other European centers is carefully noted, and Humphrey's profusely illustrated text also gives a vivid sense of the stylistic changes that occurred in both typography and prints. There is also commentary on the change in character of the books published, but the analysis remains specific and is not connected to vaster unconscious shifts in the organization of knowledge. For example, when Luther is discussed with respect to his utilization of printed materials, it is within the context of a specific political history rather than as a consequence of the general technological evolution of communications. It would remain the task of the social evolutionists to elaborate technological criteria into a series of sequential stages.

5   *Social Evolution and Social Theory*

> We are dealing with the technology of communicative acts, a study which enables us to make a bridge between various branches of knowledge interested in the science of society, in its cultural products, and in the instruments of cultural production that it has at its command.
> —Jack Goody

The univeral history of the Enlightenment, which fell into such disfavor in the early nineteenth century, enjoyed a rebirth shortly after mid-century. A new field, known as social evolution, inherited this Enlightenment legacy. Despite the label *evolution* and the fact that this inquiry rose to prominence following the contributions of Charles Darwin (1812-1882), Darwinism was not the direct cause of this development. Although a number of twentieth-century commentators have tried to make a direct link between Darwin and social evolutionary theory, most recent studies have emphasized that the case is rather one of parallelism.[1] New field work in anthropology and archaeology, more detailed studies of the early history of civilization, and the erosion of traditional religious beliefs, which were all occuring prior to Darwin, contributed to the establishment of social evolution. The Enlightenment concept of progress as a measure of historical development was reapplied using more detailed criteria. As a result, the eighteenth-century model of historical sequence, based on stages such as savagery, barbarism, and civilization, or hunting, pastoralism, agriculture, and commerce, became further subdivided and revised in response to new data.

What was less readily appropriated from the Enlightenment by the social evolutionists was the notion of the good or noble savage. Human nature was not regarded as being the same everywhere, although Tylor's position can be seen as an exception. However, rather than being strident racists most social evolutionists took a somewhat paternalistic attitude. They regarded the darker skinned peoples as representative of early stages in the development of humanity, therefore fully human and potentially capable of civilization. Although in a broad intellectual-historical sense the social evolutionists can be seen as apologists for civilization and progress, their attitude toward non-Western peoples often entailed considerable respect. The seemingly bizarre behavior of primitives was often held to be logical in terms of the circumstances to which these peoples had adapted. Also, most of the social evolutionists overtly criticized the genocide of aboriginal peoples, the plunder of their lands, and wholesale interference with their way of life, an edict nineteenth-century imperialism often disregarded.

The three key figures in the pantheon of nineteenth-century social evolutionists are, according to Burrow, Maine, Spencer, and Tylor.[2] This group can be easily enlarged to five if we include Marx and Morgan, whose contributions in this area have been at least as, if not more influential, than those of the first three, especially since both include brief but suggestive thoughts on communications. Of the first three, Tylor shows extensive interest in the communications/history question within the context of non-Western civilizations; Spencer's primary concern is with social organization; and Maine concentrates on the history of institutions allied to law and custom.

During the period when social evolutionary formulations were the hallmark of social thought in England and the United States, a tradition of social inquiry that gave significant consideration to communications was developing in Germany. It derived from previous political and philosophical thought and a consideration of the changes brought about through industrialization. Communications, especially the press, was seen as crucial in the formation of public attitudes and the maintenance of society. It is in large measure this tradition that Hanno Hardt is referencing when he notes that the "history of communication and mass communication theory in the United States emerges as a chapter in the history of philosophical, social, and political thought in Europe and North America during the last hundred years."[3]

This German tradition directly influenced North American interest in the role of mass communications and journalism, particularly as evidenced in the work of Robert Ezra Park (1864-1944). Today the sociology of mass communications is less historical than its antecedent perspectives of a hundred years ago, partly as a result of the division of labor between sociology and history outlined by Park. Also, both then and now, concern has been directed primarily toward basic information—the way it is gathered, distributed, and aligned with commercial interests and technological biases. Knowledge writ large, the way a civilization comes to interpret and understand the world, has not been a primary focus. When this subject was broached by the sociology of knowledge early in this century it was done so without serious consideration of the role of communications technology.

It should be noted that at mid-century Harold Innis was at the University of Chicago at the same time as Park; he was influenced by him and therefore indirectly by the German tradition of social theory of the latter nineteenth century. Innis attempted to relate both the character of knowledge in a given epoch and the basic information necessary for societal maintenance to a historical vision that emphasized reciprocity between prevailing institutions and the dominant medium of communications.

KARL MARX

In considering Marx as a social evolutionist who dealt with communications we should not overlook the fact that he is perhaps the most monumental and controversial figure in the history of social thought. Today perspectives influenced by the work of Karl Marx are used extensively in both the study of mass communications and, to a lesser extent, the history of communications. Indeed, some would argue that a book such as this should devote at least an entire chapter to assessing his contribution. Although Marx is influential to contemporary communications studies, the influence does not derive from what he said about communications per se, but from his materialist perspective on history, analysis of capitalism, and concept of ideology as they relate to media studies. His discussion of specific communications media and their role in historical change is minimal, but it is significant and worth considering. Hardt also appears to be of this persuasion when he stresses that for Marx the study of history must include language, public opinion, and the press.[4] Therefore it is somewhat inaccurate to contend, as McLuhan has, that Marx missed communications entirely.

Although by the time he died in 1883, Marx's work was known and revered in socialist circles around the world, his theoretical contributions, particularly his view of history in terms of the evolution of economic and social processes, were virtually unacknowledged by the British intellectual milieu that surrounded him after 1849 and developed so extensively the social evolutionary perspective.

The first work in which Marx and Frederick Engels (1820-1895) outlined their materialist perspective on history is the *German Ideology* (1845-1846).[5] In this text they view historical change as beginning with the way men procure their means of subsistence through real life processes, constrained by material limitations. History is held to be underwritten by laws of economic development deriving from the mode of production and subject to scientific scrutiny, which have given rise to tribal societies, ancient civilizations, feudalism, and the modern bourgeois state. Nevertheless it must be noted that these laws of historical development are not fixed laws as in the case of physics, but laws subject to alteration given changes in the circumstances through which societies develop. This is an aspect of Marx frequently misunderstood by both critics and supporters.[6] Marx's view of historical development, or "evolution" as he called it, even prior to Darwin, foreshadowed discussions that would take place on a less economic but more social and cultural level, by social evolutionists such as Morgan and Tylor. And despite the important and oft cited influence on his work of Hegel, Feuerbach, and classical political economy, Marx's understanding of history owed a considerable debt to the philosophical vision of both the French and Scottish Enlightenment, especially to Rousseau.

Communications are not central to Marx's historical studies, but they do constitute an essential matrix for the social relations that arise in response to productive activity in any epoch. His view of language is illuminating in this respect. In the *German Ideology* he follows an Enlightenment tradition by referring to language as "practical consciousness that exists also for other men . . ." and claims that it is as old as consciousness itself, having arisen from "the need, the necessity, of intercourse with other men."[7] Several years later in an important series of notebooks for his major project *Capital*, known as the *Grundrisse* (1857-1858), he again addresses the question of language. It is declared not to be the result of individual creation. Rather, its origins are said to reside in the context of community, where it is both the "product" and the "presence."[8] In other words, for Marx language is the essential communicative bridge between the thoughts and feelings of individual human beings and social necessity. While the content of linguistic communication is historically derived, the capacity of human beings to interact in this way is generically given, an aspect of human nature. The various forms of linguistic usage that arise from social needs, and consequent human interaction, are important to understand because as an aspect of ideology—the values and attitudes that particular interest groups, especially classes, conceive to legitimate their situation—they act back on their producers helping them create an identity and definition of themselves and others.[9]

But what does Marx say about communications other than spoken language? Recent work by Canadian political economist Ian Parker is interesting and provocative in this respect, though not entirely convincing.[10] Parker has compared Marx to Innis on economics and communications. The case he makes for parallels between them regarding their alleged "dialectical materialist," "ecological," and "systemic" approaches is not nearly as persuasive as his contention that there is a complementary relationship in several of their general concerns.

Parker concentrates primarily on Marx's major work, *Capital*, the first volume of which was published in 1867, the remaining three posthumously. He argues that there are at least five ways in which Marx incorporated communication related topics into his analysis of the way a historically produced economic system, such as capitalism, is maintained. The first is consideration of the transportation through time, and between spatially separate centers, of material goods or commodities. The second is a special case of the first and includes "translation" through time of material goods or commodities without change in location such as "storage activity" and "inventory management"; the third entails transportation of persons between various centers including such things as immigration and military involvement; the fourth deals with the movement of property claims to real resources and considers "monetary transfers" and "capital flow"; the fifth is the transmission of information through space and time, which takes into account education, science, ideology, and technological and cultural change.[11] It is argued that Marx's interest in these topics, coupled with Innis's development of the history of communications as a field of inquiry, can allow such concerns to be understood to a much greater degree than would be possible using neoclassical economic theory.

Marx's interest in communications is clearly apparent in his observation, in volume 1 of *Capital*, that in certain independent branches of industry, "the product of the productive process is not a new material product, it is not a commodity. Among these only the communications industry, whether engaged in transportation, proper, of goods and passengers, or in the mere transmission of communications, letters, telegrams, etc., is economically important."[12] Parker contends that Marx recognized communications as both an independent branch of production and a process in the sphere of circulation. The latter is in evidence both in the "semiotic" analysis of money in volume 1 of *Capital* and the circulation of men and goods considered in volume 2. This is clearly foreshadowed in Marx's early writings, such as the *Economic and Philosophical Manuscript of 1844*, where he discusses the importance of exchange in the social process; and money is dealt with in this context in *A Contribution to the Critique of Political Economy* (1859), a text Parker does not cite.

Despite the discussion of communications in Marx, his direct consideration of it is not as important as are his observations in the general sphere of economic and social analysis. Today we can apply them to a wide range of communications concerns that did not appear significant in the nineteenth century—for example, consideration of the role of advertising in the creation of commodities and associated needs, a field recently explored by Leiss, Kline, and Jhally.[13]

LEWIS MORGAN

Lewis Henry Morgan is considered to be one of the founders of American anthropology. He was a lawyer by profession but devoted much of his time to being an ethnographer and protector of the Iroquois, and scholar of the growing nineteenth-century literature on non-Western and primitive societies. Less well known is his work as a naturalist. His research on the beaver is a pioneering effort in the naturalistic study of animal behavior and was favorably cited by Darwin.[14] Morgan's anthropological studies, particularly his landmark book *Ancient Society* (1877), was enthusiastically received by Marx who made extensive commentaries on it. Morgan's work also provided a basis for Engels's important social evolutionary study *The Origin of the Family Private Property and the State* (1884).[15]

Ancient Society is an extensive treatise on social evolution, focussing on the problem of kinship, kinship terminology, and social organization in general. The classic Enlightenment categories of savagery, barbarism, and civilization are reassessed and further subdivided using extensive new material. Much of this material derives from studies of the American Indian, perhaps partly as a response to traditional histories of civilization, which gave Amerindian peoples only slight consideration. Although the book is primarily an account of the social stages of human development from earliest times to Greece and Rome, Morgan applies some overarching technological and conceptual criteria that, consciously or not, demonstrate indebtedness to the Enlightenment tradition of Turgot and Condorcet.

Social evolution in Morgan's scheme is fostered by two lines of development: one materialist the other ideational. The materialist includes inventions, discoveries, and institutions; the ideational, ideas relating to subsistence, government, language, the family, home life, architecture, and property. Morgan was appreciated as a materialist by Marx and Engels and is still regarded as such in certain quarters due to his observations such as the one dealing with the division of humanity into stages of growth or "ethnical periods": "the successive arts of subsistence which arose at long intervals will ultimately, from the great influence they must have exercised upon the condition of mankind, afford the most satisfactory basis for these divisions."[16] However, a case can also be made for Morgan placing strong emphasis on certain ideas, such as the "idea of property," as the primary agent for historical change. There is clearly ambivalence in his historiography.[17]

The ethnical periods Morgan outlines consist of lower, middle, and upper stages of both slavery and barbarism, and the beginnings of civilization. Although both the forms of the family and subsistence techniques are considered, the criteria used for delineating these stages have sometimes been criticized for being singular. For example, each stage culminates with achievements that demarcate transition to the next: lower savagery ends with fishing and fire; middle savagery with the bow and arrow; upper savagery terminates with pottery; similarly, lower barbarism ends with domestication of animals and cultivation through irrigation; middle barbarism yields iron; and upper barbarism develops writing using the phonetic alphabet, a trait that goes on to become the hallmark of civilization. Problems resulting from the use of such criteria have been readily pointed out by later commentators, especially Morgan's placement of the Hawaiians into lower savagery owing to the absence of the bow and arrow and because of their kinship terminology, which used the same term for father and all of his male siblings, and mother and all of her female siblings—this in spite of the fact that they had a complex kingdom verging on a state.

In Morgan's scheme the Homeric Greeks are located in upper barbarism; civilization is said to have commenced in Greece with the development of the phonetic alphabet and the keeping of written records. Little or nothing is said pertaining to the Mesopotamian or Chinese empires. The Aztecs, who had ideographic writing, are relegated to middle barbarism on the basis of their use of native metals, cultivation by irrigation, and absence of iron and money. Modern civilization, although not Morgan's primary concern, is characterized by its principal contributions, which include the "telegraph; coal gas; the spinning-jenny; and the power loom; the steam-engine with its numerous dependent machines, including the locomotive, the railway, and steam-ship; the telescope; the discovery of the ponderability of the atmosphere and solar system; the art of printing; the canal lock; the mariner's compass; and gunpowder."[18] These are criteria that would, in the next century, be scrupulously reexamined, and their long-term effects carefully assessed, through the work of Lewis Mumford.

Although less priority is given by Morgan to communications factors in the evolution of society than is the case, for example, in the work of his eighteenth-century predecessors Turgot and Condorcet, it nonetheless receives consideration: "The use of writing, or its equivalent in hieroglyphics upon stone, affords a fair test of the commencement of civilization. Without literary records neither history nor civilization can properly be said to exist."[19] Morgan observes that civilization is cumulative, adding to and building on what barbarism developed—in fact, upper barbarism had almost all the essential elements of civilization. Although little is said about the Egyptians, Morgan believed that the latter stages of their hieroglyphic script produced phonetic characters, which in turn were transformed into a rudimentary alphabet by the Phoenicians. Nevertheless, he still regarded the Greeks as the first truly civilized people.

According to Morgan, just as civilization stands as a cumulative advance over what went before, rather than being separated from other social forms by a qualitative gap or discontinuity, so its dominant form of communications, the phonetic alphabet, has a long, continuous development. He charts a series of communicational stages:

1. Gesture language, or the language of personal symbols;
2. Picture writing, or ideographic symbols;
3. Hieroglyphics, or conventional symbols;
4. Hieroglyphics of phonetic power, or phonetic symbols used in a syllabus;
5. A phonetic alphabet, or written sounds.[20]

He perceptively notes that native Americans developed the first three, and were proceeding in the direction of an alphabet prior to contact, a view that coincides with some contemporary opinions regarding meso-American scripts. However, except for consideration of the role of the alphabet and written records in the establishment of civilization, there is little attempt to connect modes of communication to the character of ethnical periods. A more thorough effort in this direction was provided by Morgan's English contemporary and sometimes rival for the title "father of anthropology," Edward Tylor.

SOCIAL THOUGHT AND COMMUNICATIONS IN GERMANY

A number of German social theorists in the nineteenth century broached the communications/history question. They were not part of the legacy of social evolution we have been examining, but had roots in an indigenously Teutonic tradition of historical research and political thought. Their contributions played a significant role in the formation of early American sociology, particularly as it concerned itself with the study of mass communications. One of the most eminent of the American sociologists influenced by this group was Robert Park. Until recently there has been considerable neglect of these German theorists and their work. But thanks in large measure to Hanno Hardt's *Social Theories of the Press* (1979), we have the beginnings of a communications focussed appraisal of these writers, and much of the following assessment is indebted to Hardt, especially when the particular work being discussed is not available in English translation.

One of the most sociological of this German circle was William Schaffle (1831-1903). His work contributed to the organismic theory of society, a concept better known through the contributions of Spencer, Durkheim, and the functionalist tradition in twentieth-century sociology and anthropology. Schaffle spent part of his early life as a journalist and in 1860 he became a professor of political economy at Tubingen. A decade later he retired to private life and in 1875 published *Bau und Leben des Socialen Korpers* (literally translated as *Construction and Life in the Social Body*). In this work he made some comparisons between communications and the nervous system. He advocated studying the communication of ideas by examining the process of production of symbols and their means of external transmission through appropriate institutions. He categorized symbols into two domains: the personal, which includes sounds, words, gestures, and facial expressions, and the material, those pertaining to what we would today refer to as media, such as writing, printing, pictures, and monuments.

Although grandiose historical considerations were not Schaffle's main concern, he did point out how cultural and economic progress were tied to the alphabet, mathematics, and improved methods of reckoning time. As Hardt notes, Schaffle "treats communication as a necessary condition for the development of civilization and progress of mankind."[21] This includes concern with issues pertaining to public opinion and the press, topics that would be more fully elaborated by his successors. Nevertheless, Schaffle's work, although it has historical implications, is clearly in the sociological vein of functionalist theory. His view of society as an organism, and interest in the role of language and communications, made a significant impression on one of the founders of American sociology, Albion Small (1854-1926), who in fact had early contacts with Schaffle.

Also adhering to an organismic model of society, but more historical in his interests than Schaffle, was Karl Knies (1821-1898), a major figure in the nineteenth-century German tradition of historical and economic thought. Knies had a diverse teaching career that culminated in 1865 when he received a professorship in political economy at Heidelberg. Like other German social theorists at this time his work was partly a response to changes brought about by nineteenth-century industrialism. It deals with the railroad and telegraph and treats the press as a means of transporting information over time and space. Communications for Knies was that which breaks down the isolation of individuals, and according to him not only did it include "the celebrated inventions of the alphabet, printing, etc., but nearly everything that coincides with the history of man as a social being."[22]

In arguing that social communication results from man's need to seek contact and exchange with others, and taking a position whereby everything from face-to-face interpersonal exchange to the advent of the press and telegraph fits into this conception, Knies is heir to an Enlightenment vision of human interaction. However, in the Enlightenment view communications were looked at with respect to their role in imparting knowledge—a way of interpreting and understanding the world—to particular societies, as well as conveying basic information. Knies's work is mainly concerned with the informational aspect of media, particularly as it relates to volume and speed of exchange. He deals with the history of news as it was linked to transportation systems, such as the mail, railway, and telegraph. As Hardt notes, for Knies "the history of communication culminates in the development of occupational roles and institutional activities solely dedicated to the collection and dissemination of information."[23]

Knies places emphasis on the way communications change social relations directly, rather than through long-term, culturally mediated shifts in knowledge or cognition. Thus, factors such as changing literacy rates receive greater consideration than, for example, the nature of what was read. The role of the press is assessed, particularly as it relates to the impact of news and the creation of information needs whereby news becomes a commodity and the imparting of commercial messages. Ultimately for Knies communications media develop along with increasing social complexity as a kind of nervous system conducting information throughout the social organism. This process is partly explicable as a result of man's internal psychological need to communicate with individuals who are physically separated.

The communications concerns elaborated by both Schaffle and Knies were further developed by Karl Bucher (1847-1930). His background was in history, political science, and philology, and with the support of Schaffle he was able to secure an academic career. Bucher's major work, *Industrial Evolution*, was first given as a series of lectures in 1893 and within a decade was available in English translation. His concern was with the economic history of Western society as viewed through the development of manufacturing, transportation, and communication. Newspapers and journalism were seen as a crucial conduit between segments of modern society: "In fact, the newspaper forms a link in the chair of modern commercial machinery; it is one of those contrivances by which in society the exchange of intellectual and material goods is facilitated."[24] The importance of Bucher's work was recognized by Robert Park and Ernest Burgess who, in putting together their monumental introductory text in sociology, *Introduction to the Science of Sociology* (1921), included an entry by Bucher titled "The Extension of Communication by Human Invention."

Although a major concern of *Industrial Evolution* is with stages of economic development relating to the way labor is deployed in various industries, communications is viewed as an essential facilitator, especially in the postprint period. Bucher traces the relationship between written news sheets, printing technology, and public opinion, and even considers the precursors of newspapers that were used during the Roman Empire. In so doing, as well as in emphasizing that the history of the press and journalism should be of direct interest to political economists, he anticipated the program of study advocated nearly half a century later by Innis. For Bucher the press, like the railway and the telegraph, is seen as a vital factor contributing to the unity of modern society, through facilitating the exchange of knowledge as well as basic information and material goods. In linking communications to wider intellectual knowledge in this sense, he exhibits ties to the inclusive interest in the subject that was part of the Enlightenment vision of Turgot and Condorcet.

Bucher's appraisal of the role of the press, however, was quite critical, unlike the work of his eighteenth-century forerunners. He notes how economic interests changed newspapers into commercial "capitalist" enterprises, and argues that newspapers should be free of commercial interests and for the benefit of the general public, "like public streets and water systems."[25] This concern included advocating the study of ethics as a component in journalism courses. The press, for Bucher, ultimately constitutes more than just a means for the distribution of information and shaping of public opinion; it provides a rich source for historians to study if they wish to get a fuller understanding of the cultural currents of the period they are scrutinizing.

ROBERT PARK

Other German theorists also dealt with communications. Ferdinand Tonnies (1855-1936) was interested in signs, symbols, public opinion, and the role of newspapers. Max Weber (1864-1920) mentioned the connection between writing and bureaucracies as well as considering the role of the press on social change. Nevertheless, it was the American sociological tradition that emerged around the University of Chicago which most fully developed the study of mass communications as a sociological perspective. Robert Park in particular saw the need for a sociological view of communication studies that would see its role differently from a purely historical assessment—a position that this book must note, though the task at hand precludes following the sociological line further than considering Park as a transitional figure.

A key idea in Park is Georg Simmel's (1858-1918) distinction between the factual character of history and the generalizing, abstract nature of sociology.[26]

History, according to Park, seeks to find out what happened and how it came about, while sociology deals with the nature of the processes involved. The study of history puts emphasis on concrete events as they occurred. Sociological inquiry aims at laws and generalizations about human nature and society irrespective of time and place. Park was well aware that history and sociology pass over into each other via imperceptible gradations.[27] When the historian shifts from examining periods and events, to considering the role of institutions, he moves toward sociology. Similarly, Park notes that in Tylor's work on the natural history of culture traits, historical problems become both sociological and psychological. Park stresses that sociology originated in history, and although he traces the emergence of modern sociology back to the usually accepted beginnings in Saint-Simon and Comte, he insists that the lineage extends earlier, into the Enlightenment via the contributions of Montesquieu, Hume, and Condorcet.

Park's sociology endeavored to deal with collective behavior, the institutions that are formed as a result of it, and the forces that bring them into being. He also showed interest in problems pertaining to the relationship between the individual and society, and as a result developed concepts such as social role, self-conception, and "marginal man." In addition he was concerned with what social scientists today might refer to as his "cultural present"—the time in which he lived—and when he used historical examples it was often toward this end rather than for the sake of more fully understanding some bygone time. Although a strong proponent of empirical "scientific" sociology, Park nonetheless did make short but significant incursions into the field of historical analysis; for example, in the area of communications his *Immigrant Press and its Control* (1922) is a notable study.

Another distinction that figures importantly in Park's writing is—following American philosopher and psychologist William James (1842-1910)—the division of knowledge into knowledge of acquaintance and knowledge about. The first is knowledge that gets embedded in custom and habit; the second is composed of knowledge that is formal, rational, and systematic, whereby ideas substitute for concrete reality and words for things. These are, of course, relative terms and constitute a continuum for Park. According to him news bridges these two domains more completely than almost any other phenomenon. It does not constitute systematic knowledge in the sense of the physical sciences, yet it is concerned with concrete events. News may appear to be like history in that it deals with particular occurrences, but unlike history there is no attempt to connect these events to a grander scheme. These queries led him to further consider the role of the press and newspapers in society by assessing aspects of their history. He called this endeavor the "natural history of the newspaper."

While the press has a history (in other words, a series of specific developmental events), it also has, according to Park, a natural history which is the outcome of processes in which individuals participate without a sense of the long-term consequences of their labor—a view reminiscent of Marx's notion that men make history only to the degree that encountered circumstances permit and without a long-term awareness of what their labors will bring about.[28] "The natural history of the newspaper" deals with the conditions under which the newspaper has grown, the stages of its development, and what it comes to represent in each successive transition. It "is not so much a history as a natural history of the press— not a record of the fortunes of individual newspapers, but an account of the evolution of the newspaper as a social institution."[29]

Many forms of communication were of interest to Park, although he wrote little on them apart from his consideration of the press. Being influenced by the German tradition we have just surveyed, as well as by the work of Simmel and Oswald Spengler (1880-1936), he adhered to a view of civilization whereby social relations and communication were of central importance. This is apparent in the selections he incorporated in editing his anthology *Introduction to the Science of Sociology*. Two sections in chapter 6, "Social Interaction," are given over to the study of communication. The first is titled the "Natural Forms of Communication" and deals with what we would today call nonverbal communication (gestures and expressions); the second, "Language and the Communication of Ideas," is concerned with the techniques and technology of symbolic communication, and it considers stages in the development of writing and the impact of print.

Fortunately Park's vision did not remain confined to sociology. As McLuhan notes with reference to Park's interest in communications: "The ideas of Park seem to have appealed more to the mind of Harold Innis than to any other student of Robert Park."[30] Innis picked up and developed further Park's view of the significance of communication studies to our understanding of the history of civilization, and the belief that new technologies, especially in the area of communications, facilitate the emergence of new social arrangements.

Edward Tylor, Anthropology, Culture-History, and Communications

Myths and rites are far from being, as has often been held, the product of man's "myth making faculty" turning its back on reality. Their principal value is to preserve until the present time the remains of observation and reflection which were (and no doubt still are) precisely adapted to discoveries of a certain type.

—Claude Levi-Strauss

The contributions of Edward Burnett Tylor (1832-1917) are largely unknown outside of contemporary anthropology and perhaps comparative religion. Tylor, along with Lewis Morgan, is justly revered as a founding father of anthropology. This acceptance has belied the fact that his work deals with concerns that have been more extensively elaborated in fields other than anthropology, especially regarding his interest in the range of ways human beings communicate and the cultural-historical implications of such developments. Even anthropologists have come to recognize this. For example, Paul Bohannan in his introduction to the recent abridged edition of Tylor's *Researches into the Early History of Mankind*, notes that the book is "about the history and institutionalization of the process of communication . . ." and that the first five chapters provide "detailed accounts on the basic arts of communication."[1] However, attempts such as the present one to deal with Tylor in this capacity are virtually nonexistent.

Although Tylor is often credited with establishing the academic discipline of anthropology—he occupied the first chair in that subject at Oxford—he was heir to a more inclusive tradition: the all-encompassing universal history of mankind and comparative study of society of the eighteenth century. As he matured as a theorist, the writings of both the Enlightenment philosophes and their nineteenth-century successors such as Comte, became increasingly important. Tylor endeavored to inject new data, rigor, and method into their widespread interests. This entailed dealing more fully with the non-Western and archaic societies often neglected in previous accounts. One result is that he occupies, as does Emile Durkheim in sociology, a transitional position between the study of man, society, and culture as an overarching philosophical problem, and the institutionalization of these concerns in twentieth-century social science disciplines.

Tylor began as a self-taught independent scholar in a manner similar to his contemporary, Herbert Spencer. It was only after the bulk of his work was done and his reputation established that he was offered a university appointment, an honor never accorded Spencer. Despite the fact that Tylor and Spencer sometimes dealt with similar topics, and engaged in an infamous debate over priority regarding their minimum definition of religion, Spencer's perspective proved to be too sweeping and speculative for general philosophy; Tylor, in taking a more cautious and empirical route, managed to hone some of his concerns into the subject matter of a new academic discipline.

LIFE AND INFLUENCES

The product of a Quaker upbringing free from dogma, Tylor was born into a fairly well-to-do family in Camberwell—today a suburb of greater London. Owing to his Quaker faith Tylor could not pass the test for religious orthodoxy that was required for admission to the universities until 1872. His education was at Quaker schools, supplemented by his own curiosity and independent reading. It is possible that his older brother, Alfred, who was a geologist, influenced young Edward in scientific directions, but the sparse literature on Tylor's personal life does not mention this. At age sixteen he went to work in the family brass foundry. After several years there he had what has been described as a breakdown in health. Possibly this was a lung affliction. Partly, I would venture to suggest, it was a psychosomatically induced malaise, the result of a perceptive mind constrained by the routine circumstances of maintaining a business during that period of industrialism. The remedy seems to suggest this. Tylor travelled in search of his health. But like his predecessor and major intellectual influence, the great geographer Alexander von Humboldt (1769-1859), who also travelled for his health, Tylor journeyed to some of the remotest parts of the New World, places one would be hard pressed to perceive as health inducing.

After a year of travel in the southern United States, Tylor visited Cuba in 1856 and encountered the individual destined to alter the course of his life, Henry Christy (1810-1865). Christy, twenty years Tylor's senior and a wealthy businessman turned amateur archaeologist, was travelling on an omnibus in Havana when, so the story goes, Tylor overheard him use the Quaker term *thou*. The younger man introduced himself as a fellow Quaker and a deep friendship was born. Christy discerned in Tylor an inquiring mind and undirected enthusiasm. He invited Tylor to accompany him on an anthropological and archaeological venture to Mexico. The offer was accepted without reservation or hesitation. Tylor's description of his first impression of the part scholar, part soldier-of-fortune Christy, is laced with intrigue and would do justice to "Indiana Jones." He notes how Christy was

> leading an adventurous life, visiting sugar-plantations, copper-mines, and coffee estates, descending into caves, and botanizing in tropical jungles, cruising for a fortnight in an open boat among the coral-reefs, hunting turtles and manatis, and visiting all sorts of people from whom information was to be had, from foreign consuls to Lazarist missionaries down to retired slave-dealers and assassins.[2]

Although Tylor's sojourn in Mexico lasted only several months, it was a major turning point in his life. It led directly to his first book, *Anahuac: Or Mexico and the Mexicans, Ancient and Modern* (1861) and a long anthropological career. While in Mexico Tylor made astute observations on the inhabitants, indigenous and Spanish, and he and Christy scavenged among archaeological remains speculating on the history and achievements of Amerindian civilizations such as the Aztec. Parallels immediately come to mind with the fortuitous circumstances that enabled Charles Darwin to sail around the world on the Beagle from 1831 to 1836, an event that changed the course of his life. Darwin also published a book about his travels, first as a formal account in 1839, then later, in 1845, he released the *Voyage of the Beagle*, a more popular rendering. In both Darwin and Tylor's books description filled with insight takes precedence over the systematic elaboration of theory. That such perceptive and engaging narratives are not unknown in more recent times can be evidenced from a perusal of Claude Levi-Strauss's semiautobiographical recounting of his anthropological journeys in South America, *Tristes Tropique* (1955).

Just as when Darwin returned to England he embarked on an enduring marriage with his cousin Emma Wedgwood, so Tylor in 1858 married Anna Fox, a liaison (childless) that was to be a support and comfort to him for the fifty-nine years that remained in his life. The year 1858 was important for Tylor in other respects. It saw confirmation of Boucher de Perthes's (1788-1868) archaeological researches, which capped decades of speculation regarding the antiquity of stone tools. Boucher de Perthes had suggested a venerable ancestry for such finds as early as 1836. But subsequent research, by Christy among others, finally enabled the case to be firmly established.

In 1859, Darwin's *Origin of Species* further shocked the traditionalists. For Tylor the book was a source of inspiration rather than a direct influence. He was convinced of the antiquity of man and of a long cultural evolution prior to reading Darwin. The materials Tylor had been gathering to present his case coalesced in his *Researches into the Early History of Mankind* (1865), in which both prehistoric and contemporary anthropological facts were united in comparative interpretation.[3] *Researches* established him as a leading figure in the newly emerging

field of anthropology. The year 1865 also had a sad note to it. Henry Christy died—
of an illness contracted while digging on an archaeological site.

Further study by Tylor pertaining to human antiquity, particularly establishing the position that the foundations of familiar cultural practices can be discerned
in the belief and customs of primitive peoples, led to an amplification of *Researches*. The result was Tylor's third and most renowned book, *Primitive Culture*
(1871). Thus before his fortieth birthday he had effected an enormous contribution to the study of man and perhaps produced his best work.[4]

In 1875 Oxford bequeathed him the degree of Doctor of Civil Laws, an honor
usually bestowed on older scholars. In 1881 he published a comprehensive and
accessible survey of the discipline he did so much to develop, titled appropriately
enough, *Anthropology*. By 1883 Tylor was made Keeper of the Oxford University Museum, and 1884 saw him given the position of Reader in Anthropology,
which became a full professorship in 1896, with the appendium of emeritus added
in 1909. Other honors included appointment to the presidency of the anthropological section of the British Association in 1884, and the presidency of the Anthropological Society in 1891. One major theoretical publication appeared at this
time, a landmark paper in 1888 developing a cross-cultural statistical methodology
for the study of marriage, descent, and related traits.[5] In 1912 he was knighted.

Tall, well-built, strikingly handsome by all accounts—certainly this is evident
in the few photographs of him—Tylor's patience, thoroughness, and good humor
gave him an understated charisma. When he died in 1917 he was revered as a giant,
both by those who followed in his stead and by critics who sought to challenge
some of his key assumptions.

MAJOR CONTRIBUTIONS

Few would disagree with Marett's observation that "Tylor's anthropological
apprenticeship was served in Mexico."[6] However, those who have assessed Tylor's
legacy, Marett included, have tended to downplay the book that emerged from
that apprenticeship, *Anahuac*. Certainly it is an engaging narrative. Tylor demonstrates a flair for writing that flourished only sporadically in his other works. But
this captivating description of places and people is not without theoretical explanations. It also constitutes a precious record of the state of Mexican society
at that time and what remained of the great ancient ruins.

Tylor informs the reader early in the text that he is familiar with Humboldt's
geography and Prescott's history of the region and will evaluate some of their conclusions in light of his own observations. Among the recurring themes considered
are assessments of various architectural styles; comments on what we would today call acculturation; the clash between traditional life-styles and newly introduced elements; and opinions on the unstable political situation. Tylor happened
to be caught up in some of the military actions taking place at the time and produced a forthright critique of the Mexican army, its mode of recruitment, and

lopsided structure (top-heavy, with unqualified officers). He also had opinions on several social problems, attributing them to the inefficient transportation system. For instance, often there might be a famine in one region and surplus in another, but owing to the poor transportation network the famine could not be staved off by shipping grain from an area of greater to one of lesser productivity. As a result the overall population was not increasing as much as in the United States or England.

With reference to anthropology and archaeology, Tylor broached several concerns that he would more thoroughly elaborate in subsequent works. He was fascinated with ancient artifacts, and his study of Aztec stone tools led him to comment on their similarity to stone tools unearthed in prehistoric Britain. In addition he ran tests on the uses of such tools. When back in London he would often take several artifacts of uncertain purpose to his neighborhood butcher to have the man test them and surmise their possible use and effectiveness.

While in Mexico Tylor also began a lifelong interest in the study of numbers and counting. He observed how the contemporary Mexican Indian has only a sparse idea of notation compared to the intricate mode of his ancestors, which was capable of solving complex problems. *Anahuac* includes several linguistic comparisons of number systems in European, Asian, African, and North American languages, especially regarding how the terms employed in counting relate to parts of the body, a line of inquiry that would be greatly expanded and developed in *Primitive Culture*. In *Anahuac* Tylor uses the question of number to develop a technique that would persist in later works—the forwarding of hypotheses in an equivocal manner. He convincingly suggests, in the way one would propose a firm hypothesis, that in many nations the art of reckoning by fives, tens, and twenties resulted from counting on fingers and toes, but refuses to explicitly commit himself to the hypothesis without further evidence.

One of the most striking and thought provoking features of Mexico has always been the similarity of the Aztec pyramids to those of Egypt. Tylor used this observation to embark on a discussion destined to recur in almost all of his later work, the question of diffusion versus independent invention. He always remained open to both possibilities. However, in his early work there is a definite leaning toward independent invention, which by his later studies developed into the position that if clear and certain evidence of culture contact, and therefore diffusion, could not be demonstrated, then independent invention must be assumed. Both processes are predicated on the principle of psychic unity established by Tylor and fundamental to most of his work—although this principle seems to have first arisen as a defense of independent invention. One of the earliest expressions of psychic unity to be found in Tylor occurs in *Anahuac* when he is commenting on the similarities of Aztec dances to those of the Old World. He notes how "human nature is similar everywhere, and the same wants and instincts often find their development in the same way among nations totally separate from one another."[7]

   Humboldt's hypothesis regarding the diffusion of Aztec customs from Asia is assessed. Although Tylor does not dismiss it, he urges the elimination of any trait that might be independently explained by "the same outward causes at work in both hemispheres, and from the fact that the mind is fundamentally the same everywhere."[8] Nevertheless, Tylor, in not wanting to be dogmatic, constantly hedges between the two hypotheses. In one case he extensively comments on the Toltec and Aztec calendars, their cycles, divisions, and similarities to the Gregorian calendar. However, although similarities between the Mexican calendars and those of other civilizations are said to be independently derived, their cosmological vision of destructions and regenerations of the world may, he concedes, have resulted from some remote connection with Asian civilizations such as the Indian. Not altogether convinced of this possibility he goes on to wonder how these esoteric traditions could have come to the New World from the Old without being accompanied by more basic traits such as bronze weapons, beasts of burden, oil and wax, and the art of weighing. Even contemporary archaeologists might duly ponder Tylor's puzzlement over how "a people ignorant of some of the commonest arts had extraordinary knowledge of astronomy, and even knew the real causes of eclipses, and represented them in their sacred dances."[9]

   Clearly *Anahuac* is not a masterpiece of theoretical interpretation. But it did more than merely lay groundwork that would receive full and proper treatment later, as most Tylor interpreters suggest. It presented perspectives and debates that are amplified but not necessarily more fully resolved in subsequent works. *Anahuac* does not deserve the obscurity and neglect that has befallen it. The range of concerns and illuminating references would be impressive enough for any writer of the period, let alone one with no formal schooling beyond sixteen and a trip to Mexico that lasted just over three months.

   When Tylor published *Researches into the Early History of Mankind* in 1865, the book that established his anthropological career, it represented the inspiration derived from *Anahuac*, coupled with considerable knowledge of the growing archaeological and anthropological literature. His facility with French and German aided the task. Appropriately enough John Murray was the publisher. Murray also published Darwin's *Origin of Species*, Henry Maine's *Ancient Law*, and Charles Lyell's (1797-1875) *Principles of Geology*. Tylor was in select company.

   Researches deals with the culture-history of civilization, focussing on oft neglected prehistoric and non-Western examples. Much of the book is given over to a study of the nature and development of various modes of communication. However, several basic assumptions provide grounding for the variety of topics discussed. They include the psychic unity of the human race, the affirmation of the progressionist or developmental view of civilization, and the respective merits of independent invention versus diffusion.

   The psychic unity principle is championed using all manner of evidence, from nonverbal gestures to techniques of fire making. The Tylorian thesis is that the human mind throughout the world shares basic mental operations, to the degree that when environmental circumstances and social life are similar, then like cultural activities and products will result. Tylor notes how this "mental uniformity" is apparent when we consider how difficult it is to find, in a list of twenty traits "of art or knowledge, custom or superstition taken at random from a description of any uncivilized race, a single one to which something closely analogous may not be found elsewhere among some other race, unlike the first in physical characteristics, and living thousands of miles off."[10] This is not to suggest that Tylor's view is synonymous with the twentieth-century anthropological position on racial equality. In his later work, *Anthropology*, he notes how there "seems to be in mankind inbred temperament and inbred capacity of mind," and that this can partly explain the accentuated development of particular societies.[11] It is, however, extreme to label Tylor a racial determinist, as has been done, on the basis of this observation.[12] It was merely his way of allowing for all factors. The bulk of his studies clearly favors a culturalist position.[13] Although Tylor's view of mental uniformity among races falls short of contemporary standards, it was a major achievement in light of its nineteenth-century context.

The progressionist argument presented in *Researches* seems obvious to us today. It assumes that all civilizations developed from primitive circumstances not unlike those found amongst the aboriginal tribes of Asia, Africa, Australia, and the New World. Tylor was quick to point out similarities between the artifacts unearthed by prehistorians and what ethnographic researchers had observed. Other traits, such as the customs of primitive people studied in recent times, were held to be similar to those that must have existed in prehistory. The analogy between both primitive and non-Western societies, and hypothetical stages in the development of civilization as a whole, became the basis of his comparative method. He used it to stridently counter the theologically inspired degenerationist or degradationist position. It argued that man was originally created in a moral and civilized state, and while some continued on, contemporary primitives are remnants of those who had fallen from grace, incapable of progress and destined for an everlasting position of inferiority. In challenging this position Tylor contended that evidence for it is scanty. He also affirmed that the mind everywhere is capable of development. Even within primitive cultural traditions evidence exists for progressive development of the technological arts. Liberal optimist that he was, he wanted to show that given "world enough and time," the lowly savage is potentially an English gentleman, and that the course of human development, in whatever condition we find it is, despite periodic setbacks, forever upward.

The third major theme in *Researches* is the respective merits of independent invention versus diffusion, an inquiry that began in earnest in *Anahuac*. While Tylor uses the evidence cited earlier in support of mental uniformity to establish a strong case for independent invention, he was aware that despite the fact that "man does the same thing under the same circumstances will account for much . . . it will not explain everything."[14] Being respectful of Humboldt, Tylor considered cases where diffusion seemed likely, such as the recurrence of certain mythic themes in both Asian and New World narratives, themes that he believed were too idiosyncratic to have been independently elaborated. Diffusion seemed to be the answer. However, why these traits diffused while others did not is never explained. At this time in his career the psychic unity principle was aligned with independent invention and not used to support diffusion. Later, he more fully realized that certain traits diffuse easily because the mental proclivities of different peoples are often similar, and that the initial emergence of such traits is more the result of cultural circumstances than the genius of particular human groups.

The most widely read and commented on of Tylor's books is *Primitive Culture* (1871). This is the work in which he explicitly elaborates many of the concepts and perspectives that have fueled anthropological research and debate for over a hundred years. From the point of view of the present study it is the least relevant of his four books. But it is undeniably his major work and a brief familiarity with some of its key concepts is necessary for our understanding of Tylor's cultural-historical legacy.

Primitive Culture opens with one of the most cited passages in anthropology: "Culture or civilization taken in its wide ethnographic sense, is that complex whole which includes knowledge, belief, art, morals, law, custom, and any other capabilities and habits acquired by man as a member of society."[15] This is generally taken to be the first definitive social science framing of the culture concept, though Tylor used the term *culture* in this very way in *Researches* without providing an explicit definition. What is important about the above formulation is the way it differentiates culture, as the totality of lifeways of any given people, primitive or modern, from humanist notions of culture—what we might today designate as high culture, for example, the arts, literary and intellectual life, and religious spirit characteristic of advanced civilization.[16] Although *culture* is used synonymously with *civilization* in Tylor's definition, and in many of his writings, he does adhere to subtle differences between the two terms that are more apparent after a closer examination. Culture is always the blanket referent, the universal, while civilization is characterized by degrees of development depending on how technologically and scientifically advanced a particular society might be.[17]

At the beginning of *Primitive Culture* Tylor also makes clear what he only intimated in his earlier writings, that he is studying the "laws of human thought and action" and that the "history of mankind is part and parcel of the history of nature, that our thoughts, wills, and actions accord with laws as definite as those which govern the motion of waves, the combination of acids and bases, and the growth of plants and animals."[18] In other words, he believed that not only must the study of mankind appropriate the models and methods of the natural sciences, it *is* ultimately a natural science. His quest for recurring features of human activity attributable to laws of operation is an expression of an ideal of the eighteenth-century philosophes and Scottish moral philosophers. In the twentieth century this task became scaled down to the concerns of psychology, although sociology, with its occasional attempt to glimpse laws of society or social behavior has kept alive the Enlightenment vision and that of several of its nineteenth-century heirs, such as Marx, Spencer, and Tylor. Also, in believing that the most basic expression of these laws of thought and action can be effectively studied in the behavior of primitive peoples, Tylor is part of a grandiose tradition in the study of the human pysche, which in the twentieth century has included Freud, Jung, and Levi-Strauss.

A good deal of *Primitive Culture* repeats observations that Tylor made in *Researches*, but this time the data base is considerably larger. In a manner not unreminiscent of Darwin's *Origin of Species*, a given point is illustrated with page after page of cases. After a time the reader is so overwhelmed with details that the initial point being made is often forgotten.

Using many new examples from various non-Western and primitive societies, as well as historical studies, Tylor again champions the progressionist view at the expense of degeneration theory. A major tenet of his argument is the concept of survivals. Several chapters are devoted to showing how seemingly quaint customs, practices, and superstitions are carried over, or survive into a later time. They give indication of an earlier period where such modes were more dominant and represented a maximization of human capacities. An important methodological tool in this, and other aspects of Tylor's inquiry is what he called the "test of recurrence." It simply refers to his unwillingness to use, for instance, a particular primitive behavior or custom to illustrate his argument unless corroboration of it could be found in several, ideally unrelated accounts. This is to circumvent the pitfalls of earlier writers, such as Monboddo, who sometimes uncritically based entire theories on a single, questionable ethnographic account.

In *Primitive Culture* the nature and origins of language are taken up again in light of more examples and an ongoing critique of Wilhelm von Humboldt. Related to this concern is Tylor's discussion of the fundamentals of number and counting, an interest that began in *Anahuac*. *Primitive Culture* contains a valuable assessment of many non-Western and archaic systems of numeration, which is revealing even in light of contemporary knowledge. Tylor argues, on the basis of a comparative study of many different modes of mathematical reckoning, that number had its beginnings in experience and experiment, not in the discerning of some universal truth. He notes how though a given primitive people may not have numbers beyond five—frequently the term *hand* signifies five—they are often fully capable of elaborating their system to count much higher.

Perhaps the most renowned contribution of *Primitive Culture* is to the study of myth and religion. Tylor contends that the seemingly absurd aspects of primitive and archaic myths belie the fact that they possessed a meaning and an irreducible logic for people who conceived them in circumstances radically different from our own. In a position that foreshadows contemporary anthropologist Levi-Strauss—who has paid homage to Tylor on several occasions—he argues that myth is an "organic product of mankind at large, in which individual, national, and even racial distinctions stand subordinate to universal qualities of the human mind."[19]

Out of his interest in myth emerged Tylor's (or Spencer's, depending on whom you side with in their debate) concept of animism, the belief in spiritual beings as the minimum definition of religion. According to twentieth-century anthropologist Paul Radin, Tylor, in Part 2 of *Primitive Culture*, was the first to "give us a well-thought-out history of religions from the beginnings up to the time of the great Egyptian and Sumerian-Babylonian civilizations."[20] This is a contribution that has been appreciated by both anthropologists and scholars of comparative religion.

In *Anthropology* (1881), the last of his four books, Tylor draws the wealth of his research together to create a program of study for the discipline. This program not only considers the nature of culture and history of civilization, it also deals with human evolution, the relationship between man and other animals, and race—in other words, what we would today call physical or biological anthropology. Although a good deal of his coverage seems dated, the sections comparing human and animal behavior are especially insightful in light of recent research. When dealing with these subjects Tylor pays appropriate homage to Darwin. Interestingly, in the preface to the second edition of *Primitive Culture* (1873), Tylor notes that the similarity between his evolutionary view of civilization and the ideas of Darwin and Spencer is a case of parallelism rather than direct influence. However, by the time he wrote *Anthropology* his conception of the anthropological domain included the Darwinian approach to human evolution.[21]

Whether it is a case of parallelism or unconscious influence, certain principles fundamental to Darwin and the geological work of Charles Lyell are apparent in Tylor's view of civilization as outlined in *Anthropology*. He notes how civilization results from a cumulative, steady growth of the arts, knowledge, and social institutions, with no stage coming into being spontaneously. This is an echo of Lyell's uniformitarian geology, especially since Tylor continually refers to uniform results from uniform causes when talking about culture, and it certainly recalls Darwin's view of evolution as the slow, gradual result of the production of innumerable variations. In addition there seems to be an appropriation of the concept of natural selection to the cultural domain whereby those traits and institutions that are more efficient succeed those less endowed. This has caused at least one commentator to refer to Tylor's approach as "cultural Darwinism."[22] The influence of Darwinian gradualism can also perhaps be discerned in Tylor's unwillingness to delineate particular stages having set criteria in cultural-evolutionary development, as his American contemporary Lewis Morgan had done. Although Tylor does talk of the three great divisions, savagery, barbarism, and civilization, he does so in very general terms. He always assesses the widest array of cultural phenomena, from subsistence technology to musical instruments, without attempting to hierarchize related clusters of traits in a diagnostic way.

A good deal of *Anthropology* is given over to a discussion of language, communication, and the development of science and technology. Rather than confining himself to the major breakthroughs that we would today regard as epoch-making,

Tylor takes long forays into what sometimes appear to be trivial interests, such as different techniques for fire making, brewing, various games, minor points of music, and so on. The grand system and major societal characteristics that typify, for example, Spencer's work, are sacrificed to a scrupulous examination of data and detail. Tylor shared the belief, as did a number of nineteenth-century thinkers and several in the Enlightenment as well, that he was following the path of Baconian inductionism. All generalizations approaching theory were said to derive from the facts at hand. This may seem naive and impossible from the point of view of contemporary philosophy of science. But Tylor remained closer to this ideal than any of his contemporaries.

COMMUNICATION, HUMAN NATURE, AND CIVILIZATION

Researches is the work in which Tylor most fully elaborates his thoughts on communication. However, a glimmering of this interest can be discerned in *Anahuac*, when he briefly discusses Aztec picture-writing as a clue to their social life and extrapolates on the cultural implications of language and number.

Tylor believed in the eighteenth- and nineteenth-century quest for origins. This led him, in *Researches*, to begin his history of civilization with an inquiry into what he thought was the most basic aspect of human nature, communication. The bedrock of this examination is not language per se, which he held to be a cultural construct, but gesture, a mode of exchange that is regarded as more universal and deeply rooted than the spoken word. Two key chapters in *Researches* deal with the subject and several perceptive observations derive from his own field work experience among deaf groups in England and Germany. On the basis of this work, and what he accomplished in Mexico, it seems rash to regard Tylor as "not a field worker" and to locate him in the "armchair theory tradition" of nineteenth-century anthropological thought, as has often been done.[23] If we judge the quality of his field work, not the amount, and the insight derived from it, he can be favorably compared to several twentieth-century anthropologists considerably more renowned in this area.

The concern with gestural communication for Tylor represents an attempt to establish an aspect of the nature of the mind which acts as a universal substrate of language and culture. He notes that through such study "we can realize to ourselves in some measure a condition of the human mind which underlies anything which has yet been traced in even the lowest dialect of language if taken as a whole."[24] Using the "gesture-language" of the deaf as a model for the most basic kind of human communication, Tylor is utilizing that renowned eighteenth-century method, the quest for the irreducibly human in a model of natural man. In opposition to Muller and other linguists, Tylor contends that the sign language communication of the deaf indicates that spoken language is not necessary for thought. This view was also insisted upon by Condillac and Rousseau—although Tylor appears to be unaware of their observations—who marvelled at the abilities of the deaf but did not have enough reliable accounts to fully develop a place for it in their theories.

Tylor argues that gestural communication is such a primal mode that similarities can be found in it between the deaf in Europe and native peoples around the world, and the plains Indians are examined regarding the degree to which they have developed this capacity. Today we might find Tylor's affirmation of the universality of gesture plausible, but somewhat extreme, especially when he insists that there would be a ready mutual understanding between the deaf in Western civilization and many native groups.

The key differences between primitive and civilized peoples are to be found, according to Tylor, in spoken language and cultural orientation. That the human mind underlying these differences is similar is evidenced through the study of gesture. But why is this form of communication so minimally developed in his English homeland? Tylor's interesting, provocative, and almost Rousseauistic contention is that it is because the English have become dependent to a great degree on reading and writing.[25]

Does gesture, then, antedate spoken language in the evolution of human communication and is Tylor subscribing to the gestural origin theory of language? His answer appears to be negative: "The theory that gesture-language was the original language of man and that speech came afterwards, has already been mentioned. We have no foundation to build such a theory upon, but there are several questions bearing on the matter which are well worth examining."[26] This is a frequent Tylor ploy, especially in his earlier writings—citing evidence in support of a theory without forthright commitment to that theory. Perhaps he is trying to avoid the excesses of Monboddo on language origins, whose observations he found interesting, but overstated. Without doubt gesture plays a major role in Tylor's view of language origins. He says considerably more about it than he does about the origin of spoken words. In the latter area he betrays his rationalist leaning by insisting that words could not have come into being on a purely arbitrary basis. He notes that the reasons for particular selections are long lost, except in the case of onomatopeia; imitative words are regarded as a form of gestural communication.

The importance of gesture surfaces again in Tylor's consideration of the earliest form of writing, "picture-writing." He follows Humboldt's view that gesture minus sound is a species of writing and notes how in many societies, especially native North America, extensive use of gesture and picture-writing are often found in association. Tylor also perceptively observes that many examples of picture-writing are not, in fact, self-contained texts, but suggestions of key events, therefore requiring informed narration—not unlike certain written signs used in our own commercial transactions. As a result we should not attempt to archaeologically read too much from messages inscribed in this mode.

Basic picture-writing is seen as similar worldwide. However, in certain archaic civilizations it received sophisticated development. Among the ancient Mexicans picture-writing gave rise to notational systems and also the situation whereby a sign could stand for the spoken sound, not just as a visual indicator of an object. This is similar, he notes, to the rebus writing games of contemporary children. It becomes a basis for his comparison, following the universal history of the eighteenth century, of the evolution of knowledge in the history of civilization as a whole with the psychological development of the individual in modern times. Nevertheless, Tylor remained cautious when using this approach: "The trite comparison of savages to 'grown-up children' is in the main a sound one, though not to be carried out too strictly."[27] This psychological/historical version of "ontogeny recapitulates phylogeny" also figured prominently in twentieth-century psychoanalytic theory.

In his history of writing Tylor compares the Aztecs to the Egyptians: "We thus see that the ancient Egyptians and the Aztecs made in much the same way the great step from picture-writing to word-writing."[28] The Maya are also considered in this context but are regarded as insufficiently studied to yield conclusive results. The Egyptians are also credited with the first transformation of word-writing into an alphabet, which was later developed and added to by the Phoenicians. The similarities between early Mexican and Egyptian writing, of course, gave Tylor a strong case for independent invention and the developmentalist thesis. Nevertheless, he did not ignore diffusion, or the fact that a form of alphabetic writing could be elaborated by a people who had not passed through all of the antecedent stages of its development. He notes how this is evidenced by the Cherokee of North America and the Vei of Africa, who borrowed the idea of writing using sound characters from the white man, although they developed completely different and original scripts.

Ultimately, picture-related writing systems are, Tylor believed, displaced by the word-writing mode. Nevertheless survivals exist, as evidenced in our retention of Roman numerals. Had Tylor lived into the mid-twentieth century he would have seen an interesting return of the picture mode in all manner of international and local signs, readable by young children, non-native speakers, illiterate adults, and even anthropologists. His thesis regarding the universality of gesture would receive strong support.

In *Researches* Tylor goes on to show how, in societies that do not have fully developed writing systems, myths narrated orally serve to maintain continuity between past and present by keeping a record of important events and personages in the culture-history of the group. Tylor did not regard myth as a flight of frivolous, imaginative fancy. Although myth does not constitute science or history in the strict sense, it takes its point of departure from some factual occurrence. To facilitate memory, and therefore transmission from generation to generation, myth utilizes the embellishments we usually associate with poetic form. The myths of savages, far from being an alien form of communication, are not unlike aspects of our own literary tradition, such as the Homeric epics. In both cases Tylor remarks how the scenarios depicted may not be historically accurate in the strict sense; however, important attributes of the respective societies are often faithfully depicted. In *Primitive Culture* he notes how the mythic sensibility survives into the nineteenth-century literary tradition, especially in the work of poets such as Wordsworth.[29]

Primitive Culture goes on to examine an enormous number of myths in scrupulous detail. Tylor was one of the first scholars to extensively compile and assess non-Western myths, folktales, and legends. He directly influenced the next century of research in this area, from the work of his immediate successor and follower, Sir James Frazer (1854-1941), to the contemporary treatises of Claude Levi-Strauss.

In *Researches* Tylor observes how the historical-fictional interplay in myths can be seen in such narratives as the one about Quetzelcohuatl, who is alleged to have originated aspects of Aztec culture. A similar story in Greek mythology concerns King Cadmus, the Phoenician who sprouted the alphabet from a dragon's teeth. A particularly interesting narrative, especially from the point of view of the history of communications, is the one Tylor mentions regarding the Chinese emperor Suy-jin, who it is claimed invented the quipu in the period before the Chinese acquired written characters. Although Suy-jin's role might be exaggerated, the story probably expresses a historical truth regarding the knotted cords of different length, thickness, and colors that make up quipus. It asserts that the quipu was used for records in China before it was superseded by writing, and Tylor argues that the quipu, or devices like it, were most likely independently invented around the world as necessary precursors to writing. Among the Incas the quipu reached an extraordinary level of development and "served as the regular means of record and communication for a highly organized society."[30] Tylor notes how it was suitable for reckoning and statistical tables dealing with crop production, taxation, and both military and civilian censuses.

Nevertheless quipus and devices like them, according to Tylor, required informed interpretation and commentary—making it difficult for later generations to read them. He notes that they constitute a technology fundamental to societies, such as the early Chinese and the Incas, in transition from a tribal myth dominated level of development, to written records and full-fledged civilization.[31] This is more an observation than the forwarding of a bold hypothesis. We must remember that Tylor was hesitant to delineate specific stages of cultural evolution, or to strongly champion singular criteria. However, in *Researches*, in his meticulous and cautious way, he lays foundations for such an endeavor, foundations that are always well thought out and restrained by their own limitations.

By the time he wrote *Anthropology* in 1881 Tylor had absorbed most of the new accounts relevant to his areas of interest, but while he added several interesting new details to the view of communications in culture-history outlined in *Researches*, there is no major reworking of the initial project. His position on gesture now allowed for signs which are indirectly representational. An example of such an "artificial sign" might be the deaf gesture of chopping off a head to indicate a Frenchman; although this kind of sign is a degree removed from direct representation, it nonetheless has a reasoned connection to what it signifies. It seems that Tylor's rationalism and belief in the orderliness of nature and culture was a strong impediment to his acceptance of the possibility of arbitrary signs in either gestural or spoken communication. In the following passage, although he challenges the arbitrary nature of the linguistic sign that would be strongly promoted by Saussure after the turn of the century, he seems to anticipate the latter's view that the study of language is one branch of a more inclusive field, the science of signs, which Saussure called semiology:

> Language is one branch of the great art of sign-making or sign-choosing, and its business is to hit upon some sound as a suitable sign or symbol for each thought. Whenever a sound has been thus chosen there was no doubt a reason for the choice. But it did not follow that each language should choose the same sound.[32]

In *Anthropology* Tylor also came to realize that gesture-language is not as absolute as he first thought. It is often expressed through culturally mediated dialects with their own idiosyncrasies, such as the sign language of the plains Indians. However, the underlying motivation and process involved in this form of communication, predicated as it is on the making of reasoned inferences, remain the same worldwide.

With respect to spoken language, particularly the question of origins, Tylor is somewhat more commital than in earlier works. Imitative sounds made with the voice—a form of gesture—are said to be among the oldest utterances, and universally understandable. He is here referring to words such as *bow wow* and *meow*. However, far from being universally understandable such imitative words are specific to the sound structure (phonology) of particular languages and contemporary linguists are fond of citing studies where such "obviously" representative terms to native speakers, baffle foreigners. Also, Tylor's vagueness in *Researches* regarding what the earliest languages may have been like gives way in *Anthropology* to the firm, but not dogmatic position, that what he calls "natural language" (not to be confused with what contemporary linguists mean by natural language: any native tongue from English to Innuit) is made up of "gesture-actions" and "gesture-sounds" and "must have belonged to our race from the most remote age and most primitive conditions in which man ever existed."[33]

As in the case of language, Tylor's position in *Anthropology* regarding writing is that it did not emerge through sudden creation, but as a result of our long continuous development in the use of signs. Although he was generally hesitant to attribute what we might today refer to as "prime-mover" status to any invention or technology in culture-history, such status is granted to writing: "The invention of writing was the great movement by which mankind rose from barbarism to civilization."[34] People who are dependent on memory for the transmission of their traditions can only develop to a certain degree. For Tylor writing is the factor that gives permanence to history and laws. It also greatly facilitates the expansion of science. Characteristically his perspective on culture led him to virtually exclude discussions of economic organization in this context, save for the passing mention of a few inventions. Writing brought with it a class of "copyists" or "transcribers" that endured until the Middle Ages.

As a result of assimilating new material on the history of writing after he wrote *Researches*, Tylor added some additional discussion of the subject in *Anthropology*. More detail is included on the techniques involved in Egyptian hieroglyphics, particularly how this script operated in keeping records of church and state. Cuneiform, the wedge-shaped script of the Babylonians and Assyrians, is also considered. Tylor regarded it as a cumbersome preface to the alphabet. And, in reappraising the alphabet, he gives much more credit to the Phoenicians than he did in *Researches*.

Although Tylor's approach to culture-history is primarily devoted to non-Western and archaic civilizations, he does give brief consideration to an invention of paramount importance to European history, the printing press. True to his vision that cultural evolution, like its biological counterpart, proceeds through gradual accumulation, he sees printing as a development that began in Babylonian times with imprints made from signet rings and cylinders. This was followed by the Chinese development of block printing, which was in widespread use in tenth-century China. The Chinese also developed moveable type characters, but although Tylor notes this, he observes that such characters are not conducive to the Chinese system of writing and were understandably discarded. When moveable type printing was invented in fifteenth-century Europe, Tylor reminds us that it was after all "the practical application of a Chinese invention."[35] However, its importance cannot be underestimated, for it is the art of printing "to which perhaps, more than any other influence, is due the difference of our modern life from that of the Middle Ages."[36] Thus, Tylor kept alive the view of the eighteenth-century philosophes, such as Turgot and Condorcet, a view destined for futher elaboration in our time.

Part III

The Twentieth Century

7 Archaeology, Technology, and Civilization

As soon as one man was recognized by another as a sentient, thinking being similar to himself, the desire or need to communicate his feelings and thoughts made him seek the means to do so.
—Jean-Jacques Rousseau

Up until Harold Innis published *The Bias of Communication* in 1951 and created a virtual subfield for the study of communications media and history, discussions of the subject in this century were, as they had been for the previous two, part of a more general historical and social evolutionary inquiry. Nevertheless, several renowned scholars devoted specific attention to the question. Two of the most notable have been Gordon Childe (1892-1957), an Australian archaeologist who relocated to England; and American polymath Lewis Mumford (1895-   ).

Although neither Childe nor Mumford give communications the preeminent focus it enjoys in the work of Innis, there are intriguing parallels of personae and context between the three. Innis, as the next chapter will highlight, was Canada's foremost interdisciplinary scholar. He was part of the mainstream of Canadian intellectual development, but manifested creative idiosyncracies that made him at the same time a scholar espousing a view from the margins. He ultimately produced a legacy that transcended his national origins when he created a global program for assessing the comparative history of civilization, accentuating communications.

Childe also came from a colonized nation and went on to become the most widely published and translated Australian author. He worked in the archaeological mainstream in England, but his colonial origins, flirtation with Marxism, and attempt to use archaeology to pursue some of the broadest questions in comparative and theoretical history, led to perennially marginal status.

Mumford emerged from the American urban heartland, New York, at the dawn of the twentieth century. One of the most prolific American writers, his critique of what his country represented in the context of world historical developments in technology, and interdisciplinary vision, consigned him to marginal status as well.

Discussions of the role of communications figure importantly, if not centrally, in the work of Childe and Mumford. In the case of Childe, communications are diagnostic rather than causal with respect to the character of an epoch. In his view, no matter what happens in the realm of demography and subsistence technology, major historical shifts require the embodiment of new knowledge, ways of understanding and controlling the natural world. He argues that to understand how new forms of communication, such as writing, enabled such knowledge to be constituted and deployed, is an important question for both the prehistorian and the historian. Mumford's view is similar, though the scenario he examines and his overall methods differ. When dealing with prehistory he tends to see communications less as technology per se, and more as the manifestation of the informational capacity inherent in the nature of different forms of social organization. With later developments, such as moveable type printing, he *does* assess communications in terms of its role as technological innovation, but always within a nexus of other innovations that both prefigure the new element and enable its distinctive potential to be realized.

CHILDE'S BACKGROUND AND MAJOR STUDIES

There are only a few contemporary appraisals of Childe's legacy. The majority are confined to archaeology and occasionally anthropology—the latter discipline uses his materialist perspective and social evolutionary framework as point of entry. However, during his lifetime he was read by a wide audience and appreciated in many disciplinary contexts. His most renowned and perhaps significant book, *Man Makes Himself* (1936; revised in 1944 and 1951), an accessible account of the rise of civilization, sold exceptionally well. True, some colleagues were disdainful of his popularization of the esoteric subject matter they jealously guarded, but others were more appreciative. One of Childe's admirers was Innis, who praised both Childe's research and his attempt to make more accessible the results of scholarly study, thereby helping to break down what Innis referred to as academic monopolies of knowledge.[1]

Born in Sydney, Australia, Childe studied classical philology and archaeology at Oxford. Although the latter became his dominant concern, the influence of the former, rarely acknowledged, perhaps played a role in the way he conceptualized social evolution and placed emphasis on the organization of knowledge in particular epochs. Much of what is known about Childe's personal life is from secondhand observation. He rarely reflected on it in his work and his correspondence generally lacks intimate revelations. We do know that as an Australian in Britain he felt himself somewhat of an outsider in both the personal and professional contexts, which he compounded with his eccentric behavior. In a sympathetic evaluation Bruce Trigger notes that among these eccentricities was a tendency to flaunt his left-wing politics by signing letters in cyrillic script, asking for a copy of the *Daily Worker* at posh hotels, prominently displaying that journal in his office, and occasionally using quotations from Stalin in his public lectures.[2]

Despite a fairly conservative upbringing, Childe was influenced by the radical ideals he encountered while growing up in Australia. He became highly critical of war and religion, and when his peers were enlisting in the European conflict he went to Oxford instead, returning to Australia in 1916, the year of conscription in Britain. During his stay at Oxford he had frequent contact with R. Palme Dutt who later became a key figure in the British Communist party. The two often engaged in lengthy discussions of Hegel, Marx, and the situation in contemporary society.[3] Childe's first book grew out of these political interests. In 1923 he wrote *How Labour Governs: A Study of Worker's Representation in Australia.* It expressed the disenchantment he was feeling over the co-optation of the original ideals of the labor movement. As a result, he returned to England to pursue archaeology full-time.

His illustrious career as an archaeological researcher, writer, and teacher earned Childe academic appointments at Edinburgh and London, and took him to many parts of the world. He taught at Berkeley in the summer of 1939 and influenced an entire generation of American prehistorians concerned with Old World prehistory. Childe himself gave scant consideration to New World prehistory, believing that the civilizations it studies are located outside the mainstream of world social evolution, which was his primary concern. His dubious view of their achievements and failure to include them in his great comparative study, *What Happened in History* (1942), has been justly critiqued by Glyn Daniel.[4] Similarly, Innis's comparative history of civilization evidences the same neglect of New World examples. For both men, however, there is much in the archaeology of the Americas capable of enhancing and challenging their major contributions.[5]

After World War II several attempts were made to appoint Childe to a visiting professorship at the University of Chicago. They were impeded by funding problems, the situation in the archaeology department, and his ill health.[6] During the same period the department of economics at that university tried unsuccessfully to secure the services of Innis, who had earned his doctorate there twenty-five years earlier. In 1953 Childe went on a tour of Russia, several years after Innis made a similar journey. In 1957, with his health deteriorating, he returned to his native Australia after an absence of many years. While hiking alone in the Blue Mountains near Sydney, he fell to his death—perhaps accidentally, possibly intentionally.

A prolific writer, Childe's reputation resided primarily in his ability to synthesize on a grand comparative level, rather than from the discovery and excavation of particular noteworthy sites. Nevertheless, he began his career with several specific studies partially based on original field research. Two are particularly significant. In 1925 he published the *Dawn of European Civilization*, and in 1928 *New Light on the Most Ancient East*. Both books anticipate the broad perspective on economics and technology that would characterize his more renowned *Man Makes Himself* and *What Happened in History*. They also provide a brief glimpse into the social structure and organization of knowledge in archaic civilizations, which would receive fuller treatment in later writings.

In *Man Makes Himself* Childe attempts to deal with nothing less than the development of the human species from its earliest prehistoric beginnings, to the emergence of food production and a settled way of life (the "neolithic revolution") to the rise of the world's first civilizations in the Near East (the "urban revolution"). His use of these terms has been repeatedly critiqued. Nevertheless, it is a tribute to the significance of his work that they are still discussed and occasionally employed. Whether or not Childe was aware of it, two hundred years earlier Rousseau, in his *Discourse on Inequality*, used similar labels. He referred to the "first revolution," which created agriculture and metallurgy, and the "second revolution," which brought towns and civilization. Both the *Discourse* and *Man Makes Himself* range over similar terrain. Childe, however, makes a case for progress, a historical direction Rousseau disavowed, which puts Childe more in sympathy with the philosophes who were Rousseau's contemporaries. Without mentioning a possible link to Rousseau Trigger points out that Childe's understanding of progress and cultural evolution is grounded in the Enlightenment vision of Turgot, Condorcet, Montesquieu, Voltaire, Feguson, Millar, and Robertson.[7] This foundation was in turn updated by new discoveries in anthropology and archaeology, which comprised the nineteenth-century tradition of social evolution that immediately preceded Childe, a tradition he drew from on numerous occasions.

Having captured a wide audience with *Man Makes Himself*, Childe went on to expand aspects of his general synthesis in *What Happened in History*. There is considerable overlap in the two books. Despite the inclusive title of the latter, it does not encompass all of history. Rather, it takes the initial perspective on the origin of civilization in *Man Makes Himself* to Greece and Rome, barely mentioning the Far East and completely omitting ancient New World civilizations. As in the earlier book, emphasis is on major technological innovations such as the wheel, pottery, metallurgy, and writing. These breakthroughs are seen as gounded in a Marxian perspective on relations of production, which according to Childe do not determine ideology (belief system) in an absolute sense, but modify it to the degree that it is consonant with the function of the economic foundations.[8] This approach allows for the influence of factors such as trade, transportation, and the development of abstract principles in science leading to new knowledge, but always within a deliberate materialist framework. Little significance is given to the arts or religious practices, as other than responses to the economic and technological circumstances. It should also be noted that despite the importance of Marx to this perspective, Childe's use of the term *revolution* as a qualifier for *neolithic* and *urban* does not derive from his influence.

The success of *Man Makes Himself* and *What Happened in History* prompted several follow-up studies, less designed to expand the scope of Childe's historiography than to clarify particular points regarding the origin and meaning of the insights that led to his major works. In 1944 he published *Progress and Archaeology*, a book that tried to outline the field, establish a series of key questions it should consider, and suggest methods for pursuing both concerns. In 1947-1948 he gave a series of lectures, which in 1952 became a book titled *Social Evolution*. This project tried to clarify how he used the term *social evolution*, given the traditions Childe both drew from and critiqued.

In 1956 Childe published his last major work, *Society and Knowledge*, as part of Unwin's World Perspective series. A year later Lewis Mumford's the *Transformation of Man* also became part of that series, a tribute to the broad critical vision in the work of both men. *Society and Knowledge* is an archaeologist's attempt to deal with questions of philosophy, the sociology of knowledge, and human communication in general. The book is noteworthy, not because it puts forth definitive arguments, but through the way it reveals a major archaeologist's wide-ranging insight and humanist commitment.

PREHISTORY AND SOCIAL EVOLUTION

Historical development, according to Childe, is an evolutionary process akin to, but not identical with what happens in the natural world. It is characterized by a series of adaptations leading to successive stages of advance, explicable with respect to regularities that are subject to scientific observation. Cultural innovation, as evidenced through new technologies and processes such as diffusion, differentiates social evolution from biological evolution and renders it a more rapid phenomenon. Childe disavows the notion that organic change in individuals, or populations, played any role in the emergence and development of civilization. In this regard he stridently attacks notions of racial determinism used in the kind of historical interpretation that accompanied and was sustained by the rise of fascism.

Childe traces his social evolutionary roots back into the universal history of the eighteenth century. In *Social Evolution* he specifically mentions Adam Ferguson for his delineation of the differences between savagery, barbarism, and civilization, which Childe's work greatly updates. Perhaps this reverence for Ferguson was also motivated by the fact that both men once occupied a chair at the University of Edinburgh.

In the nineteenth century Childe indicates familiarity with the ethnographically informed work of all the major social evolutionists. In general he contends that their schemes lack the elaboration of comprehensive principles capable of explaining the order and development of societies. Although it could be argued that Spencer is an exception, Childe accuses him of being too prejudiced by bourgeois values. Tylor's effort is said to be excessively piecemeal in its failure to see societies as functioning wholes, owing to his stress on isolated elements and institutions. In contrast, high regard is expressed for Morgan, who it is argued avoided the fragmented approach of his contemporaries and discerned social evolution as a whole by delineating ethnical periods based on technological criteria compatible with archaeological discovery.[9] Childe also notes that when Marx needed ethnographic augmentation of his historical perspective he turned to Morgan; likewise Engels, who made some significant revisions to Morgan's *Ancient Society* in his *Origin of the Family, Private Property and the State* (1884), bringing in important new data on European prehistory.

For Childe, the study of prehistory is grounded in the human use of technology. Manufactured artifacts are the most easily discerned remnants of past societies and constitute definitive criteria for establishing evolutionary sequences, and ultimately the chronological order for the development of society as a whole. At one time or another he used, but not without reservation, prehistoric cultural-technological stages based on stone, bronze, and iron, in addition to traditional categories of savagery, barbarism, and civilization. He nonetheless recognized that congruency between the two schemes is far from perfect and the range of societies possible within any specific division quite variable. Eventually he settled on a typology of paleolithic, mesolithic, and neolithic.[10] With respect to the rise of civilization, his work follows Morgan in accepting writing as the diagnostic element. He regards it as a crucial technology, one that led to a series of further adaptations that drastically increased human capacities, especially in the realm of harnessing nature.

A central theme in Childe's vision of prehistory is a concern with the totality of circumstances that constitute the foundations for the emergence of civilization. Although the tenets of social evolutionism guide his interpretation, he avoids the earlier unilineal assumption that regards this process as taking place through a series of fixed stages. Civilization was arrived at, he repeatedly stresses, in different geographical areas and via different routes of development. Nevertheless, certain recurring elements characterize each case: a large population; full-time specialists such as merchants, priests, and rulers; and the concentration of economic and political power. These features were coordinated through the use of conventional symbols in writing, which served to record and transmit essential information, particularly regarding standard weights and measures used in production, trade, and building. It would be interesting to see how Childe would have accommodated into his scheme Andean civilizations such as the Inca, which lacked written communications. Generally averse to considering New World cases, he does make an exception in *Social Evolution*, mentioning the Mayas when arguing against the unilineal approach. Their society was without the plow and domestic animals, but he grants that it was a civilization because other criteria such as external trade, the production of surplus, and writing, provide the necessary parallels with the Near Eastern examples his work favors.

Childe carried into the twentieth century the legacy of nineteenth-century social evolutionism at a time when this legacy was being roundly critiqued in most sociological and anthropological quarters. The grand evolutionary vision gave way to functionalist studies of specific societies, studies inspired by Durkheim in France, and eventually by A. R. Radcliff-Brown (1881-1955) and Bronislaw Malinowski (1884-1942) in England. In the United States Franz Boas (1858-1942) and his followers also eschewed the evolutionary approach, substituting instead the historical particularist method for careful, and some would say unsystematic, scrutiny of a number of aboriginal cultures. Childe was quite aware of the criticisms levelled against evolutionism. Nevertheless, in an interesting way he managed to hold on to the best features of it, and also to utilize the influence of Durkheim and the functionalist tradition in order to understand the operation of select societies located in the grand scheme.

One way in which Childe deviated from both the mainstream of nineteenth-century social evolutionary thought, and from the concerns of the twentieth-century functionalist tradition, was in his emphasis on diffusion. He believed that people naturally preferred established ways of doing things, and as a result major technological innovations, such as the wheeled cart, should reasonably be assumed to have been invented only once unless archaeological evidence exists to the contrary. Similarly, he thought that isolated societies rarely progress without culture contact—a position Trigger calls "moderate, empirical diffusionist."[11] This is almost the converse of the stance taken by Tylor. In fact another recent commentator, Glyn Daniel, cites Tylor's judicious argument for parallelism as more consonant with contemporary knowledge than the "modified diffusionism" of Childe.[12]

Doubtless the emphasis Childe placed on diffusion was made more secure by his failure to consider New World civilizations. It was also motivated by his attempt to distinguish social from biological evolution. Although he adhered to a Darwinian model of variation and adaptation, when it came to the process of social heredity, diffusion rendered human culture unique and allowed it to change at a rate unparalleled in the natural world. It also dispensed with the invocation of any sudden or miraculous factors to explain major historical transformations. Childe's diffusionism might seem extreme in light of contemporary assessments of the same case studies. However, it represented a balanced counter to the hyper-diffusionist tradition in archaeology that gained notoriety at the time he wrote.[13] For Childe diffusion is never an indiscriminant process. Before any society can utilize a particular diffused element it must have reached the appropriate stage in its development.[14]

KNOWLEDGE AND COMMUNICATIONS

Of all the innovations that facilitate the transformation to civilization, Childe puts the elaboration of new modes of communication, such as writing, in a singularly privileged position. In *Man Makes Himself* he refers to it as precipitating a "revolution in human knowledge," which becomes an important subset of the earlier food producing revolution and is virtually coterminous with the later urban revolution.

Childe regards writing as a technology, an intellectual tool that became the necessary instrument of exact science, accounting, mathematics, and astronomy. In the archaeological record it is a convenient index of the change in size, economy, and social organization of any given population. Writing, for Childe, is a hallmark of civilization, but not an absolute determinant. Other factors must facilitate its introduction and influence. In *Social Evolution* he points out that Mycenaean Greece falls short of being a full-fledged civilization, despite the presence of writing among merchants and specialized craftsmen. In this society the general scale of settlement and level of productivity precluded writing from having the dramatic effect it had in Egypt, Mesopotamia, and the Indus valley.

When we look today at the writing systems of the great ancient civilizations we deem such communications to be important because of the way they provide access to the mental and cultural world of a bygone time. However, the true significance of writing, according to Childe, resides in the way it affected the more practical situation of economics, administration, and trade, where "it was destined to revolutionize the transmission of human knowledge."[15] The great changes of the urban revolution were only possible because the societies in question were able to develop a body of accumulated experience and applied knowledge. In *Man Makes Himself* he notes how writing influenced the knowledge produced through earlier craft lore and oral tradition. It made such knowledge more retainable, by a reordering process that rendered it permanent in a systematic, specialized manner.

In Childe's analysis, the invention of writing was not merely an idea whose time had come. It was an innovation forced by productive circumstances. Vast resources had to be monitored by the temples, revenues accounted for, and some unitary control imparted to the expanding resource base. Memory no longer sufficed, even memory enhanced by the use of the mnemonic devices that became increasingly prevalent as the threshold of civilization was approached.

Citing the Mesopotamian city states as examples, Childe notes how accounts were first kept using shorthand pictures, pictograms, which in turn led to ideograms, whereby a picture-sign could stand for an idea rather than the object, as in the case of the sign for jar being a unit of measure. Ideograms could also be conventionalized so that they no longer resembled the familiar, a process that accentuated the exclusivity of writing and led to the emergence of an entrenched scribal class. In Mesopotamia the wedge shaped cuneiform script was the result of this tendency. Difficult to read and write, it required a long apprenticeship for mastery but had the advantage of recording more information in a smaller space to a degree unparalleled in earlier communications. Although Egyptian hieroglyphic and hieratic writing followed a somewhat different path of development, Childe argued that it was created in response to economic and social factors similar to Mesopotamia's.

In early civilization, according to Childe, writing was not geared toward the production of widespread literacy among the populace. It was the preserve of specialists and therefore consonant with the growth of an increasingly complex division of labor and social stratification. In a sense a scribe was like a weaver or a smith; in a sense he was not. The craft of embodying knowledge conferred a more advanced status on its practitioners than was the case with other specialists. As custodians of accounts, medicine, and astronomy, they perpetuated the class divisions and exclusive nature of the new elitist culture, a situation that Innis would later describe and analyze using his "monopoly of knowledge" concept.

Perhaps the most thorough and revealing feature of the discussion of knowledge and communications in *Man Makes Himself* is Childe's examination of the way writing, and associated developments in mathematics, led to the resolution of practical problems, such as those pertaining to weights and measures. With considerable perception, he notes how this enabled the great ancient civilizations to construct vast edifices and coordinate complex agricultural cycles. For him, as for Innis, these activities provided the foundations on which high level abstraction and modern science were later elaborated.

LEWIS MUMFORD: AMERICAN CONTEXT, GLOBAL CONCERNS

Born in the U.S.A. in 1895, three years after Childe and one after Innis, Mumford remains one of the most difficult twentieth-century scholars to evaluate. The simple question of what he is, and represents, can receive no appropriate answer: a scholar who held no regular academic appointment and had a limited, though rich university education; a writer who sustained himself by delving into myriad topics; and a teacher who conveyed by example to a classroom without walls that had parameters extending to whoever was influenced by the aura of his thought. Out of synch with his age, Mumford nonetheless understood and evaluated its dominant trends with great critical skill. In a rare moment of vanity, while not yet thirty, he expressed in his memoirs, a revealing sense of personal location:

> I think that every person of sensibility feels that he has been born "out of his due time." Athens during the early sixth century B.C. would have been more to my liking than New York in the twentieth century after Christ. It is true that this would have cut me off from Socrates, who lived in the disappointing period that followed. But then, I might have been Socrates.[16]

Mumford has been an extraordinarily prolific writer. More than thirty books and innumerable articles have emerged from his inquiring mind.[17] The subjects range from literary and cultural criticism, to urban and architectural studies. Most of these concerns are embedded in an all-embracing history of civilization and technology steeped in a humanist commitment. And unlike Childe, he has written several autobiographical reflections, which are themselves revealing ethnographic accounts of the times and places of his life journey. To summarize each of Mumford's main works would require the remainder of this chapter and then some. Instead, the focus will be an examination of the way his thought led to and coalesced around the theme so aptly used as the title of what many consider to be his best and most important book, *Technics and Civilization* (1934). Although this theme is readily identifiable in many of his other works, the perspective which guides it seems forever elusive. When British art historian and critic, Herbert Read, reviewed *Technics and Civilization*, we can sense both frustration and admiration in his words: "Too diffuse to be science, too disconnected to be history, too concrete to be philosophy, it is difficult to fit into any category".[18]

Mumford saw himself as a generalist, breaking down barriers between academic disciplines and unifying theory, experience, and practice. This has been a mixed blessing. It freed him from formal academic constraints and provided unparalleled breadth of vision; but it also impeded the acceptance of his work by particular disciplines reticent to consider any ideas, no matter how relevant, which do not derive from an acknowledged academic tradition.

In several revealing memoirs Mumford presents us with a sense of the dominant influences that shaped his destiny. For anyone not versed in his more established writings the portrait that emerges is one of artist-writer rather than historian-scholar. This is because many influential situations he describes are of a non-intellectual kind; when scholarly sources of inspiration are cited it is with a brevity that, as general reader, I found refreshing, but as would-be commentator, frustrating. Without going into detail, a few points about his background and influences, appropriate to the rest of this analysis, should be mentioned. Of particular note is his New York upbringing. Then, as much or more than now, this put him in close proximity to the major technological and intellectual developments of the age. Mumford witnessed the creation and initial impact of major innovations in construction, transportation, and communications. The world that unfolded in conjunction with his personal and intellectual growth was one of bridges, skyscrapers, the subway, air travel, radio, television, the military and personal holocaust of two world wars, and several wars of lesser magnitude.

Although Mumford never obtained his B.A., he availed himself of New York City's institutions of higher learning, accumulating numerous courses at the City College, Columbia University, and the New School for Social Research. He dispensed with the ritual of collating these credits and going through the bureaucratic process of petitioning for a degree. Shortly thereafter, in 1919 he served in the navy as a radio-electrician, a practical situation that doubtless gave him insight into the wide implications of communications technology. An intriguing parallel with Innis comes to mind. A few years earlier, during the war, he served in the signal corps of the Canadian army. After his military stint Mumford embarked on a full-time writing career, which included being editor of the *Dial*, a noted literary journal, and publishing the first of his many books, *The Story of Utopias* (1922).

Tracing the vast range of influences on Mumford's thought can be a sketchy matter at best.[19] Unlike several other renowned writers in the social sciences and humanities he does not conceal major sources or feign originality by slightly altering already established ideas to suit his needs. Rather, his major works are bibliographic treasure troves, often annotated to give the reader a sense of what was important and the strengths and limitations of allied studies.

In a sense there is classical Americana underlying part of Mumford's vision. Ralph Waldo Emerson (1803-1882), Henry David Thoreau (1817-1862), Walt Whitman (1819-1892), Nathaniel Hawthorne (1804-1864), and Herman Melville (1819-1891) inspire his understanding of nature, culture, and the human condition. They get recurring mention throughout his work, and one of them, Herman Melville, became the subject of a full-length study by the same name in 1929.

Philosophically, Mumford has claimed influence by, and alliance to, the work of Samuel Butler (1835-1902), Henri Bergson (1859-1941), Petr Kropotkin (1842-1921), and Alfred North Whitehead (1861-1947). Although he is not specific as to what is derived from these sages, or why he chose this grouping, they all share an affirming humanism derived from a firm rejection of mechanism, and the adoption of an organicist vision that emphasizes life as an ongoing process. In a more immediate sense, two of his teachers at the New School for Social Research, Thorstein Veblen (1857-1929) and Graham Wallas (1858-1932) sharpened his critical eye. Both also profoundly affected Innis.

The most intriguing influence on Mumford comes from the man he refers to as his master, Scottish biologist-ecologist and urban theorist, Patrick Geddes (1854-1932). It was Geddes, whose writings he first encountered at age nineteen, that inspired Mumford to follow the generalist as opposed to the specialist path, and provided him with the beginnings of a historical typology. When Mumford eventually met Geddes, and developed as a scholar, disagreements between them began to surface. This is an understandable process, as the disciple matures to become a master in his own right. Nevertheless, Mumford's reverence for his Scottish mentor never abated.[20]

CIVILIZATION AND MECHANIZATION

The method through which Mumford cohered the multiplicity of influences affecting his thought into a revealing and original perspective is a difficult one to chart. The extreme personalism of his approach increased as he matured. His last tour de force, the *Myth of the Machine*, is much more opinionated and critical than its precursor, *Technics and Civilization*. The work is also broader in scope, being divided into two volumes: volume 1, *Technics and Human Development* (1966), which ranges from prehistory to the dawn of the modern age, and volume 2, the *Pentagon of Power* (1970), a consideration of the technological and conceptual foundations of our current era and crises. A short but important transitional work between the two major projects is the oft neglected *Art and Technics* (1952), a book that has relatively more to say about communications than either its forerunner or successor.

One of the most strident critics of progress, technology, and mechanization, Mumford is nonetheless hostile toward those who would advocate an all-consuming pessimism. Nevertheless, the hint of pessimism present in *Technics and Civilization* becomes a full leitmotif in the *Myth of the Machine*. Needless to say recent prophets of the redemptive power of technology—such as Marshall McLuhan and Buckminster Fuller—have severely tried Mumford's patience. But the one writer on technology to whom he has truly ambivalent feelings is Marx.

As in the case of Childe and Innis, for Mumford there is something in Marx necessary for a genuine critical history of man and technics; but there are also directions that would be futile to follow. As early as 1934, in the first edition of *Technics and Civilization*, he notes that "it was Marx's great contribution as a sociological economist to see and partly to demonstrate that each period of invention and production had its own specific value for civilization. . . ."[21] In recent years he has again addressed Marx and again affirmed his importance as a humanitarian and student of the role of technology in history, worthy to stand beside Vico and Comte.[22] However, reservations are also expressed. The later Mumford is less convinced of the priority of the technological—that material relations are the basis of all relations. He emphasizes language, the arts, and politics, chastises Marx for not giving them fuller acknowledgement, and concedes that Marx was right in assuming that all man's creations have a material basis, but wrong in confusing basis with cause. Marx is also seen as holding the view that "economic institutions are self-begotten and all social changes are the by-products of that automated technological development."[23] It could be argued that this reaction is more appropriate as a response to the Marxist tradition than to Marx himself.[24] It doubtless emanates from the dwindling belief in technology as the driving force in history that characterizes Mumford's later works.

The preeminent but not absolute role of technology in affecting historical direction is most forcefully expressed in *Technics and Civilization*. It is the machine age, beginning for Mumford in the tenth century rather than the eighteenth or nineteenth, which must be thoroughly and critically assessed. How did the machine come into being? What forms did it take? Why has our fate been so inextricably linked to its development? These are questions he endeavors to resolve in a landmark study of the psychological as well as practical consequences of machine technology and its interplay with the rest of culture. This perspective is not technological determinism, but a view whereby what he calls technics is a powerful element within human culture, constraining its development and key features. More than three decades later, in the *Myth of the Machine*, technics would still be stressed, but not so insistently. Mechanization is now regarded as an outgrowth of aspects of the nature of human social organization, with machines a material consequence of this tendency rather than a first cause.

Technics and Civilization was elaborated around a typology that all but disappears in the *Myth of the Machine*, although elements from it are extrapolated further in a more inclusive context. In contrast to Innis and McLuhan, who would later base their historical periodization on what we can refer to as the dominant mode of communication, Mumford uses more general technological criteria, particularly features relating to the production of energy. His scheme consists of three overlapping and interpenetrating phases: the eotechnic, paleotechnic, and neotechnic. The latter two were appropriated from Geddes, the first is his own elaboration. The eotechnic ranged from approximately A.D. 1000 to 1750, and was characterized by a cultural-technological complex based on wind, water, and wood. The paleotechnic stretched from mid-eighteenth to mid-nineteenth century and was grounded on the widespread use of coal and iron. The neotechnic followed, and has continued to the present, based as it is on electricity and alloys. The vulnerability of this typology to criticism might have been a reason for Mumford's decreased reliance on it. For example, to treat the period from A.D. 1000 to 1750 as a single culture seems extreme. Even if we discount ideational movements such as the Renaissance, and view social life solely in accordance with technological criteria, we can discern crucial shifts occurring in the mid-fifteenth century traceable to the invention of moveable type printing. Mumford does give this invention considerable significance, but not enough to create a new historical division.

Mumford's consideration of the printing press illustrates that his analysis is not limited to energy technologies. Indeed, some of his finest passages deal with other developments. Perhaps the most renowned and oft cited is his consideration of the mechanical clock. In *Technics and Civilization* extensive commentary is devoted to tracing its origin and its influence on social structure and psychology. It is to him, the most all-pervasive of our technologies, the machine which, directly or indirectly, regulates all other machines. Other provocative passages assess the implications of glass, glasses, mirrors, the telescope, and microscope in entrenching a dominant visual bias. This bias has also been discerned by McLuhan, who links it exclusively to print, and by Foucault, who connects it to shifts in cultural perception deriving from changes in the discourse embodied in the dominant texts of the time.

Technics and Civilization warns us of the dangers of the machine, but ends on an optimistic note. The *Myth of the Machine* sees less promise in technology, and therefore the future. The position Mumford takes recalls, no doubt unintentionally, what Camus said regarding the one authentically heroic response possible to the contemporary world of the absurd: to confront it without hope, but also without resignation, through an unyielding, self-reflective struggle.

The situation assessed in the *Myth of the Machine* is one Mumford describes as megatechnics. He now adds, to the list of all the technologies considered in *Technics and Civilization*, nuclear energy, supersonic transportation, cybernetic intelligence, and new modes of instantaneous electronic communication. The human lot, he argues, has not been bettered by these developments. Technological progress does not equate with moral progress, rather, it suppresses cultural autonomy and emphasizes uniformity. To substantiate this assertion requires a sense of what humankind inherently is, and why our creations have been disengaged from full and reasonable control. In establishing this scenario Mumford uses the metaphor of the sorcerer's apprentice, who casts a spell that he cannot stop to animate domestic objects to do his labor, and the example of a runaway locomotive minus its engineer.

The anthropological, archaeological, and historical-philosophical perspective of the *Myth of the Machine* recalls the one put forth by a writer whom Mumford cites favorably on several occasions—Jean-Jacques Rousseau. I would go further and say that Mumford's project constitutes a recasting of the *Discourse on Inequality* in light of the resources in data and theory available to mid-twentieth-century inquiry. There is a similar consideration of humankind's emergence out of a state of nature, and a history of civilization and technology as one, not of progress, but of progressive alienation.

A key to Mumford's negativity toward the recent technological imperative resides in his rejection of the established anthropological view that accords tools the definitive role in human evolutionary development. Although not dismissing their importance, he emphasizes the greater significance of play, mimesis, ritual, and imagination as modes of self-discovery and self-transformation. Considerable multidisciplinary research informs this perspective. Interestingly, a major source is Tylor, whom Mumford regards as the founding father of anthropology. One of only several nonanthropologists to appreciate Tylor's work, Mumford credits him with being one of the few early anthropologists who did not overrate the importance of stone tools.[25] In a contrasting vein, while greatly appreciative of Childe's contribution, he regards it as leaning too much in the direction of technologism.

In Mumford's scheme, early human evolution was characterized by a vast array of communicational modes such as language, myth, art, and ritual. Accompanying these developments were vast changes in the realm of social organization, first with cooperative hunting, then with agriculture, and finally with full-fledged civilization. The latter transformation occurred in the third millennium B.C. and had profound and far-reaching repercussions. It yielded the megamachine. This is not a technology but a mode of human organization, a vast social machine. It first arose in the great archaic civilizations under the auspices of divine kingship, and served to restructure human productive life and labor. Human components were arranged in a regular, mechanical way and provided a basis for later technological machines. This major social occurrence is of course invisible to archaeologists and historians. In looking at the consequences of it, such as the pyramids, they have been too quick to make reference to technological criteria. Mumford convincingly argues that when we look back at the monuments of ancient civilizations, the technology they had at their disposal to effect them pales in comparison with the great feats of human organization required to do the job.

The megamachine was not only effective for projects of civil labor, it provided the basis for the military machine, which has been with us ever since: *"Through the army, in fact, the standard model of the megamachine was transmitted from culture"*[26] (Mumford's italics). The military is a system of specialized, interchangeable, but functionally differentiated parts. Like other forms of the megamachine, its purpose is not labor-saving, but labor-enslaving. In more recent years megamachine operation has been consciously modelled on the technological machines that it once predated and inspired. Mumford's analysis here converges remarkably with that of Foucault, who in *Discipline and Punish* independently develops a perspective on the mechanistic regimentation of the human body in military, disciplinary, and educational arenas, which he claims has been a neglected but important aspect of our social history over the past two centuries. Finally, bringing the megamachine into the twentieth-century world of instantaneous communication, Mumford notes how under Hitler and Stalin it led to a rebirth of archaic divine kingship, and new forms of anonymous regimentation.

COMMUNICATIONS AND HUMAN DEVELOPMENT

The study of different facets of human communication has always been a significant aspect of Mumford's writings on technology. In a sense, it is unfortunate that although he wrote in the years after Innis's death, as well as before, there appears to be no influence or even mention of that Canadian scholar. Rather, it was McLuhan who caught Mumford's eye and ire—initially, because of McLuhan's optimistic paean to new technologies, eventually because Mumford came to the realization that certain ideas about new media, credited to McLuhan, had in fact been broached in his own writings. In one of Mumford's autobiographical studies, *Findings and Keepings* (1975), he includes a persuasive section titled "Thirty Years Before McLuhan." In it he cites several quotes from *Technics and Civilization* that address the implications of electronic media, including one that anticipates the "global village" concept of McLuhan, only in more cautious language.

There is, in Mumford's writings, a kind of discontinuous history of communications. In *Art and Technics* and the *Myth of the Machine* he discusses the nature and origin of language and the symbolic capacity in general. In the latter book he considers the role of writing in the rise of civilization and deployment of the megamachine. The implications of moveable type printing are examined in *Technics and Civilization* and *Art and Technics*. And finally, reflections on electronic media are scattered throughout all of the above writings. Let us consider each of these subjects in turn, beginning with language.

Following the linguist Otto Jespersen (1860-1943) Mumford notes that spoken language was "probably a source of emotional communion long before it became a useful instrument of practical communication."[27] The vagueness and ambiguity of language indicate its origins in subjectivity and emotional reaction to experience, rather than in the formation of abstract concepts or the translation of observations into precise messages. Following in the romantic tradition, he notes that although practical considerations such as cooperative hunting doubtless played an important role in the emergence of spoken communication, the needs of these activities are not as complex as the language they helped bring into being; even today children are ready for language and ritual long before they are ready for work. Also, in technologically primitive societies spoken language is far from primitive. In complexity it rivals any tongue spoken in the cultures of advanced civilization.

These views are not original to Mumford. He claims location in the tradition of Vico and Muller. Muller, he argues, properly stressed the expressive aspect of early language, whereby it was steeped in metaphor and myth in order to cope with the mystery of existence. Rational uses of language, such as numbering, sorting, and defining, came much later. Mumford also downplays tools as the essential criteria defining our humanity during early epochs. Like Vico and Rousseau he sees human beginnings in an age of poetry and song, where dreams, ritual, and new social arrangements, rather than technological achievements, enhanced and defined our existence. What tools actually accomplished during this time was far less substantial than generations of researchers have believed. The meagre tool repertoire was not as significant as what developed on the psychological and social planes: a powerful retentive memory, imaginative intelligence, and group strategies.

It is unfortunate that in the many pages of the *Myth of the Machine* devoted to language Darwin receives only the briefest mention, despite the fact that his view of language origins is grounded in emotional expressiveness. Although Mumford makes a good case for not overrating tools, the crucial issue of early human evolution *is* Darwinian survival, and whatever is being considered in the area of behavior, be it song or the manufacture of a hand axe, must enhance it through conferring selective advantage. Muller, one of Mumford's main sources, rejected the Darwinian theory. Mumford of course does not. Nevertheless, the provocative views on language in the *Myth of the Machine* need to be further elaborated in the crucible of evolutionary thinking. For example, consider Mumford's astute observation: "In collecting food man was also incited to collect information."[28] (It is here, as French anthropologist Levi-Strauss insightfully shows, that the aesthetic and poetic is fused with the logical and rational in primitive thought and in the nature of mind underlying all human thought.) This view needs fuller contextualization using the calculus of evolutionary theory, which need not preclude accepting the mythopoetic as an adaptive survival strategy.

Like several other researchers in the field of prehistory and anthropology, Mumford waxes eloquent over the bygone days of hunting and gathering. With the agricultural revolution of the neolithic a certain freedom and spontaneity was lost. The new security provided a new regularity of life, with more drudgery and boredom than ever before. The domestication of plants and animals was a direct result of man domesticating himself.[29] (Again, this is a view that, intentionally or not, echoes Rousseau.) The neolithic produced societies of higher potentiality and diversity than ever before, but the new modes of labor it engendered also provided the basis for elaboration of the megamachine. Writing greatly facilitated this occurrence: "If one single invention was necessary to make this larger mechanism operative for constructive tasks as well as coercion, it was probably writing."[30]

In his assessment of the role of writing in ancient civilization, several of Mumford's views either parallel or were influenced by Childe. However, he has a stated preference for the work of Henri Frankfort on the ancient Near East. Frankfort dealt more with human organization, Childe with technology, and Mumford credits the former with inspiring his concept of the megamachine. For Mumford, writing made possible the transmission of vast amounts of information throughout the system. It also fixed accountability, which went hand in hand with organizing the obligations of vast numbers of people. As in the case of earlier generations of researchers, perhaps going as far back as Condillac, Mumford points out how early writing was developed for purposes of record keeping, and the communication of such records through time and over space, not for expressing conceptual, mythical, or historical ideas. But for him, writing also gave rise to an institution, the bureaucracy, which in turn functioned as a form of communications: "The bureaucracy was, in fact, the third type of 'invisible machine'—one might call it a communications machine—co-existing with the military and labor machines, and an integral part of the final totalitarian structure."[31] This reciprocity between power, knowledge, and communications, which Mumford reveals in the *Myth of the Machine*, to a degree parallels aspects of Innis's research. One key difference is that Mumford usually deals with the origin as well as function of particular historical scenarios, whereas Innis is primarily concerned with function. Nevertheless, Mumford could have benefited from a familiarity with Innis's work.

Regarding the printing press, there is a good deal of coverage in Mumford's writings, and observations similar to those that become full-blown hypotheses in McLuhan's oracular pronouncements. For Mumford print, with its standardized interchangeable parts, lent itself to large-scale production and continued the process of mechanical replication that began socially with the megamachine. Print released people from the domination of the immediate and local, contributed to the collapse of medieval society, and disrupted the balance between the sensuous and the intellectual—a major McLuhan theme. With print, authority in knowing became the authority of books; face-to-face communication diminished in importance. The new intellectual world view accompanied an increasing personal autonomy and alienation: "abstracted from gesture and physical presence the printed word fostered the process of analysis and isolation."[32]

In *Art and Technics* printing is discussed with reference to the scribal tradition that preceded it. Print took over the mechanical aspect of book reproduction, at first in a way that acknowledged the aesthetic dimension of earlier manuscripts, but after a long struggle full mass production forced the technical to override the aesthetic. However, Mumford's assessment is not a nostalgic longing for a more artistic age. He also notes how print: freed writers; transferred the mechanization of the worker (scribe) to the work process; broke the class monopoly on the written word; gave the common man greater cultural access; and "accentuated man's natural eyemindedness" by freeing "mind from a state of irrelevant concreteness."[33] These are views that hark back to the celebration of print found in the eighteenth-century writings of Turgot and Condorcet. For example, the following passage from the *Myth of the Machine* could just as easily be transplanted to Condorcet's great historical overview: "The enrichment of the collective human mind through the printing and circulating of books is comparable only to that linking together of individual brains and experiences brought about through the invention of discursive language."[34]

Less positive words are directed at modern electronic media. In *Technics and Civilization* Mumford notes how the telegraph commenced a series of inventions —the wireless, the telephone and television—which speeded up exchange over space. As a result modern communications verge on returning us to an instantaneous person-to-person situation, as long as the required perfection of the apparatus can be attained. But negative aspects of this development include a weakening of the kind of reflective thought involved in reading and writing, and ultimately a tendency to render people more passive and susceptible to coercion by a dominant minority. These dangers are reiterated in the *Myth of the Machine*, as he launches a full assault on what he calls McLuhan's "audio-visual tribalism." For Mumford a situation of polytechnics in communication, utilizing all available media, is preferable to the monotechnic world McLuhan envisions. McLuhan, he notes, fails to recognize that real communication is between people sharing a common culture. Also, Mumford cites research to show that a medium such as the radio, far from retribalizing the planet, has been more effective on the local level.

Mumford takes McLuhan's views on communications quite literally—too literally in fact. The result is a harsh critique. However, this situation is preferable to McLuhan's attempt, in *Understanding Media*, to chastise Mumford for failing to consider communications, when the American polymath has hardly ignored this area.

8   *The Canadian Connection I: Harold Innis*

> The arbitrary signs of language and writing provide men with the means of insuring the possession of their ideas and of communicating them to others in the manner of an inheritance. . . .
>
>   —Turgot

In the later writings of Harold Adams Innis (1894-1952) communication becomes not merely an aspect of a sweeping epochal history, but its central theme. Arrival at this position came after a long sojourn through political economy, accentuating Canadian historical development within a global framework, and a closely attuned sensitivity to the major events and crises of the first half of the twentieth century.

Generally regarded as Canada's foremost interdisciplinary scholar, Innis's marginal/mainstream relatedness to his country's culture and intellectual life somewhat parallels that of Gordon Childe and Lewis Mumford. Although Innis had considerable international renown at the time of his death, his communication studies were not widely known. He drafted them hastily and in a cryptic but suggestive style during his final years. These stylistic difficulties doubtless impeded recognition of his work, along with the fact that it does not fit comfortably into any formally established disciplinary tradition; even close colleagues were and still are uncomfortable with his research. A major factor behind recent increased interest in this aspect of Innis—although a number of Canadian scholars may choose to ignore or deny it—has been McLuhan. His citations of Innis and claim of discipleship, while contentious and rife with misunderstanding, have led more than one student to discover Innis in the original.

Innis began making direct inroads into communication studies about 1945. His major compilation was a thousand-plus page manuscript titled the *History of Communication*. From this base emerged *Empire and Communications* (1950); *The Bias of Communication* (1951); and *Changing Concepts of Time* (1952). These contributions are suggestive rather than definitive. They attempt to frame distinct areas of research rather than hand down a specific theoretical perspective. This is not to say that the theoretical component is minimal. However, it is never rigidly cast, and a main contention of mine is that acceptance and further development of the field as Innis conceived it is not necessarily contingent on accepting his particular explanatory formulations.

In opening for investigation a full-fledged perspective on the relationship between communications and history, Innis argued that the orientation of any one discipline would be insufficient. What he labelled "academic monopolies of knowledge," a subset of his sweeping monopoly of knowledge concept, had rigidified the viewpoint of the social sciences and humanities. His criticisms were not directed so much at the structure and focus of traditional disciplines, but on their unwillingness to exchange insights and collaborate on relevant problems. As a result he called for an interdisciplinary perspective in his communications researches well before the idea became fashionable in the late sixties and early seventies.

In a number of circles a traditionalist view persists that regards Innis's communication studies as an idiosyncratic preoccupation of his later years, not worthy to stand beside his earlier work in political economy. Recent commentary has been critical of this two Innises notion and more inclined to view his research as a developmental continuum.[1] Even a brief glimpse of his life and influences will reveal events and circumstances that prefigure the communications concerns of his final years and the methodology he brought to that subject.

PERSONAL AND INTELLECTUAL DEVELOPMENT

Born and raised in the farm country of southwestern Ontario, Innis's early life was very much tied to the land.[2] Farming experiences, including the reality of a fluctuating market, doubtless impinged on his consciousness at an early age. He attended a classic one-room schoolhouse and was greatly encouraged in his educational pursuits by the atypical situation of having a college educated mother. In 1905 he went to high school, in part because his family had three other children to help with the chores. His commute there was on the Grand Trunk Railway, not an insignificant fact. Exposure to this mode of transportation and communication, and the impromptu narratives about it that he gleaned from railway people, opened his mind to historical/geographical ideas that would resurface more fully in his as yet unglimpsed academic career. Other commentators have also pointed to the significance of these early years. For example, Havelock has stressed that Innis's upbringing in a primary rural context affected considerably the nostalgia for the oral tradition evidenced in his later communication studies.[3]

One of Innis's early goals was to be a teacher, and after graduation from high school he taught part-time in his old one-room elementary school and worked in the general store to earn enough money for college. Again, the situation can be construed as influential to his later years when we think ahead to his disdain for obsessive specialization and compartmentalization in the world of academic learning. Eventually he went to McMaster University, located then in Toronto, and graduated prior to World War I. Although his original goal was to be a teacher, his family hoped he would become a Baptist minister, an ironic choice given his eventual skepticism toward inflexible institutions. At this point in his life, however, a career in law seemed an amenable compromise. The prelaw university studies had revealing moments, particularly in history and political economy, his favorite subjects. Several inspiring teachers inculcated in him a sense of reflective questioning regarding the nature of knowledge. He also learned that although the economic interpretation of history is not absolutely definitive, it is indeed a powerful tool.

After graduation from McMaster Innis enlisted in the army to fight in the war. His military involvement was with the signal corps, an appropriate calling in light of the contention that early life experiences can influence later intellectual directions. (World War I was a veritable history of technology in microcosm, utilizing everything from horses to aircraft for transportation, and carrier pigeons to the radio for communication.) Innis saw front line duty at Vimy Ridge, suffered a wound to his knee from an artillery shell, and during convalescence began work on an intriguing M.A. thesis, "The Returned Soldier."

After returning to Canada and completing his M.A., Innis finally entered law school. Still interested in political economy, however, he decided to take a few summer courses in the subject at the University of Chicago. He was enthralled by the intellectual spirit there, which included the likes of Thorstein Veblen, Robert Park, and George Herbert Mead. Although Innis did not take courses with these luminaries, he appears to have been influenced by the environment they created. The law career went on what would become permanent hold and he enrolled full-time in the Ph.D. program in economics. The result was a dissertation, which eventually became a book in 1923, titled *A History of the Canadian Pacific Railway*. This led to a teaching position at the University of Toronto and continued research and teaching in the economic history of Canada, a field in which he was a true pioneer. In 1930 he published another major work, the *Fur Trade in Canada*. Fundamental to this study, as with the previous, was a firsthand exploration of the country as an accompaniment to the obligatory archival researches. He also established the viewpoint that Canadian history could be approached through examining the development of trade, transportation, and communication networks, an anticipation of what he would later elaborate on a global level.

Further studies on the economic history of Canada led to a third book, *The Cod Fisheries: The History of an International Economy*. To this point, Innis's political-economic studies championed what has become known as the staples thesis.[4] It deals with the way dominant features of a country are related to the exploitation of staple resources such as minerals, fur, timber, fish, grain, oil, gas, and hydroelectric power. The thesis contends that the way regional development occurs, as a result of extraction of such staples, is through a pattern that serves the interests of major centers of power leading to one-sided development of the exploited regions. Social disparity and instability often result. In his later years, when Innis shifted to global communications concerns, staple commodities were no longer of prime concern. Nevertheless, certain features of the staples thesis persisted and were applied to the new situation where information took on the role of a commodity, and its link to monopolies of knowledge created another kind of dependency relationship between the center and the margins.

Innis had many honors bestowed upon him. He was appointed to several commissions dealing with regional economic planning, which was certainly consonant with his "get out of the ivory tower at every opportunity" approach. In 1937 he was appointed head of the department of political economy at the University of Toronto. In 1943 he was offered a prestigious position at the University of Chicago, which he graciously declined. He also helped establish the Canadian Social Sciences and Humanities Research Council and the Association of, and Journal of, Economic History. Innis died of cancer in 1952, just prior to delivering his presidential address to the American Economic Association. Doubtless his impending death prevented him from imparting more coherence to his later communication studies. If anything, it spurred him to map out the field as broadly and convincingly as possible, at the expense of a careful elaboration of part of this vision, which would have been more accepted in traditional academic circles.

THE HISTORY OF COMMUNICATIONS

Innis's history of communications is a kaleidoscopic fusion of outlines for a new field of study and specific hypotheses pertinent to that field. At least a partial separation of these two aspects can perhaps further clarify the context of development and ongoing relevance of his later works.

First, the issue of style must be addressed. It has created a considerable impediment for both the scholar and educated layperson who attempt to grapple with Innis. To describe the way Empire and Communications and the Bias of Communication are elaborated is almost as difficult as reading these works. Often whole arguments are encapsulated in a single sentence or phrase. At best, insightful aphorisms can be frequently discerned. At worst, contradictions overwhelm the reader hoping for at least a modicum of scholarly consistency. There is considerable ambiguity and meandering narrative; a promising insight or argument will be raised and suddenly disappear, only to resurface later in the text.

McLuhan has claimed that Innis intentionally cultivated such a style, that it is a major strength of his work, and that the insights Innis achieved can only be presented in this way. This is questionable. The mystery of Innis's writing can be partially resolved if we look at it as a series of notes, or a draft, that provides foundations for further elaboration—almost as if we were to have Marx's economic and philosophical manuscripts or Darwin's early notebooks without further qualifying texts. Interestingly, when some of Innis's primary notebooks were actually published, for example, his *Idea File*, similarity between it and the formal texts is striking.[5] In a sense all his later communication studies constitute an idea file. They represent an effort of self-clarification regarding a new field of study and the key insights pertaining to it. The disjointed, or "mosaic-nonlineal presentation" as McLuhan refers to it, is not necessary for a full appreciation of the results of Innis's research. Another format could have been used. But it was essential for Innis, in the early stages of thinking about the subject and pressed for time, to work with a notelike style. As in all note compilations personal idiosyncracies abound. To raise Innis's style to the status of a new method of historical writing is misleading. What resulted is more a glimpse of mind in process than a new and deliberate research strategy.

Despite the complexity of Innis's writings, the basic ideas are accessible.[6] History is perceived as a series of epochs separated by discontinuity. Each is distinguished by dominant forms of media that absorb, record, and transform information into systems of knowledge consonant with the institutional power structure appropriate to the society in question. The interaction between media form and social reality creates various biases, which strongly affect the society's cultural orientation and values. This is not a monocausal process. For Innis, communication technology never determines the character of an epoch. To use his words it "hastens," "facilitates," or "helps to define" that character. *Interplay, formation*, and *interaction* are terms that can be used to describe his view of the historical process. Reflexive determinism is as inappropriate to Innis as it is to Marx. True, Marx once said that the "hand mill will give you society with the feudal lord and the steam engine society with the industrial capitalist."[7] But he did not base a theory of history on such illustrative one-liners, and few would, except perhaps McLuhan, who has raised Innis's aphorisms, as well as his own, to such a status.

In Innis's historiography communications function as a first and last point from which we can assess the character of a civilization. To understand any epoch we of course have to take into account a considerable amount of material. However, to grasp its basic processes and dominant cultural patterns, a communications perspective can be more revealing than one solely based on relations of production or the system of beliefs, in part because it crosscuts so many features of the social fabric.

The historiography of Innis is not one where details predominate. Concern is with broad configurations in cultural form as they are related to major technological features. Personalities and events are subordinate to movements in the macrostructure. It is not surprising that he cites Hegel on several occasions, and indicates a clear debt to the historical vision of twentieth-century writers such as Spengler, Toynbee, and anthropologist Alfred Kroeber. Like these scholars Innis had a penchant for seeing the historical process as an organic one governed by tendencies of growth, decay, rise, and fall. Although Innis remained within a humanist or interpretive tradition, never explicitly delineating laws of development or necessary recurrences, as did social evolutionists such as Childe, he clearly pushed this tradition to its explanatory limits.

In developing his history of communications, Innis elaborates a framework of epochal divisions that are linked to the dominant mode of communication. From the oral tradition of preliterate cultures, through different types of writing and print, to the electronic media of our own time, communications have been integral to the functioning of all social institutions. This perspective and the associated analysis are far less simplistic than it appears at first glance. Unlike McLuhan who makes direct leaps from media to cultural traits, Innis acknowledges the complexity of the interplay. For example, in understanding a particular society from a history of communications perspective, the dominant medium has to be considered in terms of its inherent properties, be that medium spoken language in a primary oral culture; stone, clay, papyrus, or parchment in early civilization; or printed paper and electronic media in modern times. This consideration must be accompanied by an assessment of the form of communication utilized by the medium in question. For instance, if the medium is used for writing, what type of script is employed: pictorial, cuneiform, hieroglyphic, syllabic, or phonetic; also, what are its characteristics and how do they articulate with the potentialities of the medium? Finally, any analysis of culture and communication must be grounded in the economics surrounding both the production of the dominant medium and the institutional framework that will incorporate it.

Needless to say, Innis did not carry out this project in its entirety. But he did make programmatic inroads capable of being elaborated further. His landmark text in this area remains *Empire and Communications*. It traces the interplay between communications and civilization from the Near East through Greece, Rome, and medieval Europe to the beginnings of the modern era. There are, to be sure, major omissions, such as New World and Asiatic civilizations. However, we must remember that the work is an outline, not a definitive history. In this sense it can be seen as similar to Rousseau's *Discourse on Inequality*. Both works ask fundamental and enduring questions about the human consequences of social and technological change, and lend themselves to being rewritten in subsequent generations in response to new data and research developments.

As in the case of Rousseau's *Discourse*, acceptance of Innis's historical vision, it can be argued, need not be predicated on acceptance of the way Innis rendered specific interpretations within his programmatic scheme. To use features of his overall method, in light of further data, to challenge some of his own theoretical conjectures, would be to pay him high tribute. Can a perspective this flexible and self-corrective be construed as a paradigm in humanities and social science research? Perhaps. A possible parallel can be drawn with the natural sciences, where such accommodation is not unknown.[8] A case in point is the Darwinian paradigm in evolutionary biology, which in response to new research can challenge and refute several of Darwin's more imaginative theoretical conjectures, without diminishing his pathbreaking research program.

THE ORAL VERSUS THE WRITTEN TRADITIONS

Much of Innis's history of communications is given over to the elaboration of a number of concepts that range from general themes to key hypotheses. Their originality complements the originality of his overall map of the field. They also have a contentious and speculative dimension that invites challenge and extrapolation. Unfortunately there are those who find Innis's concepts problematic, and reject his entire project on that basis, when what the concepts illustrate are only several lines of possible inquiry within the field as a whole.

True to the general pattern of his late work, Innis's exploratory formulations are not systematically elaborated and then applied, but woven throughout his texts, leaving the reader to draw more implications than are spelled out. This creates perils for the commentator, who risks being accused of misrepresentation. However, if we acknowledge that access to what Innis really meant is forever beyond recall, and try to remain faithful to the general spirit of his texts, then a reasonable attempt at interpretation can be made.

A fundamental notion that runs throughout Innis's vision of communications and history is the importance of understanding the oral tradition. The contrast between orality and literacy, central to the work of recent scholars in communication studies such as Goody and Ong, is used in Innis as a starting point for numerous general discussions, and as a lead-in to an elaboration of several key concepts. Although reasons for this emphasis are never rendered explicit, the logic behind it appears direct and plausible. If we are to understand as fully as possible the transformations brought about by complex technological developments, especially in the realm of communications, then we must have a sense of the way things were before this occurred. Such a perspective can help us see ourselves in revealing and unconventional ways, and enable us to assess the losses as well as the gains that are the price of civilization. This vision is anthropological—more precisely, it constitutes a philosophical anthropology and has roots that can be traced back to eighteenth- and nineteenth-century social thought in the primitive/civilized dichotomy of Rousseau, Marx-Engels, Morgan, Maine, and a host of others.[9] Nevertheless, Innis's immediate source in this area appears to have been twentieth-century classical scholarship.[10]

For Innis, the important feature of an oral tradition is not its aural nature, as McLuhan would have us believe, but the fact that it emphasizes dialogue and inhibits the emergence of monopolies of knowledge leading to overarching political authority, territorial expansion, and the inequitable distribution of power and wealth. Writing, in contrast, yielded a "transpersonal memory." It facilitated abstract thought giving rise to science and mathematics, and although it freed thought from the subjective realm of the oral tradition, it rendered explicit social obligations in law and economics. Innis, of course, did not use this oral/literate contrast to advocate a romantic return to the former. Rather, it functioned as an element in a critical theory of knowledge, whereby recapturing something of the spirit of the oral mode, with its attendant "elasticity" would, he believed, foster intellectual exchange and generate a skeptical attitude toward entrenched dogma.

There are a number of problems with Innis's formulations on orality. For one, inequities of wealth and power are possible in such cultures. A case in point are the early Greeks that served as his model; and as the anthropological record shows there have been numerous nonliterate societies engaging in territorial expansion. This does not invalidate his analysis, provided we appreciate it with the flexibility in which it was conceived. To use a structural-linguistic kind of reasoning, we can say that in Innis's perspective orality is never defined discretely, by absolutes, but always in contrast to what writing entails, as a series of opposed historical tendencies. It could be construed that this illustrates the dialectical nature of his approach. It is probably no coincidence that *The Bias of Communication* opens with a quote from Hegel.

Perhaps the most limiting feature of Innis's concept of the oral tradition is that his ideal type, or model of it, is based on the Greek experience, particularly prior to Aristotle where the nondominating presence of writing imparted balance (another favorite Innisian notion) to the social scene. Innis's discussion of orality evidences no consideration of the phenomenon as it pertains to the native cultures of Africa, Asia, or the New World. Discounting the obvious limitations of model building from one source, the real oversight resides in Innis, the Canadian nationalist, looking for enlightenment outside of Canada where illustrations could have been drawn from the home front. For example, the oral tradition and democracy among the Iroquois were subjects elaborated by two well-known nineteenth-century American writers, Francis Parkman, the historian, and Lewis Morgan, the anthropologist. Both favorably compared the Iroquois to the early Greeks, Innis's primary source. Even in Innis's regional studies of Canada and elaboration of the concept of marginality, native peoples get virtually no mention.

An interesting point of contrast is to look at the concept of the oral tradition as espoused by McLuhan. Although McLuhan's view of the phenomenon is laced with misunderstandings, and almost any comparison of Innis and McLuhan is bound to be to the detriment of the latter, it is nevertheless worth noting that his acknowledgement of oral cultures is substantially more inclusive than Innis's. For McLuhan, African, native American, as well as early Greek peoples, all validly represent the oral mode. Yet, like Innis, and despite the concern both evidence toward the implications of new technologies, neither discuss issues pertaining to racial and cultural genocide on this continent facilitated by the introduction of these technologies.

Further understanding of Innis's view of the oral tradition can be derived from consideration of his concept of culture and attendant notion of balance. In this area his roots are clearly in the humanist as opposed to social science tradition.

Instead of subscribing to a social science definition of culture such as Tylor's, whereby it is seen as the totality of lifeways of any given social group, he uses a concept considerably more value laden. The humanist use of the term is usually associated with an enlightened, privileged, or balanced state of individual being; also to those transcendent outpourings of society such as art, religion, and intellectual life.

Innis seems to have been aware of the pitfalls of the traditional humanist associations of culture, especially when he notes that "writings on culture can be divided into those attempting to weaken other cultures and those attempting to strengthen their own."[11] Nevertheless, in a case of "do as I say, not as I do," he partially succumbs to what he warns us against. This is evidenced in his ideal, but certainly not utopian, model of a culture whose extremes are balanced by the presence of a democratically grounded oral tradition inspired by the Greek example. It serves him as a measure of the shortcomings of recent times: "In contrast with civilization dominated by Greek culture with its maxim 'nothing in excess,' modern civilization dominated by machine industry is concerned always with specialization which might be described as always in excess."[12]

Although aware of problems with the Greek situation, such as slavery and the low status of women, Innis, trained as he was in a humanist tradition, nonetheless sought the best of culture, as well as indicting the worst, in the Western lineage. This orientation is also reflected in his overall perspective on the development of civilization. What is deemed significant is not the nature of the process in its own right—as it might be studied by an archaeologist or anthropologist—but the chronological transformations that led to our present age. As a result, the analysis in *Empire and Communications* covers Egypt, Mesopotamia, Greece, Rome, and Europe, whereas civilizations outside of the mainstream of this evolution, for example, those in the Indus valley, ancient China, and Central and South America are not assessed. Pointing to this gap in Innis is to be critical in a positive sense, not by indicating deficiencies in his work, but suggesting areas where it can be further developed and tested.

The attempt by Innis to use a concept of culture to gain critical insight on Western civilization was paralleled by a writer of his generation who was also a part of the University of Chicago scene, American anthropologist Edward Sapir. In 1924 Sapir wrote a landmark article, "Culture, Genuine and Spurious."[13] Although it is difficult to say whether or not Innis was influenced by Sapir—there is brief mention of him in *Empire and Communications* without a textual citation—the themes Sapir raised in his paper are similar to those Innis elaborates in the essay "Industrialism and Cultural Values" in *The Bias of Communication*. What makes Sapir's effort extraordinary, and worth considering in this context, is the way he succeeded in synthesizing the best features of the humanist and social science concepts of culture, thereby avoiding some of the limitations that characterize Innis's efforts.

TIME, SPACE, AND THE MONOPOLY OF KNOWLEDGE

Perhaps the most recurring, frequently cited, and ambitious of all Innisian formulations regarding the history of communications and civilization, are those pertaining to time and space. His contentions in this area are sweeping. Just as each civilization has it dominant form of communications, so too it has a resulting bias in cultural orientation toward either time or space. Rarely does a situation of balance and stability occur. According to Innis, the way time and/or space are accentuated through communications is a crucial factor behind the rise of a civilization and its eventual collapse.

Time-biased or time-binding societies tend to be those dependent on durable media that are difficult to transport; examples cited are the ancient empires reliant on stone or clay, and medieval Europe employing parchment. Like oral societies, which Innis also deemed to be time-bound, these civilizations were tradition-oriented. They emphasized custom, continuity, community, the sacred and moral, which impeded individualism as a dynamic for innovation, but allowed it to flourish in terms of expressive communication, especially in the language used to convey dominant ideas. In the case of the major civilizations, as opposed to purely oral cultures, the time bias led to hierarchical social orders that allowed an elite group, be it Egyptian or Babylonian priests, or the Catholic clergy of the Middle Ages, to form a powerful class with exclusive access to a monopoly of knowledge. Such monopolies, as Innis points out with numerous but at times disconnected examples, became a powerful tool in regulating the division of labor of the populace. This resulted from their interpretative hold on time connected to the calendrical reckoning of seasonal cycles.

Frequently, according to Innis, civilizations that overemphasized durable media and time became subject to challenge and eventual collapse as a result of the introduction of lighter, more portable space-biased media having a quite different institutional emphasis. In Egypt, papyrus challenged stone and eventually facilitated the expansionist Roman Empire. In medieval Europe, paper and later print, both espousing the vernacular, challenged the Latin entrenched scribal culture dependent on parchment. Space-biased media were able to do this because the rigidity of the time-bound empires created a tension that left them susceptible to major upheavals. Again, there is perhaps more than a hint of the Hegelian dialectic in these formulations.

Unlike the tradition-oriented, time-binding media, those oriented toward space tend to be present and future directed. They facilitate expansionist empires that subjugate marginal groups. Such empires are characterized by administration over great distances, complex political authority, the growth of secular institutions, and the creation of abstract science and technical knowledge. These features entailed the loss of a sense of place, community, and gave rise to a whole new configuration of monopolies of knowledge.

For Innis, in today's world, space-biased media in the form of modern electronic communications have assumed unparalleled influence. In the guise of giving greater access to, and democratizing information, they subtly entrench modes of domination that in some ways resemble what took place in previous epochs. It is the rich and powerful nations like the United States which can afford to exploit this technology to its limits, who in the guise of making it available to others, extend their information empire. It is interesting and unfortunate to note that a major Innis-influenced theorist, McLuhan, who has dealt extensively with new communications, expresses no interest in Innis's insistence on the importance of media orientation toward time and space, or the critical vision that nurtured it.

In the work of writers who have addressed Innis recently the general attitude toward his formulations on time and space has been either critical rejection based on the vagary and inclusive application of the concepts, or acceptance of them as the foundation of historiography. A more balanced (to use an Innis phrase) appraisal is perhaps necessary.

On the negative side, to argue as Innis does that the tendencies of time or space bias constitute a principal dynamic in the rise and fall of civilizations is a grandiose and naive extension of an interesting aspect of cultural orientation. It is subject to the same criticisms that the discipline of history, as well as the social sciences, have levelled at other epochal historians. However, in brief passages Innis does apply the time/space model to concrete historical situations with some effectiveness. A case in point is his analysis of the struggle for the control of time between church and state in the history of Western Europe, a focus that can enrich traditional studies of the conflict between these institutions. Similarly, his concern with space bias is more revealing when, instead of making sweeping generalizations about the rise and fall of civilizations, he deals with specific relationships between communications technology, concepts of geographical space, and the use of space in architecture. In the latter area there are some intriguing parallels with the recent work of Foucault, especially *Discipline and Punish*, which deals with the way power and social control is manifested in the physical structure of nineteenth-century disciplinary and educational institutions.

Specific applications of Innis's concept of time bias and space bias can also be incorporated into an area he never considered: the history of New World civilizations. This has already been done with the Incas by Marcia and Robert Ascher in their book, *Code of the Quipu*.[14] The expansionist Inca empire, although it lacked writing, utilized the quipu, a series of cords of different length, thickness, and colors, which could be knotted, braided, and tied together, with all of these features indicating a certain kind of information. The quipu served as a form of ongoing census. It tallied population, crop production, taxation, and a host of other data. Light, portable, and suitable for administration over distance, it fulfills Innis's requirements for a space-biased medium. Ascher and Ascher, citing Innis, elaborate on these points, and also effect a comparative assessment of the quipu with respect to the role of writing in other archaic civilizations.

Another New World civilization amenable to an Innisian appraisal, though not yet considered in this way, is the Mayan. Their use of the durable medium of stone and obsession with sacred rituals pertaining to an astronomic and calendrical system of staggering complexity, are highly consonant with Innis's model of a time-biased civilization. Not an expansionist society, like the Inca, classic Mayan civilization collapsed suddenly in the ninth century A.D. The cause of this collapse has been a source of recurring speculation. Famine, disease, political insurrection, and a host of variations on these possible occurrences have been postulated. Perhaps Innis might have argued that overemphasis on time was a key element. However, without accepting such an ideational cause, we can nonetheless apply parts of his analysis to the Mayan case to further understand the role of media, temporal concerns, and ritual tradition in the maintenance of a major archaic civilization.

This link between Innis and archaeology is not just a recently conceived possibility. Over a generation ago it was glimpsed by no less an authority than Gordon Childe. An interesting exchange began when Childe reviewed *Empire and Communications*.[15] Innis replied in a rejoinder titled "Communications and Archaeology".[16] Childe praised Innis for dealing with the history of communications in terms of the media that convey information rather than making reference to the linguistic content of particular periods. He also brought to light several of Innis's inaccuracies and misunderstandings, graciously noting that they were the result of Innis's unavoidable distance from firsthand sources and expert advice and praised the Canadian scholar for pursuing and awakening anew Childe's own interest in such an important line of inquiry. Innis responded by thanking Childe both for the review and for being kinder than necessary—quite a contrast to the ego posturing so typical when academics respond to critical reviews of their books. He complimented Childe for being a lucid writer and popularizer in the best sense of the term (Innis was neither and must have recognized this deficiency), thereby helping to break down entrenched monopolies of knowledge. In concluding, Innis stressed the strengths and limitations of firsthand research in archaeology and highlighted the importance of Childe's contribution to his own sphere of interest.

No matter what the civilization Innis considered, or the dominant medium it employed, one prevalent characteristic was a monopoly of knowledge controlled by a privileged group. In his analysis of this phenomenon he claimed to be applying the economist's concept of monopoly to the field of knowledge. His basic assumption in this area, as David Crowley has pointed out, is that the media of communication through which the conceptual systems of an epoch are formed "disclose as well the blueprint for its domination."[17] The properties of the dominant medium, along with the preexisting institutional structure, facilitate knowledge, and therefore power, being localized in such a way that it serves particular interests and is always beyond access for a large segment of the population. This is as true of capitalist Europe emerging along with and utilizing moveable type printing as it was in the case of Babylonian theocracy incorporating cuneiform writing on clay tablets. Even in the contemporary university, Innis argued that this trend was leading to what he called academic monopolies of knowledge. He attacked this situation personally by critiquing obsessive specialism through his interdisciplinary work and also by involving himself with practical social issues, such as regional planning and engaging in various writings about, and programs in, adult education.

There is a strong pessimistic streak in Innis's writings on the monopoly of knowledge concept. He views the phenomenon as an almost inevitable process of historical formation. At the very moment when monopolies seem to be shattered, they reassert themselves. His most telling example, dealt with at length in both *Empire and Communications* and the *Bias of Communication*, is the way the dominant control of knowledge by the parchment-wielding clergy of the Middle Ages was challenged by print, which through the mass production of competing points of view, opened access to world understanding for larger numbers of people than ever before. Nevertheless, despite the ideology of a free press, this technology, like others before it, developed restrictions on what was acceptable content, and fostered a particular kind of social control, which in turn led to a new series of monopolies of knowledge. Innis has no utopian vision of an egalitarian future free from such restrictions. Neither does he advocate resigning ourselves to the situation. Rather, what should be cultivated is an ongoing challenge to the extremes and inequities that result.

An interesting aspect of the monopoly of knowledge concept is the way it independently recurs in the work of several other writers working in allied areas. For example, Foucault has used the term *knowledge monopolies* with reference to the "will to truth" in the West being accompanied by wholesale strategies for the control of knowledge, such as libraries, publishing houses, and learned societies. He emphasizes the importance of studying the conditions governing the formation of learned discourse and the rules of its employment that deny access to others.[18] Similarly, Lewis Mumford uses the term *monopoly of knowledge* to assess the situation whereby class formation and bureaucracy led to communications being used in political and military attempts to hierarchize power and limit access to knowledge.[19]

Finally, what Innis ultimately presents is an overarching but imprecisely formulated plan for the study of communications and culture within a comparative history of civilization. His work cannot provide us with an ongoing theory or even a methodology that can be used to any extent beyond the way he himself operated as a scholar. Yet he outlined the field of communications/history more inclusively than anyone before or since. It is this project that can provide a point of reference to which the diversity of recent contributions in the field can be profitably related. Within this domain the Innis legacy can help foster multiple and contrasting hypotheses, and allow new data and research to substantiate or challenge them.

9   *The Canadian Connection II: Marshall McLuhan*

Few new truths have ever won their way against the resistance of established ideas save by being overstated.

—Isaiah Berlin

Few names have been associated with the field of communications to the extent that Herbert Marshall McLuhan's (1911-1980) was in the 1960s. His sudden rise to the status of pop culture guru and oracle of the electronic media, resulted in him becoming a direct manifestation of the very conditions he was diagnosing. Unfortunately, his wide-ranging speculations on contemporary culture often obscured the fact that he was advocating the importance of an overlooked area of study, media, and culture, as much as he was generating hypotheses, which he called "probes," to explain it. Also, a good deal of his understanding of contemporary communications derived from a serious, if often exaggerated historical sense of how information technology operated in the past to produce widespread changes in thought and perception.

McLuhan has claimed affiliation to the pioneering studies of media and history elaborated by Innis. This is a controversial declaration, especially in Canadian circles where Innis and McLuhan are sometimes viewed as being diametrically opposed in intellectual spirit, politics, and in terms of the way they promulgated their work—though it is conceded that they share common subject matter. It is significant that their paths crossed when both were at the University of Toronto in the late forties and early fifties, but little evidence exists, or has been revealed, regarding the nature of that exchange. McLuhan has claimed it entailed mutual admiration; others, more skeptical, contend that there was more friction than affinity. Several crucial similarities and differences will be proposed in the following pages. Any such consideration would do well to follow James Carey's point of departure: that although both Innis and McLuhan bequeath primacy to communications technology, for the former it is the effect of media on social organization and culture which is crucial; while the latter's concern is in the area of sensory organization and thought.[1]

An important hint that the legacy of McLuhan should be reappraised for its relevance to the history of communications has recently been made, though somewhat unintentionally, by Elizabeth Eisenstein. In her monumental study, *The Printing Press as an Agent of Change*, she points out how McLuhan inspired her initial entry into this area. And, although she experiences considerable discomfort with his mosaic approach and wide-ranging generalizations, she grudgingly concedes that he was one of the few scholars to insist on a serious study of the historical importance of communications media, such as print. What she fails to point out is that there were crucial precursors to McLuhan and that his work can be situated in the unacknowledged communications/history tradition we have been examining, a tradition in which her own project comprises a major recent chapter.

LIFE BEFORE *THE GUTENBERG GALAXY*

In 1962, McLuhan published *The Gutenberg Galaxy*, a work many consider to be his most impressive achievement[2] —although others have sarcastically noted that this honor should be reserved for his reputation. With this book McLuhan entered the communications/history field, a field that for a brief period would be thought of as almost synonymous with his name. He entered this domain with an expertise in literature that at times took him close to his future area of notoriety.

It is not easy to chart the influences that molded McLuhan from childhood to the point during the sixties when he exploded into public prominence. This is partly a result of the fact that he has been vague and reticent to discuss aspects of his personal history. Memoirs are lacking, and to date it appears as if no biographical study is in the works, which is puzzling given the plethora of commentaries on his thought and influence. McLuhan has eschewed exposing his background for any number of reasons. The most frequently cited is his contention that the very idea of authorship and biography is a dangerous artifact of the written tradition entrenched by print. It bespeaks specialism and individualism, which violates the anonymous, inclusive, and public nature of knowledge that is characteristic of primary oral cultures. Yet on the other hand, he has done nothing to impede the establishment of his own privileged reputation as author, including legal action against those who allegedly pilfer the exclusive stock of *his* ideas.

McLuhan was born in Edmonton in 1911 and moved to Winnipeg in his early youth. He was of Scottish-Irish and Methodist-Baptist background. It has often been said that the prairie background induced in him a nostalgia for the agragrian based small-scale community (sentiments shared by Innis), which his later notion of the "global village" endeavored to recapture. He completed his B.A. in English literature at the University of Manitoba in 1933, after a brief early stint in engineering, and earned his M.A. at that school in 1934. Shortly thereafter, he continued his literary studies at Cambridge University, distinguishing himself both as a scholar and oarsman. In 1936 he earned another B.A. and in 1940 another M.A. He finally garnered his Ph.D. in 1942 with a dissertation titled "The Place of Thomas Nash in the Learning of His Time," which solidified his reputation as a scholar of the Elizabethan period.

McLuhan's sojourn at Cambridge was not continuous. In 1936 he returned to North America to begin a teaching career with a brief stint at the University of Wisconsin. Two important events occurred in his life at this time. He underwent a much commented on conversion to Catholicism—perhaps influenced by similar conversions taking place on the literary scene in England; and feeling somewhat alien in the role of teaching American youth of that generation, he decided to try and understand their world by immersing himself in the study of popular culture. The result of this latter preoccupation was the publication, in 1951, of a pathbreaking but largely unheralded book, *The Mechanical Bride*. Doubtless he was influenced in this pursuit of the academic study of popular culture by the fact that in England Wyndham Lewis and F. R. Leavis were beginning to give it newfound legitimacy.

His conversion to Catholicism caused McLuhan to gravitate toward institutions of higher learning so affiliated. Eventually, in 1946, he took a post at St. Michael's College at the University of Toronto, where he became full professor in 1952. In 1963 he became director of the newly established Centre for Culture and Technology, which was set up by that university partly in response to a decade of McLuhan's communication studies. Besieged with worldwide notoriety for having written *The Gutenberg Galaxy* and *Understanding Media*, he was honored in 1967 with a year-long appointment to the Albert Schweitzer Chair in the Humanities at Fordham University in New York, after which he returned to the University of Toronto until his death in 1980.

As a literary scholar, McLuhan was both traditional and unconventional. He became fascinated by poetry, which explored the limits of language rather than accepted it as given, poetry that provided a sneak preview of new directions in cultural orientation and sensory awareness. Among his favorites were Gerard Manley Hopkins, T. S. Eliot, Ezra Pound, and most preeminently, James Joyce. When he noticed that some of the techniques of word play used by these poets also appeared in the media of popular culture, where they voiced a wholly different content, it launched him in earnest into the research that would yield *The*

Mechanical Bride. In the twentieth-century context this study has been regarded, not without justification, as the "single most important book published on popular culture."[3]

Only a brief appraisal of *The Mechanical Bride* will be attempted here. However, it should be noted that although frequently cited, the *Bride* has rarely been commented on at any length. A full evaluation is long overdue. Not only is it a pathbreaking study, many themes relevant to McLuhan's later perspective on the history of communications were first aired in this book. Perhaps McLuhan himself has dissuaded would-be commentators through his later dismissal of the project with the claim that it has been rendered obsolete by the emergence of television—an understandable strategy geared no doubt to focus attention on his more recent work. Nevertheless, the *Bride* has relevance to media studies of all kinds. As Leiss, Kline, and Jhally note in their definitive study of advertising, significant parallels exist between the semiological perspective applied to contemporary culture by renowned French theorist Roland Barthes and what McLuhan attempted in the *Bride*, which "anticipated much of the later interest in advertising from the perspective of its relationship to the media system and popular culture."[4]

In the *Bride* we find McLuhan entering the domain of modern sociology through the door of one of its most recent concerns, mass communications. In a sense it is quite understandable that John S. Blacking would jointly review *The Mechanical Bride* and C. Wright Mill's *White Collar*. The review appeared in the Jesuit magazine *America*.[5] Both books, according to Blacking, deal with the effects of modern industrialism, on values in the case of McLuhan, and on class domination in Mill's study. Furthermore, both writers argue for a demystification of the choices and stereotypes pervaded by media. It should perhaps be added that this is about as close as McLuhan would ever get to Marx's concept of ideology.

For a work so close to being social science which deals with the cultural present, the *Bride* ignores major theoretical sources capable of informing this project. Weber, Durkheim, Marx, Simmel, and G. H. Mead are not cited. McLuhan seems to prefer writers who are more contemporary. Margaret Mead's name appears often, especially for her *Male and Female*; Swiss art historian Siegfried Giedion, whose influence would continue into McLuhan's later work, is heavily praised for his *Mechanization Takes Command*; and Lewis Mumford's *Technics and Civilization* is respectfully referenced, though the future would see a more hostile attitude. Other probable (in other words uncited) sources for the *Bride* include the dystopias portrayed by Aldous Huxley's *Brave New World* and George Orwell's *Nineteen Eighty-Four*, coupled with the concept of "brainwashing," which was just entering the public discourse of the time.

McLuhan was acutely aware that even in a democracy public opinion could be significantly manipulated by the very technologies that purport to accentuate diversity. Innis had been grappling with this issue for years, but is uncited, perhaps because his relevant published statements in this area, *Empire and Com-*

munications (1950) and *The Bias of Communication* (1951), were released too late for McLuhan to have taken them into account—it appears as if 1949 were the cutoff date for sources used in the *Bride*.

The style of the *Bride* is reminiscent of the infamous mosaic approach employed in *The Gutenberg Galaxy* and *Understanding Media*. There is no conventional linear sequence (chapters can be read in virtually any order), no bibliography (even the two later works include excellent concise bibliographies), no index or footnotes, and chapters are unnumbered. Nevertheless, a well thought out preface lucidly states the goals of the study. It opens in convincing fashion: "Ours is an age in which many thousands of the best trained individual minds have made it a full-time business to get inside the collective public mind."[6] In exposing the way this situation operates, McLuhan tries to avoid moralistic criticism—though his disdain for some of the examples cited is obvious. He adopts the perspective destined to resonate throughout his later work, that of Edgar Allan Poe's mariner in "Descent into the Maelstrom," who, in the face of imminent chaos does not rail against the awesome power that engulfs him, but becomes a perceptive observer of the swirl and thereby escapes its worst effects. In his later works some might say that rather than escaping the worst effects of media, McLuhan succumbed to them, with his unabashed proselytization and work as a consultant to industrialists and politicians.

Doubtless part of the reason for the minimal recognition of the *Bride* when it first came out was, in addition to the newness of the subject area, McLuhan's unorthodox semipoetic writing style. The *Bride* is clearly a work in which original insight cleverly expressed takes precedence over systematic exposition. In the margins of each chapter are flashy one-liners that employ the very techniques of popular culture discourse utilized in the media situations the primary text endeavors to critique. Several examples should perhaps be cited of these early forerunners of what would, during the sixties, become known as "McLuhanisms":

"Will Capp be the first stripper to get a Nobel prize?"

"The face that launched a thousand hips?"

"You'll never hit the jackpot unless you first become a slug for a machine?"[7]

Although the *Bride* deals with the content of the media of popular culture, such as advertisements, comic strips, and paperback novels, considerations of media form are not altogether absent. For example, McLuhan's assessment of the newspaper prefigures the way he would examine other types of media in his later books. He refers to it as a collective work of art that utilizes narrative discontinuity in ways similar to the technique of spatial discontinuity elaborated by artists such as Picasso. The overall effect of this structuring of text and illustration "has been to develop the image of the world as a single city."[8] Clearly, this is an anticipation of the "global village" concept belabored so frequently in his later work, but in the *Bride* it is used in a more critical and less optimistic way.

A primary concern of the *Bride* is with how the techniques used in newspapers, advertising, and mass media in general, consumerize and mechanize deep emotions, trivialize the profound and render profound the trivial. A world is presented where each part of our physical and emotional being must be dealt with separately by the appropriate product or agency. Organicism, the human whole, is replaced by a configuration of cultural fragments—hence the title of the book. The influence on this theme exerted by Siegfried Giedion's *Mechanization Takes Command* is significant, as is Samuel Butler's *Erewhon*, an early brilliant attack on the new mechanical culture produced by industrialism. Throughout the *Bride* McLuhan warns us about the tyranny of a "so-called" democratic culture—a tyranny that does not rule by brute force, but nevertheless coerces conformity through the promise of material comfort. To proclaim this vision is to be a direct heir, although McLuhan does not acknowledge it, to the tradition of Rousseau.

CREATION OF *THE GUTENBERG GALAXY*

It might seem trite or flippant to say that *The Mechanical Bride* was ahead of its time. Most important books are. But in this case it is possible to be specific and say that it was about ten years ahead of a cultural situation that would have given it grateful recognition. The sixties saw myriad studies emerge that were critical of the values of Western civilization, technology, and consumerism. At the very moment when the *Bride* could have garnered a widely sympathetic audience, McLuhan was immersed in another area, the history of media disembodied from content, and rapidly gaining recognition for this project. *The Gutenberg Galaxy* and *Understanding Media*, although not critical works in the sense of the *Bride*, nonetheless in their own way appealed to and fueled the sensibilities of the sixties. And in so doing they virtually eclipsed the message and spirit of their precursor.

When *The Gutenberg Galaxy* was published it was greeted with mild academic interest. Not until 1964, when *Understanding Media* was unleased on the world, did a wider audience, curious to know where else this "medium is message" philosophy was being dispensed, looked toward the *Galaxy*. Nevertheless, it never enjoyed the widespread notoriety engendered by its sequel. Although the *Galaxy* is written with catchy chapter glosses and in the McLuhanesque "mosaic" style, it remains a dense, scholarly study. Almost every idea is bolstered with numerous and often lengthy quotations, whereas *Understanding Media* strives for a less pedantic and seemingly more original and accessible presentation.

For many readers, the emergence of McLuhan during the sixties as champion, or charlatan, of a history of communications perspective was rather sudden. Nevertheless, it had been ten years in the making. The major impetus behind McLuhan's new quest was a project seminar and journal that he edited along with anthropologist Edmund Carpenter and the occasional collaboration of artist Harley Parker: *Explorations: Studies in Culture and Communication.* It was irregularly published in eight issues between 1953 and 1959 and assisted by a Ford Foundation grant.

Explorations was a major interdisciplinary forum, bringing together scholars from diverse fields who shared a concern for the phenomenon of human communication. Several participants, such as sociologist David Riesman and historian Siegfried Giedion, would become frequently cited sources in McLuhan's later work. In a rare moment of candor, McLuhan has readily acknowledged the importance of Giedion during the period of *Explorations*, referring to the latter's *Space, Time and Architecture* (1954) as "one of the great events of my lifetime."[9]

The influence of Carpenter was no less profound. His work in cultural and linguistic anthropology among the Avilik Inuit, and sensitivity to a wide body of literature on non-Western cultures, helped McLuhan develop a sense of comparative history not limited to the tradition of the West. Carpenter's own originality and contribution to McLuhan's cause can be clearly discerned in a book they jointly edited in 1960, *Explorations in Communication*, which brought together some of the more notable contributions from *Explorations*. In a sense the bond between McLuhan and Carpenter can be likened to the one between Marx and Engels, though the parallel is of course a loose one. In each dyad the senior partner was difficult to access, seemingly deep and intolerant of divergent opinion, while the junior evidenced an accessibility, intellectual and personal, human compassion and loyalty that at times obscured the orginality of his own unique insights.

To say that the *Explorations* project was unorthodox is an understatement. As Theall has pointed out in his still definitive study of McLuhan, it was "one of the more interesting intellectual events of the decade. . . ."[10] *Explorations* also contributed to the eventual establishment of the Centre for Culture and Technology at the University of Toronto, which became McLuhan's eventual base camp. Although characterized by the participation of numerous renowned scholars, the journal endeavored to disseminate its message in an unconventional mode. It employed the disjointed discontinuous style—later to become the notorious "mosaic approach"—and utilized typographic resources in new and unusual ways. Almost all the major ideas and themes of *The Gutenberg Galaxy*, either original to McLuhan or emanating from his collaborators, were field tested in the *Explorations* arena.

The Gutenberg Galaxy opens with an affirmation of the "mosaic approach" as the only means to reveal the "causal operations" in history. At the outset we have a major contradiction. Though the purpose of this chapter is to contextualize McLuhan, not to point out the various paradoxes and contradictions that abound in his work—they have been well criticized in previous commentaries—this particular one cannot be ignored. "Mosaic" implies, as McLuhan acknowledges, simultaneity and interplay, while causality is a concept born of the very lineal/literate/sequential mode of thought he disavows. It is this very insistence on championing a causal technological determinism grounded in media, which has led several critics to refer to his work as "McLuhanacy." Nevertheless, the "mosaic" strategy does allow for other factors. Essentially it is a style of exposition that juxtaposes divergent observations, moves back and forth across history in a comparative way, and cites relevant observations from authors in a wide range of disciplines. To the degree that it is interdisciplinary, it can be seen as linked to the tradition of Innis.

It is not surprising, therefore, to find the name of Innis mentioned several times in the text, including the respectful claim that the *Galaxy* is but a footnote to his work. At best the book is an amplification of several themes elaborated by Innis, at worst it raises these themes to the status of an autonomous field severed from the social, historial, and institutional concerns that Innis would have thought essential to the task. Other sources are used less controversially. Indeed, it is a major strength of McLuhan that almost every idea of significance in the *Galaxy* is shown to have been expressed in some way in a host of other studies. The reader becomes acquainted, through extensive quotes and gracious lead-ins, with the texts of genuinely insightful but not often mainstream writers. In addition to those already mentioned in conjunction with *Explorations*, frequent use is made of the work of Walter Ong regarding the educational reforms induced by print; H. J. Chaytor on the transition from script to print; William Ivins on the visual shifts created by print; and Lucien Febvre and Henri-Jean Martin for their landmark study on the history of the book.

Despite McLuhan's disavowal of traditional sequential typologies, and his claim that the order of presentation of topics in the *Galaxy* is irrelevant and could easily be otherwise, he nonetheless follows a venerable historical scheme. History is divided into four phases characterized by the prevailing means of communication. In the first phase, rule and logic are dominated by the properties of the spoken word; examples in more recent times include the nonliterate cultures studied by twentieth-century anthropologists. This oral phase is followed by the emergence of the phonetic alphabet, the scribal tradition. Unlike Innis, McLuhan shows no interest in civilizations using nonalphabetic scripts—he classifies the great empires of the East as large-scale tribes still within the oral mode. Innis was more respectful. He concluded that writing, not just alphabetic writing, was *the* major historical-technological development. It conferred on its practitioners a particular kind of visual bias, whereas the early alphabet, particularly in Greece, retained several aspects of orality—a position diametric to McLuhan's. The third phase McLuhan highlights is the Gutenberg revolution utilizing printing via moveable type. This is followed by the electric age, which although mentioned in the *Galaxy*, receives fuller treatment in *Understanding Media*.

The oral tradition, according to McLuhan, is based on a multisensual, nonlineal orientation to the world steeped in magico-religious sentiment. Phenomena are not perceived in one fixed way, as they are in typographic culture. Rather, they are held to contain several possibilities with respect to form and meaning. This leads him to emphasize the verbal (and visual) punning common in such societies. There are interesting parallels here with French anthropologist Levi-Strauss's "science of the concrete" and notion of *bricolage*: the nonliterate primitive's way of looking at objects in terms of a repertoire of possible meanings and uses.[11] However, Levi-Strauss sees this as a fundamental aspect of our generic mind, which becomes restricted as cultures attain increasing complexity, while McLuhan links it to a particular kind of communication, the spoken word. It should also be noted that McLuhan tends to overstress the acoustic and understress the visual orientation of nonliterate societies, a bias that can be tempered by Levi-Strauss's insights on the intricate and nonlineal visual component of the modes of classification employed by these people. Finally, to make a comparison with Innis on orality, McLuhan uses a wider range of examples than his predecessor, who relied mostly on the early Greek experience for his generalizations. But while Innis explored the full social ramifications of orality, McLuhan confines his emphasis to its acoustic (aural) properties and psychological implications.

Although the *Galaxy* argues that an important and unparalleled revolution occurred with the invention of moveable type printing, the development of alphabetic writing formed the essential prelude. As with most historians who employ typologies, McLuhan talks about changes that took place continuously over several centuries as if they happened with dramatic suddenness. For example, the alphabet, with its emphasis on lineality, abstraction, and specialism (Innis saw these qualities arising with writing per se, not just alphabetic script), is said to have effected a dramatic break with the wholeness and inclusiveness of the oral tradition. He makes minimal use of archaeological sources that map the details of this transformation. Preference is given to highlighting the renowned Greek achievement in science, philosophy, and logic, which he ties directly to phonetic literacy. One important source appears to have been unavailable to him, Havelock's *Preface to Plato*. It was first published in 1963, less than a year after the *Galaxy*, and eventually exerted a significant influence on McLuhan's subsequent work, especially *Understanding Media*.

The aspect of preprint culture that is most thoroughly elaborated in the *Galaxy* is the medieval period. Although characterized by alphabetic script and known sometimes as the manuscript tradition, McLuhan deems it to be a transitory phase, incorporating features from traditional orality, along with the kind of literate perceptions that would dominate with the rise of print. Clearly, McLuhan is describing a situation that, in a sense, represents a reversion from the state of philosophical thought and culture which the alphabet had earlier brought to Greece. This is never explained. Nor is the fact that with the rise of print many areas of Greek thought suppressed during the Middle Ages acquired newfound interest and application. The problem, of course, is that causality in history, if it exists at all, cannot be attributed to any single factor such as media, especially through the vast expanses of time dealt with in the *Galaxy*.

Nevertheless, McLuhan's analysis of the scribal world of the Middle Ages is probably the most astute and well thought out aspect of the *Galaxy*. He makes judicious use of the highly regarded work of H. J. Chaytor, Walter Ong, and Istvan Hajnal. His own conversion to Catholicism seems to have led to a passionate identification with this period. Just as Innis's ideal of a harmonious and balanced culture was newly literate Greece preserving key aspects of earlier orality, so McLuhan's ideal seems to be the manuscript era, where oral ritual and an inclusive sensorium coexist with a mode of permanent preservation of revered wisdom.

With the advent of print things changed—overnight if we read McLuhan's statements on print in his later more popular writings. However, a careful reading of the *Galaxy* will reveal that he is considering a sequential transformation that occurred over several centuries. Like Michel Foucault in *The Order of Things*, he sees the ideas of Descartes in the mid-seventeenth century, two hundred years after Gutenberg, as a definitive statement expressing the newly emergent conceptual system destined to influence later European thought; Foucault attributes it to a mutation in the discourse, McLuhan to print. Both see Cervantes's *Don Quixote* as a figure straddling this great cultural divide. Both elaborate on the stress on visuality that took place at this time. For McLuhan, print/visuality constitutes *the* axis around which post-Renaissance, pre-electric culture revolved. It obliterated the more inclusive world views of the oral and manuscript traditions, giving rise to the fixed objective point of view, an emphasis on quantification, serial order, the uniformly repeatable commodity, a stress on repeatability in science, individualism, nationalism, and doubt.

And the above list is only a partial one! As noted, McLuhan does concede that this cultural avalanche did not occur instantaneously. For example, he takes great pains to show how early printed books were attempts to replicate the form and content of what was already available during the manuscript era. Eventually the potential of the new technology led to structural changes in texts (the book as a work of reference rather than a sacred compendium of wisdom intended for at least partial memorization), new subject areas, and individual authorship. What he rarely, if ever acknowledges, is that several aspects of cultural modernism were on their way prior to Gutenberg. For instance, emphasis on quantification increased significantly with the introduction and increasingly widespread use of the Arabic system of numeration in the twelfth and thirteenth centuries, accompanying burgeoning commercial interests. Similarly, nationalism, in the form of regionalism, began exerting itself several centuries prior to the emergence of nation states in the sixteenth century. Its early growth was tied not to print, but to the introduction of paper, which facilitated the spread of writing in the vernacular during the later Middle Ages and contributed to the decline of the Latin-parchment monopoly on written communication held by the Catholic Church. Paper enhanced the diffusion of Arabic numbers, and it eventually also led to a situation whereby specific authors were acknowledged and supported.

In *The Gutenberg Galaxy* McLuhan ultimately fails to establish the intended case for historical causality based on print. Instead he convincingly shows how it was a great facilitator, often giving rise to new aspects of cultural orientation, and also, as we have just seen, amplifying trends already present in a historical constellation too complex to be explained by any one factor.

UNDERSTANDING MEDIA AND BEYOND

Throughout *The Gutenberg Galaxy*, McLuhan makes leaps from whatever historical period he is assessing to the situation of modern electronic communications. He consolidates a number of these observations in the last chapter, and in a traditional manner suggests that the interested reader check out the forthcoming sequel, *Understanding Media.*

Whatever its merits, *Understanding Media* was one of **the** books of the sixties: the main forum for the ideas of one of the few North American academics to gain a cult following. It has been said of the eighteenth century and Newton that no writer was more discussed by so great a number of people who never read his work, that his ideas were "in the air" as much as in print. The same could be said about McLuhan during the psychedelic days of the sixties. Anyone who can recall the memorable scene in Woody Allen's film *Annie Hall*, where McLuhan makes a cameo appearance as himself, gains an immediate sense of the phenomenon that he was. The scene involves the discussion of a basic McLuhanesque dualism, hot versus cool media, terms he first introduced and tried to explain in part 1 of *Understanding Media*. It is a vivid statement as to the elusiveness and imprecision of these terms. For although the would-be McLuhan interpreter in the film spells out in convincing fashion why television is hot and film is cool, the astute McLuhanite knows he has the polarities reversed. In any case, McLuhan quickly appears to denouce this pretender.

Understanding Media is a book of history. Like Foucault, McLuhan claims that he is not interested in history for its own sake, but in a history of the present. This entails looking at recent developments and events with an eye to sorting out those that are the most pervasive and influential. It also entails examining the past to see both the extreme contrast with our own time and charting precursors of what would become more permanent in later epochs. The book is written in a semipoetic style, laced with repetition, overstatement, and contradictions. It is also packed with as many quotable quotes as can be found in any English language writer since George Bernard Shaw or Oscar Wilde. In addition to the immortal "the medium is the message," other gems include "art is anything you can get away with," and, "the electric light is pure information." Perhaps *Understanding Media* is best approached as a list of such provocative aphorisms, designed to stimulate thought and provoke discussion.

Numerous critics have written exceptionally engaging essays denouncing *Understanding Media*, blissfully unaware that their own stylistic accomplishments were being fueled by the ingenious perceptions they were disavowing. Many have never written as well or as insightfully since moving on to other issues. Perhaps it is an unintentional high tribute to McLuhan's coolness, in this sense something that compels involved creative participation for resolution, that it should be so capable of inspring eloquent arguments of completely diametric persuasion.

Since almost everything in McLuhan contradicts something he said somewhere else, it would be an easy exercise in sniping to systematically elaborate a comparative list of such statements. At this juncture, however, it is more important to see if any enduring and consistent insights emerge from his inconsistent exposition.

In a sense, assessing McLuhan is not so dissimilar from trying to fathom Rousseau, although there is at least one important distinction: Rousseau was readily aware of the paradoxes and contradictions that seem prevalent in his work and encourages the reader to get beyond these surface impediments and seek the deeper truths. McLuhan denies that his writing is ever at odds with itself. One of the ironies of his work is the claim to be effecting nonlinear tentative "probes"—explorations that he is readily prepared to scrap should they no longer illuminate— and the fact that he has never renounced a single such "probe." Not infrequently he has protected them with a fervor and defensive posturing worthy of the most dogmatic conventional academic.

From the perspective of historical methodology perhaps the one contradiction in McLuhan's work that cannot be bypassed is his disavowal of linear causal models, which in *Understanding Media* leads him to cite Hume's arguments against causality several times. Contrast this with his avowed quest for the causal operations in history at the outset of *The Gutenberg Galaxy* and his media-based technological determinism in general.

The main arguments of *Understanding Media* are divided into a two-part format. Part 1 is a statement of major concepts and methodology; part 2 deals with specific media from the spoken word to the computer. Part 2, in attempting to bring factual data to bear on the principles enunciated earlier, gives the book an orientation that is more traditionally academic than McLuhan with his advocacy of nonlineal "probes" might want to concede. What is interesting and limiting in McLuhan's presentation of methodology in part 1, is how a number of intriguing notions about communication processes are elaborated, then inflexibly bound to specific technologies. A case in point is the hot versus cool distinction. A hot medium is one that extends a single sense in high definition; it is rich in specific information and leaves little to be filled in by the audience. According to McLuhan print is hot, as is radio and film. In contrast, cool media are low definition in terms of information; they compel audience participation for resolution. This necessitates the involvement of more than one sense. Colloquial speech is cool, as well as the telephone and television.

McLuhan elaborates the play and interplay of hot and cool media on the drama of history. In a sense there is a similarity with Innis seeing history in terms of a struggle between "space-biased" and "time-biased" communication. At times it appears as if McLuhan appropriated the Innisian dualism and merely changed the labels. But there are crucial differences. Innis was an institutional economist who saw history as a complex occurrence that could perhaps be best understood from a communication perspective. His concept of a medium is basic: stone, clay, papyrus, parchment, paper, and so on; while for McLuhan a medium is an extension of some human faculty, in other words anything. Many factors entered into Innis's thinking on how a medium could be used and its eventual effect. To say that stone is "time-biased" and print "space-biased" is also to accommodate other factors responsible for their role in influencing history. This is not determinism but possibilism, or if from a certain perspective one wants to refer to it as a kind of determinism, it nevertheless differs from the predeterminism of McLuhan.

Space bias and time bias are *processes* strongly influenced by the available technology influencing culture. Hot and cool are also processes, but rigidly defined by and at one with certain kinds of technology. To talk about hot and cool the way McLuhan does is to talk about the way media allegedly are, rather than how given societies utilize them. If this rigidness can be broken, it might be possible to free up and reuse some of the perceptions that originally went into formulating the hot versus cool distinction. One might be able to look at a medium, such as American television in the eighties, and see it as a hot purveyor of political options more limited than when it was the cool voice of the sixties. With all his insistence on the separation of form and content, medium from message, McLuhan's analysis of television in *Understanding Media* is trapped in an unsuspected assumption: that the content of this medium during the sixties constitutes its universal essence.

A fundamental thesis of *Understanding Media* is that communications media constitute a pervasive environment that saturates us with a whole series of perceptions of which we are largely unaware. McLuhan argues that environments are invisible and that it takes a profound and unconventional shock to discover and understand them, the kind of challenge that has traditionally been confined to the realm of the arts, especially poetry, and which he tries to evoke with his "probes." The term *environment*, with respect to the natural environment, enjoyed wide currency during the sixties, thereby making fortuitous McLuhan's transposition of it to the realm of technology.

According to McLuhan, in addition to functioning as an environment, media also constitute a language. Like languages, particular media have their own grammar, or rules, which render them suitable for the conveyance of certain types of information. And, like language, particular media do not merely record and convey, but profoundly shape the way information becomes culturally acceptable. There are several probable sources for this perspective. Through working and collaborating with Edmund Carpenter—whose writings on media and language in *Explorations in Communication* are clearer and more well thought out than any of McLuhan's—McLuhan must have become at least indirectly acquainted with the Sapir-Whorf hypothesis. Edward Sapir and Benjamin Whorf were two American anthropological linguists whose work with native North American languages led them to conclude (or infer; they never made the hypothesis that bears their name an explicit declaration) that language is not a neutral vehicle for transmitting information and experience, rather it encodes it in very specific ways, which differ from one group of speakers to the next. For Sapir and Whorf language *is* the basis for culture and world view, just as media fulfill this role for McLuhan.

Sapir and Whorf, in turn, strongly influenced a writer whom McLuhan cites on several occasions, anthropologist Edward Hall. Hall's book, *The Silent Language* (1959), developed the notion that every culture has a language-like code that governs the way it deals with time. McLuhan adapted this notion to communication technology in general in *Understanding Media.* In subsequent work he uses another book by Hall, *The Hidden Dimension* (1966), which deals with the unconscious codes that cultures employ to define personal and public space and the sensory biases that result. Hall also champions the notion that technology constitutes an amplification and further elaboration of primary human faculties.

Much of part 2 of *Understanding Media* uses examples already cited in *The Gutenberg Galaxy*, especially when considering orality, the manuscript tradition, and print. This time there is little in the way of supportive quotes and the writing is more negotiable. But the gift for outrageous and downright wrong overstatement persists. For example, McLuhan now adds transportation to his examination of media in history and opens chapter 10 in typical oracular fashion: "It was not until the advent of the telegraph that messages could travel faster than a messenger."[12] History is rarely characterized by such clear demarcations. This pontification overlooks talking drums, smoke signals, vocal relays, the heliograph, and the semaphore towers that crisscrossed France just prior to the telegraph. Even in American history, which McLuhan is fond of citing, before Paul Revere became a messenger he first had to have a message. It was flashed to him across the harbor using a lantern code.

There is in McLuhan a maelstrom effect, but not the one he attributes to Poe's mariner. Rather, all manner of technologies are drawn into a conceptual vortex that funnels them directly toward particular modes of cultural orientation and perception. For McLuhan technology is never a series of variably related elements, but a coherent determining force in which each component acts as an extension of some human faculty and plays a role determined by the whole in configuring the way the world is seen and contemplated. Historical change *is* technological change. The possibility is never broached that culture, economics, or demography can induce certain forms of technology, which can lead to a process of reciprocal influence. The titles in McLuhan's "mosaic" always slant in the same direction.

On several occasions McLuhan rejects Marx's approach to history as overly rigid. Unfortunately, McLuhan is rejecting a perspective that, although it appears to verge close to determinism, argues for the variability of historical laws. Marx believed that each epoch was shaped by a specific equation of economic, technological, and social factors, which never remain in a static ratio.[13] They change as circumstances are changed by them. The next epoch might see such elements arranged in a different order of priority; this strategy avoids the kind of reflexive determinism characteristic of McLuhan.

Perhaps the key technology assessed by McLuhan in *Understanding Media*, the one that triggered public interest in the others he discussed, is television. A dominant feature of our cultural present, in McLuhan's sense, it is also the most invisible of environments. That someone would dare voice loud opinions about it to the effect that its effect is not as has been supposed, was bound to attract notice. Television, the archetypal cool medium, prompted McLuhan to elaborate his infamous retribalization hypothesis (or "probe"): that television and associated electronic media necessitate multisensory involvement and return us to the unified, inclusive, simultaneous space of the oral tribe from which centuries of phonetic literacy and print-induced visual specialism had divorced us.

In assessing the impact of television, McLuhan observes a superficial shift in patterns of perception, no doubt induced by a multiplicity of factors, sees its source in one medium and its effect penetrating to the deepest structural foundations of our culture. Is this hypothetical hyperbole, to borrow from the master's style? Perhaps. McLuhan has often said his goal is to shake us out of our complacent trance and get us to look at what modern technology is really about. It might even be possible to accept this contention outright if it were not accompanied by such defensive posturing and dogmatic insistence. Nevertheless, any contemporary discussion of the role of television, including one based on, "heaven forbid," content, cannot help but address some aspect of McLuhan's perspective. Even complete avoidance of his position creates a situation whereby important considerations inevitably arise in the gap between the new non-McLuhan view and the one it tries to sidestep.

Despite its theoretical shortcomings *Understanding Media* is an important book. Its significance resides not in what it says about things, but in the things it brings together for the saying. McLuhan's real gift—apart from his resonant style—is in assembling a constellation of historical artifacts that have traditionally been taken for granted, but on closer inspection appear to be, to use one of Innis's favorite phrases, "things worth attending." One need not follow McLuhan to his inevitable overstated conclusions to recognize that somehow printing, the clock, money ("the poor man's credit card"), the telegraph, telephone, typewriter, and so on, have had a pervasive influence in shaping modern civilization. Even if this influence has not been as he stipulates, rectifying his excesses can be a valuable exercise in exploring why the contemporary world is as it is.

What McLuhan had to say about modern communications he said in *Understanding Media*. A series of derivative studies followed and restated the main ideas in a number of engaging verbal and visual ways. Most are like advertisements for the arguments he previously developed. One partial exception is *Through the Vanishing Point: Space in Poetry and Painting* (1968), which he did with Harley Parker. In its reliance on extensive quotes, especially from literature, it recalls the format of *The Gutenberg Galaxy*; and its McLuhanesque captions evoke the style of *The Mechanical Bride*.

Through the Vanishing Point was published in Ruth Nanda Anshen's World Perspective series, which had earlier yielded Gordon Childe's *Society and Knowledge* and Lewis Mumford's *The Transformations of Man*. It also restates the debt to Innis. Does McLuhan then belong in the select company of scholars such as Childe, Mumford, and Innis, who have studied key aspects of the history of civilization? Absolutely. Such a pantheon should have a clown prince. This one has earned his place.

10   *History and Discourse:*
Michel Foucault

One must first observe differences in order to discover properties.
—Jean-Jacques Rousseau

Recently deceased, enormously controversial philosopher-historian Michel Foucault (1926-1983) has been a dominant intellectual presence for almost two decades. His thought provoking work spans the social sciences and humanities and has unintentionally created an interpretive cottage industry. So much has been said about his elusive texts that it appears as if space for yet another evaluation is severely limited. Nevertheless, there is one area of his thought that has gone virtually unclaimed: the degree to which his historical studies of discourse, which he refers to as his "archaeology of knowledge," interface with earlier considerations of media and history, such as those assessed in the previous chapters.

The emergence of Foucault into wide prominence was closely tied to the success of *Les mots et les choses* (*The Order of Things: An Archaeology of the Human Sciences*) first published in 1966. It inadvertently coincided with the ascendency of the predominantly French intellectual movement known as structuralism. As a methodology, structuralism endeavored to apply a linguistic model to the analysis of a variety of human information systems based on language. Its notable practitioners include anthropologist Claude Levi-Strauss, who has dealt with primitive systems of myth, exchange, and thought in general as the deep structural ground on which all subsequent human understanding is rooted; literary critic Roland Barthes, who has examined modern myths that deploy themselves through the texts and images of a variety of media; and psychoanalyst Jacques Lacan, known for his efforts to build on orthodox Freudian concepts by merging them with a linguistic understanding that was not part of Freud's strategic vocabulary. Foucault became a somewhat unwilling member of this pantheon, making it a kind of intellectual "gang of four," perhaps most embarrassingly depicted in a cartoon from the period that has the quartet rendered in caricature and sitting in a jungle clearing wearing grass skirts while engaged in discursive exchange.[1]

Why should the reticent Foucault have been included in this group, since on several occasions he has vehemently denied being a structuralist?[2] On the one hand there is his strong reliance on a linguistic, semiologically inspired perspective, especially in *The Order of Things*; also, the fact that structuralism's attempt at inclusivity made it welcome the work of someone who could, no matter how tentatively, take a large segment of history, especially of the West, and subsume it to structuralist tenets. Even Foucault himself has reluctantly admitted that his discourse is, after all, not independent of the largely unconscious conditions and rules that affect the production of related discourses at the same time and place.[3]

BACKGROUND

The affiliation with structuralism that resulted from *The Order of Things* does not mean that Foucault was not a significant writing presence prior to 1966, only that his wide notoriety began then. As a result, his previous works finally garnered a large audience. Earlier, in 1961, he wrote the book many consider to be his landmark statement, *Folie et deraison: Histoire de la folie a l'age classique* (*Madness and Civilization*). This was followed in 1963 by *Naissance de la clinique* (*The Birth of the Clinic*) and *Raymond Roussel. The Order of Things* was succeeded in 1969 by *L'archéologie du savoir* (*The Archaeology of Knowledge*). This is a confusing although provocative attempt to explain the methods and categories employed in the previous texts. However, like the visual artists Foucault seems to relate to, he is more effective when doing his renderings than when explaining them.

The Archeology of Knowledge brought to a close the first of what can be seen as a twofold division of Foucault's published thought. It also provides a convenient label for this phase.[4] Subsequent work can be more effectively grouped under a new designation, the "Genealogy of Power." To understand his development through the two phases and the continuities between them, several features of his personal and intellectual development should be noted.

The son of a doctor, Foucault was educated at both state and Catholic schools and went on to study philosophy at the Ecole Normale Superieure, France's elite bastion of higher learning. After immersing himself in the historical main currents of philosophy, he engaged in the almost obligatory dialogue with existentialism, phenomenology, and Marxism. The prospect of teaching and writing solely in philosophy held no appeal for him. He continued his studies by pursuing degrees in psychology and psychopathology, which were followed by conventional publications that he would later wish to forget.[5] Nevertheless, his curiosity in this area remained unsatisfied, especially after having spent several years studying first-hand what was being done in the name of institutionalized psychiatric practice. This led to an examination of the entrenched Western notion of reason as it governs scientific discourse and the practice of deciding what, in the sphere of human behavior, constitutes the normal and the abnormal. *Madness and Civilization* and *Birth of the Clinic* arose directly out of these concerns. Shortly thereafter, in *The Order of Things* and *The Archaeology of Knowledge*, he broadened his canvas to include the underlying conditions that govern what constitutes acceptable knowledge in the field known as the human sciences.

The second of Foucault's two phases, "Genealogy of Power," was in part a response to the political upheavals in France in 1968 and the subsequent social and intellectual polarization that followed. Although he did not renounce his earlier "Archaeology," the method of "Genealogy" exhibits an important shift in emphasis. Drawing from aspects of Nietzsche's philosophy, discourse is examined from a perspective that deals with it, not as a system of conceptual relations, but as a manifestation of power over human subjects; it is now seen as an agent that constantly defines, excludes, and constrains social relations. The glimmerings of this approach, if not the new terminology and explicit references, can be found in *Madness and Civilization* and *Birth of the Clinic*, as Foucault himself readily notes.[6] However, "Genealogy" dispenses with the position of detached intellectualism that characterizes "Archaeology." Instead, Foucault acknowledges himself, and the critical discourse he accesses and creates, as part of the very phenomenon under study.

Perhaps the major work emerging out of Foucault's "Genealogy" is *Surveiller et punir* (*Discipline and Punish*), which first appeared in 1975. It deals with both the discourse and structure of architectural space pertaining to nineteenth-century disciplinary practice: the birth of the modern prison and associated reforms. Many of the situations Foucault examines he readily generalizes to other institutions, such as schools and the military. A year later he published *La volonté de savoir* (*The History of Sexuality*), the first volume in a proposed series of six dealing with the history of discourse about human sexuality. Fundamental to this project, and the entire approach of "Genealogy," is the inextricable alliance between power and knowledge, which for Foucault constantly imply one another. Numerous shorter writings also emerged out of "Genealogy," and many have been gathered together in English translation in at least two volumes to date, *Language, Counter-Memory, Practice* (1977), and *Power/Knowledge* (1980).

THE ARCHAEOLOGY OF DISCOURSE

Although causing widespread attention in France when it first came out, *The Order of Things*, and Foucault's "Archaeology" in general, are not nearly as discussed, critiqued, and applied as the works emerging out of "Genealogy." The latter are assumed to have more immediate social relevance. They also touch on areas illuminated by the past contributions of Marx and Freud, always popular points of departure for critical intellectual discussion. *The Order of Things* does not have such noteworthy connections, either for the type of study it is or in the sources utilized. Yet it is a significant work, especially regarding the way discourse is approached as an aspect of the mode of communication. While the medium of communication, be it script or print, is of only incidental interest to Foucault, the underlying principles in the formation of the discourse within a given medium are examined in a manner considerably more detailed, and yet highly complementary, to what is presented by Innis in *Empire and Communications* and McLuhan in *Gutenberg Galaxy*. At least a brief provisional reassessment of Foucault in this regard is merited. This is not to suggest that the link between Foucault and communications has not been broached before. Mark Poster in his *Foucault, Marxism, History: Mode of Production versus Mode of Information* has made important inroads in this area.[7] Unfortunately, his otherwise excellent study is deficient in one major respect. It has an orientation to critical theory that causes Poster to confine himself almost completely to Foucault's "Genealogy," at the expense of an almost total exclusion of relevant aspects from "Archaeology."

The Order of Things at times appears to be more all-inclusive than the author's declared intentions. In fairness to Foucault we should note at the outset that the book's stated purpose is, beginning in the Renaissance, to give us a history of the underlying textual orientation in three general fields, which in turn gave birth to several modern academic disciplines. These three fields are: (1) natural history, the study and classification of life forms; (2) the analysis of language, as it was rooted in general grammar and comparative philology; and (3) the study of wealth, money, and labor, or early political economy. These significant intellectual domains and concepts had far-reaching implications throughout the rest of European intellectual history.

Fundamental to Foucault's approach is a semiological (some would say structuralist) concern, not with the subject matter of these fields per se, but the *way* it is represented in the texts of the day. How is appropriate knowledge, which he would come to refer to as "the true," deployed? The issue is not whether a particular theory is declared to be right or wrong at a particular time, but rather, the general conditions of discourse within which assertions can be made. What unsuspected, unconscious knowledge underlies the organization of the diversity of forms that legitimate knowledge takes? Even in the most vociferous debates in any age there is often an unstated agreement to disagree, based on certain unquestioned givens about the way the subject is discussed. These givens are so deep and pervasive that they reside beneath conscious, explicit declarations, such as the subject matter selected for discussion and the competing theories purporting to explain it. Foucault refers to this invisible field as the "episteme" and much of *The Order of Things* is devoted to unravelling its mysteries. In typically dense fashion he outlines his task:

What I am attempting to bring to light is the epistemological field, the *epi-steme* in which knowledge envisaged apart from all criteria having reference to its rational value or to its objective forms, grounds it positivity and thereby manifests a history which is not that of its growing perfection, but rather that of its conditions of possibility.[3]

As a concept, the episteme lends itself to comparison with Thomas Kuhn's oft cited notion of the paradigm.[9] However, the episteme, if one assumes its existence, resides beneath both theory and what is agreed to be appropriate data. For example, for Kuhn, Darwinian theory constituted a paradigm revolution: a new theory was born out of a major reinterpretation of traditional data. For Foucault, there was no revolution here at the level of the episteme. While Darwin's theory represented an important break with traditional biology, his concept of a fact and the principles of organization of life forms that his discourse subscribed to, are almost identical to those his anti-evolutionist predecessor, Cuvier (1769-1832), used nearly half a century earlier. Darwin, although controversial, was still within "the true" of nineteenth-century biological thinking, whereas for Foucault, Darwin's contemporary, Gregor Mendel (1822-1884), was speaking about nature in ways disconsonant with the reigning episteme.[10] As a result, it was not until fifteen years after his death that the significance of his work was appreciated and integrated into a rapidly changing biology.

As in the case of Kuhn's paradigm revolution, for Foucault the episteme does not change in a gradual continuous way. Instead, a discontinuity forms as a result of a rupture or epistemological break. The old codes of understanding are suspended, and within a relatively short time period (one assumes several decades but Foucault is never explicit) are displaced by a new series. How this comes about is not broached, which has led to numerous criticisms. We are simply given a situation of before and after, a history, not a change but of discursive strata suspended in time and studied using the freeze-frame approach structural linguists refer to as "synchronic analysis." Similarity with the cross sections delineated in archaeological excavation doubtless led Foucault to use that disciplinary label for his more cerebral field of study. Geology might have been an equally appropriate metaphor, though less fashionable in the twentieth century than it might have been in the nineteenth.

Interestingly, Foucault's nonevolutionary, nondevelopmental approach to history could have been influenced, perhaps unintentionally, by the geological and paleontological formulations of discontinuity espoused by Cuvier. In *The Order of Things* Foucault champions Cuvier as a benchmark of new principles of biological discourse. Perhaps he also picked up on and appropriated Cuvier's conceptual framework of discontinuity. In most histories of science, Cuvier is depicted as a tyrannical academician who persecuted Lamarck (1744-1829) for his evolutionary perspective, thereby impeding the later reception of Darwinism in France. Even today there is discomfort with the Darwinian paradigm in French science and a lingering reliance on the discontinuous model of change in natural history known as catastrophism, for which Cuvier was a seminal proponent. Nevertheless, the usual sources cited, by both Foucault and his commentators, as contributing to his concept of discontinuity, are Gaston Bachelard, Georges Canguilhem, Michel Serres, and Louis Althusser. And, despite Foucault's reluctant identification with structuralism, which seems to have intimidated a number of commentators from making connections that should be made, we might want to add Saussure to the list. Saussure's advocacy of the synchronic approach over the diachronic (movement through time) in language study, and use of the terms *signifier/signified*, are readily transposed to the study of discourse throughout the first part of *The Order of Things*.

Given Foucault's concern with discontinuities, we should note where he demarcates them, what they signify, and the characteristics he ascribes to the discursive continents separated by these divides.

In *The Order of Things*, two historical separations are elaborated. The first occurs around the middle of the seventeenth century and inaugurates the classical age, which in addition to opening up new vistas of theory construction and data gathering, embodies a discursive field entirely different from the era that preceded it. Although Foucault does not make a direct causal connection between the new discourse and shifts in theory and the definition of appropriate data, it is certainly implied that it was the epistemological rupture of the discourse that precipitated major transformations in conscious knowledge. In *Madness and Civilization* this divide saw definitions of reason and unreason arise in the judgment of the mentally ill. It initiated the great confinement, the "hospital of madmen" and "madhouse"; whereas in the previous era mental illness was a dispersed, nonlocalized phenomenon, especially through institutions such as the "Ship of Fools," and looked upon not without a degree of awe and veneration.

The second break occurs in the closing years of the eighteenth and early years of the nineteenth centuries. In *The Order of Things*, it relates to a discursive shift yielding different principles of organization in the human and life sciences, as well as new disciplines of inquiry. Earlier, in *Birth of the Clinic*, Foucault saw this divide establishing that institution. And in a later work, *Discipline and Punish*, the same transition brought in modern concepts of penology. In the last chapters of *The Order of Things*, there are numerous hints that in more recent times another break has occurred, or is occurring. However, at this point Foucault's writing attains heights of ambiguity and vagueness that make any reasonable effort at interpretation impossible.

For our purposes, in assessing Foucault's location in the tradition of the history of communication, it is the divide that separates the preclassical from the classical era that is most significant. During what he calls the preclassical episteme, which we can take to include the latter Middle Ages and the Renaissance, studies of nature and human understanding were based on a mixture of science, theology, mysticism, and rational knowledge. Inquiry incorporated principles such as "resemblance" and "analogy." In other words, the objects of the world were classified because of shared qualities, tactile, visual, their use, and mythical or historical origins, which linked them with other objects having similar properties. The laws governing signs, and therefore discourse, were predicated on establishing "likeness"; the world, according to Foucault, folded in on and reflected itself. There were direct links between the macrocosm and microcosm. For example, the conceptual structure of major buildings often reflected the assumed congruency of cosmographic and geographic space; medical remedies frequently resembled the organs they were supposed to treat—aconite for eye irritation, walnuts for brain-related maladies, and so on.

Lest we scoff at such assumptions (Foucault takes almost the opposite attitude), it should be noted that Levi-Strauss in *The Savage Mind* (*La pensée sauvage*, 1962) has, using contemporary communication theory, assessed similar conceptual processes in primitive (nonliterate) societies. He shows how, in the absence of modern scientific research methods and data gathering, this "science of the concrete" based on the association of sensible properties, frequently hits on what we would regard as objectively real connections. And even when it does not, the meaningful order imposed on the world through sensory based classification has its own therapeutic value. Although Foucault does not cite this major structuralist study, there can be no doubt that its influence on *The Order of Things* was significant.

Among the most vivid examples Foucault cites of preclassical word and world ordering are taxonomies of nature. Their rich and multifaceted semantic fields are highlighted and contrasted with the systems of the subsequent episteme, based on visually observable and measureable qualities hierarchized in gradual levels of formal complexity. In the preclassical age one reason the natural and human universe was ordered as it was had to do with the fact that knowledge was not based on seeing or demonstrating, but on interpreting. This observation has also been made by McLuhan in his assessment of the preprint manuscript period in *Gutenberg Galaxy*. However, while McLuhan tends to base his arguments on texts having a philosophical or literary orientation, neglecting important studies in natural history, it is in the latter area that Foucault is especially astute. Foucault's work also complements studies of the period by the eminent historian of ideas, Arthur Lovejoy, a writer whose approach Foucault would not find consonant. In *The Great Chain of Being*, Lovejoy's characterization of medieval cosmography interfaces with numerous aspects of the preclassical age in *The Order of Things*.[11]

One of the most revealing areas of the preclassical discourse was the way it reflected on language. During this era both the spoken and written word were held to be phenomena continuous with nature, part of the divinely created natural order. There was held to be a unity, not an arbitrary connection, between spoken and written discourse and its subject of reference. According to Foucault the search for meaning was often tied to discerning the "similitude" between signifier and signified, word and thing. As a result of this interpretive perspective, preclassical inquiry resembled what he refers to as a superimposition of hermeneutics and semiology.

In arguing this perspective Foucault's work can be profitably compared to similar studies by Hans Aarsleff.[12] Although Aarsleff has criticized Foucault for generalizing too widely, there are specific points in his own analysis that can been seen as enhancing observations in *The Order of Things*. For example, although Aarsleff does not use Foucault's concepts of *resemblance* and *similitude*, he describes a historical situation that exemplifies what they represent: the search for the Adamic or original language. This was undertaken by doing an extensive comparison of known languages. It was hoped that the Adamic language would hold the key to the original link between words and things by revealing the divinely ordained, natural homology between them. Scholars of the time believed that this primal congruency had become greatly attenuated over the centuries, not quite to the point of making words arbitrary signs of things as the classical age would come to believe, but reducing the strength of the bond between them from its original sanctified state to something barely discernible. To find the Adamic language would be the surest way mortals could attain to absolute knowledge of, and power over, the material world. Mysticism, alchemy, and the beginnings of rational scientific inquiry were fused in this quest.

From our vantage point, the quest for the Adamic language might seem like an unenlightened and overly imaginative research strategy, but in Aarsleff's sober judgment much useful empirical and comparative linguistic work resulted from using it. This judgment would no doubt delight Foucault, who takes an antiprogressive, antiheroic view of history, whereby past ages are never denigrated as ignorant nor are later times held to embody greater wisdom. If anything his work in both "Archaeology" and "Genealogy" sometimes hints at the opposite.

FOUCAULT'S ARCHAEOLOGY AND ITS LINK
TO COMMUNICATIONS

If we assume that the nature of knowledge is strongly influenced by the medium through which it is organized and transmitted—the legacy of Innis and McLuhan being an insistent recent elaboration of this position—then Foucault's observations can be critiqued and augmented by assessing the dominant communications employed in the historical situation under discussion. As it stands, he is concerned with communication rather than communications, discourse as embodied language rather than discourse in light of the context of its material embodiment. How then might a more inclusive appraisal, dealing with the medium of communication, both inform and be informed by Foucault's epistemic constructs?

First, to rethink the preclassical age with regard to this question we can note, along with Innis, McLuhan, and Ong in their assessment of the Middle Ages, that it was not a period characterized by modern-print-derived literacy. The organization of the manuscripts embodying medieval knowledge, and the printed books of the early Renaissance (which often replicated the structure and outlook of the preceding manuscripts), represented a tradition straddling primary orality and the visually oriented literacy that became entrenched after two centuries of print. As a result, many of the classic devices of primary oral communication survived, with modifications, into the scribal and early print period. For example, Foucault's preclassical age, with its multidimensional semantics and poetic range of associations recalls Levi-Strauss's "science of the concrete," the mode of organization of knowledge in nonliterate societies that live and communicate through an oral tradition.[13] In such societies sensible properties and mythological/cosmological connections, rather than abstract formal qualities, govern the classification of phenomena. This facilitates what Levi-Strauss has called a "cultural memory bank," storing information in the minds of individuals collectively, rather than externally in written texts. A loose parallel with premodern European thought can be drawn when we note how manuscripts were organized and used. Their structure often reflected a cosmographic orientation, each element part of a coherent organic whole. Rather than being used for reference like later printed books, manuscripts were arranged to facilitate memorization of specific passages and often entire texts. Reading aloud was the norm. These factors were all facilitated by the textual devices Foucault describes.

The fact that the printing press came into being during part of the preclassical episteme has not gone unnoticed by Foucault. He credits it, along with the arrival of oriental manuscripts and the appearance of a literature not created for the voice or performance, with accentuating a church-inspired notion that the primal nature of language is written: not trusting the memories of men, God introduced written words and it is thus in writing that the true word is to be found again. Foucault uses this observation to explain the sixteenth-century view whereby what was seen and read were indissociable in the knowledge of the time. But the impact of printing was far more pervasive. It drastically restructured the storage, retrieval, and organization of knowledge. Yet, according to numerous historians of technology, it was not until amost two hundred years after print's invention when most of its major effects became entrenched—the very point at which Foucault locates the divide heralding the classical age.

In Foucault's scheme, with the onset of the classical episteme there occurred a relatively sudden and deep seated shift in the dominant human science discourse. The kinship between the spoken and written word and the world, a hallmark of previous inquiry, dissolved. Words and things became separate. Analysis displaced the panorama of analogies that characterized the earlier age. Knowledge broke with theology. And perhaps most importantly for Foucault, language became conceived of as separate from the divinely ordained natural order of things. No longer regarded as being one of nature's species, like those it signifies, it was deemed to be a human creation, a tool of history and progress. Through the act of naming and classifying, in arbitrary but systematically linked ways, was the world known, not through reflecting on language as somehow congruent with that world. In the classical age representation and the analysis of differences, rather than similarities, displaced "resemblance" and "similitude" as organizing principles, especially with the emergence of a range of new taxonomies.

Perhaps the following passage from Locke's *Essay on Human Understanding* (1690), although not cited by Foucault, is as good a summary of the new view on language as was written during that time. Nevertheless, it must be noted that Locke's intention here is to address the nature and origin of language, not the epistemological suppositions of his own age, although the latter could not help but be carried over to a consideration of the former: "Words came to be made use of by men as the signs of their ideas, not by any natural connexion . . . between particular articulate sounds and certain ideas but by a voluntary imposition whereby a word is made arbitrarily the mark of an idea."[14] Locke is clearly hoping that recognition of this "truth" regarding language origins would put lingustic inquiry on a much firmer footing than it had been in past centuries. And he was also less than enamored with medieval and Renaissance formulations on the subject, such as the quest for the Adamic language.

Another major characteristic of the classical episteme, in contrast to its precursor, is the reduction in the varieties of sensory experience that went into classifying phenomena. Instead of being grouped on the basis of an inclusive semantic field, which could include heresay (legenda), texture, taste, and smell, "the area of visibility in which observation is able to assume its powers is thus only what is left."[15] Foucault puts considerable emphasis on the separation and fragmentation of the senses that occurred at this time, stressing the rise to prominence of a primary visual emphasis. He cites the development of the telescope and microscope as agents strongly contributing to this transformation, a rare instance of him acknowledging direct influence from the realm of technology. But again we must not forget, nor will McLuhan let us, the effect that moveable type printing had on this shift. Perhaps Foucault fails to argue for its importance because it was invented almost two hundred years before his classical rupture occurred. Nevertheless, as Eisenstein has shown, it took almost that amount of time for the sequence of print induced changes to cohere into a world view sharply distinct from that of the earlier manuscript period.[16]

This delay or "lag" effect of print can be better understood by assessing the earliest material it replicated. The first printed books were attempts to recapture the content and form deployed in the previous manuscripts. This recalls McLuhan's flippant, but nonetheless insightful observation about the content of a new medium usually being what was conveyed by the old. In the case of print, and with subsequent media as well, information was first processed along familiar and conventional lines that did not fully maximize the potential of the new technology. Gradually the potentialities of a new medium, print in this case, exert changes on what it conveys. Information is organized differently and new systems of knowledge arise from these changes. Usually, such media are regarded as neutral conveyors, more efficient perhaps than what went before; and when changes in thought or world view are perceived, they are held to have their origins within the realm of conscious knowledge, not in the media rendering it.

Interestingly, the mid-seventeenth century is not the only period Foucault assesses with respect to a shifting sense ratio. In a course in systems of thought that he gave at College de France in 1970-1971, he spoke about the transformation of Greek justice, and the accompanying discursive shifts, which occurred from the seventh to the fifth centuries B.C. He referred to the role of money and commercial exchange as a key factor and described the new discourse as "linked to a form of knowledge which presupposes truth is visual, ascertainable, measureable. . . ."[17] Taking a communications perspective, we can note that what he fails to stress is the contribution made to changing the discourse rendered by the establishment of the Greek alphabet and emergence of the common reader, a development extensively elaborated by Havelock.[18]

Moving back to the classical episteme, we can note how most of the changes that Foucault elaborates can be linked to moveable type printing. For example, not only did the reproductive powers of print replicate a multiplicity of well-known and not so well-known works (which he readily concedes), a conceptual as well as physical space for the production of many new kinds of texts was also created. These texts became oriented in ways that would have been inconceivable during the scribal era.

With print influenced discourse there is less reliance on mnemonic, multisensory connections and poetic allusions, especially in philosphical, scientific, and historical texts, and an increasing visual emphasis, as Foucault rightly notes. One reason is that manuscript literacy is closer to primary oral tradition: texts were didactic, designed to facilitate memorization of key passages, or in some cases the entire work. The profusion of new knowledge that accompanied the print era made such feats of learning increasingly difficult, if not impossible. Texts now had to be organized along lines that accommodated them for reference rather than memorization. The vivid dictionaries of the Renaissance were transformed into the matter-of-fact, scientifically modelled encyclopedias of the eighteenth century—information to be looked up, perhaps cited, but not recited verbatim.

Another area where print technology could have been influential in effecting the changed thought world of the classical episteme is in the area of how language itself was conceived. As noted, the preclassical view of language for Foucault was one characterized by a belief in similitude between word and thing, signifier and signified; there was believed to be a nonarbitrary, almost magical resonance between the spoken and written word and the world to which it referred. In the classical age this bond was broken. Language was regarded as an arbitrary human contrivance, a historically derived tool of understanding. Perhaps this view was prompted by typography, which employed separate neutral technological bits, which became meaningful only when strung together in certain conventional sequences. Could not this situation have helped create awareness of the arbitrary nature of the alphabet, which led to the belief that words, and therefore language, *are* actually composed of these irreducible components known as letters? It is this latter understanding that inevitably questioned the status of language as the God-given embodiment of a specific idea, a view postulated during the previous era. We know, for example, that many major thinkers of the classical age worked hand-in-hand with their printers, thereby acquiring intimate knowledge of the technology replicating their thought. Is it not reasonable to assume that this technology, in addition to giving words a new kind of permanence, also contributed to a conceptual model whereby their location in the "order of things" would be irrevocably altered?

Finally, it must be noted that whatever the range and interplay of factors responsible for the great transformation of knowledge that occurred at this time, it was still a cumulative process. Although such change appears rapid with respect to what occurred in previous centuries, it was not as sudden a shift from one epochal configuration to the next as Foucault postulates. A valid but not devastating critique of his work is that it does not explain how we get from one episteme to the next. A change is postulated between two separate end states only a few years apart; rapid transformation is assumed but never explained. This bias allies his work to the type of synchronic "freeze-frame" analysis championed by structuralists. It has also led to accusations that he is antihistorical, by those who insist that true history is a study of the past that deals with the reality of continuous change, not an exercise in mapping conceptual cross sections.

Similarly, any attempt to construct a historical typology of whatever persuasion will inevitably be subject to criticism for being too static and exclusive. Foucault has been challenged in this regard by George Huppert.[19] For Huppert, Foucault's preclassical episteme cannot accommodate the likes of Copernicus, Tycho Brahe, Galileo, and Kepler, and he contends that even in France the dominant humanist tradition at the time scoffed at the mode of thought Foucault alleges characterized the age. Yet, if we take Foucault's work as an examination of certain forms of discourse, not all discourse, and assume that the shifts he describes take place in different disciplines at different times and in different places, it might be possible to chart the transformations he describes using a temporal sequence not dealt with in his "archaeology."

DISCOURSE AND THE GENEALOGY OF POWER

After 1968 Foucault's work underwent a shift in emphasis. This constituted more a rearrangement of priorities than the dramatic break that certain critics, hostile to his earlier structuralist influenced discourse theory, would have us believe. In contrast to the earlier "Archaeology," which emphasized theory rather than practice and sought to grasp the unsuspected rules governing discourse, "Genealogy" places understanding the consequences of discourse ahead of an analysis of its internal formulations. The human sciences now become meaningful, not in terms of their relationship to an all-pervasive episteme, but with respect to the set of organizing practices that their situation produces. These practices are held to play a crucial role in history, not because of the nature of the discursive operations that configure them, but because of the way they define, constrain, include, and exclude the human subject with respect to the dominant institutions and power relations of the day.

The seeds of this vision were present in Foucault's earlier work. One need look no further than to *Madness and Civilization* and *Birth of the Clinic* to see how discourse was wielded as a tool of domination. Foucault acknowledges this in a brief but important statement made in 1970, the "Discourse on Language" ("L'ordre du discours"), and explains his new research strategy.[20] Further explication of "Genealogy" can be found in several essays in *Language, Counter-Memory, Practice*.

Two major projects emerged from "Genealogy": *Discipline and Punish*, which deals with the history of penal practice and associated technologies in the eighteenth and nineteenth centuries; and the multivolume *History of Sexuality*, a study that is concerned with how sexuality is constituted through discourse and one in which Foucault emphatically rejects the notion of it as an immutable natural category. It is the first of these two projects, dealing as it does with technology, media, space, and time, which invites comparison with the communications/history researches of Innis and Mumford.

Discipline and Punish, more than any other book by Foucault, can perhaps be tentatively labelled a historical sociology, though traditional historians and sociologists might cringe at my use of this appellation. Part of their consternation might derive from the fact that although Foucault uses Marx in an implicit way that orthodox Marxists have already disavowed, he also draws inspiration from Nietzsche's genealogical method. To combine aspects of Marx with Nietzsche in human science investigation is about as challenging as the proverbial mixing of oil and water. That Foucault is even partially successful is a tribute to his astute eye for discerning underacknowledged aspects of major thinkers, and his unwillingness to be trapped into producing a traditional response to their work.

What then does Nietzsche's genealogical method bring to what Mark Poster rightfully calls the "critical theory" of Foucault's later work?[21] At the outset, a reemphasis on the concept of discontinuity, which seems to have been as important for Nietzsche as for later structuralist inspired writers. With "Genealogy," depth analysis is shunned—meaning is to be found in readily accessible practices. "Genealogy" also assumes that much of traditional history is nothing but high sounding stories masking base motives and coercion, a view not all that distant from Marx's concept of ideology. According to Foucault, the genealogist must destroy the notion of unchanging truths as well as doctrines of development, progress, and reason. But again, lest I belabor the point, this is also an intrinsic assumption of "Archaeology." Where "Genealogy" diverges is in the deliberate quest for strategies of domination in what passes for value, goodness, and virtue. This leads to Foucault's explicit declaration of a dictum that goes back at least to Bacon—"knowledge is power." For Foucault the reverse is equally apropos: knowledge and power imply one another.

A major criticism of this aspect of Foucault is the all-pervasive and nonlocalized way in which he conceives power. For example, take the following statement: "Power is everywhere; not because it embraces everything but because it comes from everywhere."[22] This notion of power as a universal quality recalls Augustine's characterization of God as a being whose presence is everywhere and center is nowhere. It also resounds with some metaphysical aspects of the social process that are part of the legacy of Durkheim; and indeed, aspects of Durkheim's terminology, such as the "social body" and "social organism" are used by Foucault in *Discipline and Punish*. Despite Foucault's metaphysical leanings when discussing power, which can be discomforting to anyone ensconced in a more empirical social science tradition, it would perhaps be more gracious, and fair, to critique "Genealogy" by assessing what it does or does not accomplish rather than chastising the logistics of it as a research program.

A main theme of *Discipline and Punish* is how the body, through what Foucault calls "semio-techniques," becomes a medium of communication. The messages imparted and internalized are those of order, regulation, and docility. This trend becomes widely established in the eighteenth century, during the classical age. It has intellectual roots in the mechanistic side of Descartes' rationalism, which was elaborated further in the hands of numerous Enlightenment philosophes, particularly the physiocrats, who sought to understand both human life and nature with reference to mechanical principles of operation. In the practical social world, forerunners of this ideology can be traced to the organization of monasteries, workshops, and the military. In the eighteenth century many of these elements coalesced into a general formula for domination.[23]

Clearly Foucault is arguing that although all features of the new mode of regimentation were in place by the end of the classical age, the transformation was not sudden or cataclysmic: it had been cumulatively occurring at a number of different loci in previous centuries. This is a concession to history as a temperal process that he seems unwilling to make in his "Archaeology." Nevertheless, "how" these various elements came together to create the new order is of little concern. Precedence is still given to the analysis of end states expressed in certain forms of discourse. But in "Genealogy" as opposed to "Archaeology" the discursive process is seen as embodied in human subjects as well as written texts. This emphasis on human organization for purposes of social control has striking parallels to Mumford's concept of the megamachine. At times it appears to be a localized variant of the latter's more inclusive perspective. And although Mumford, like Foucault, extensively cites the medieval monastery as an immediate source for these social formations, he argues that their ultimate origin is in the methods used to deploy the laboring masses in archaic civilizations, a realm of history into which Foucault does not venture.

One of Foucault's central premises is that "discipline proceeds from the distribution of individuals in space."[24] The eighteenth century saw a proliferation of segregative techniques, many of them described earlier in *Madness and Civilization* and *Birth of the Clinic*. Now he adds military barracks, penal institutions, and schools to the list of institutions employing specific forms of human distribution to signify the location of individuals within a rigid hierarchy. In the nineteenth century these practices became deeply entrenched in architectural space. The modern prison was born and some of the features that characterize it also influenced other institutions.

In assessing the nineteenth-century prison, Foucault put considerable emphasis on observation and surveillance. Although increasing visual emphasis, partly influenced by the telescope, microscope, and scientific method, was a hallmark of the classical age, it was the nineteenth century that saw it deployed in a wide range of ways to facilitate social control and the maintenance of hierarchies. Much of *Discipline and Punish*, as a result, is given over to a discussion of the many ramifications of Bentham's panopticon. Its effect was "to induce in the inmate a state of conscious permanent visibility that insures the automatic functioning of power."[25]

However, the panopticon is but one manifestation of the use of space in the service of power, where it regulates the distribution and definition of human subjects. Foucault regards his examination of it in *Discipline and Punish* as only a beginning, not a finished project. Several years later he engaged in some programmatic reflections on the enterprise:

> A whole history remains to be written of *spaces*—which would at the same time be the history of powers (both these terms in the plural)—from the great strategies of geopolitics to the little tactics of the habitat, institutional architecture from the classroom to the design of hospitals, passing via economic and political installations. It is surprising how long the problem of space took to emerge as a historico-political problem. . . . The development must be extended by no longer just saying space predetermines history which in turn reworks and sediments itself in it. Anchorage in space is an economico-political form which needs to be studied in detail.[26]

The perspective of both "Genealogy" and "Archaeology" goes against the established grain of historical interpretation. Foucault's selection of subject matter, a-temporality, and emphasis on discontinuity, have given rise to criticisms that claim what he is doing is a static, idealized description of the symptoms of deeper processes. This is undoubtedly true. Nevertheless, his work is useful as a new conceptual model, a signpost, against which we can at times assess part of the bewildering flow of events that make any comprehensive or "true" history ultimately impossible.

Conclusion: Current Directions

> I have attempted to suggest that Western civilization has been pro-
> foundly influenced by communication and that marked changes in
> communications have had important implications.
>
> —Harold Innis

Few will deny that we live in an age of rapidly developing technology. Many established institutions are changing in response to what has been called the "information revolution." Industry in the developed world is shifting from a situation
dominated by the production of commodities to one where the information/service
sector is starting to provide the bulk of jobs and income.[1] Communications figure
significantly in this transformation. Many of us were heralded into an awareness
of this by McLuhan during the sixties. However, he was not unique in exhorting
us to study the "invisible environment" of media. He represents a tradition, hith-
erto unacknowledged, which as this book has tried to show, goes back at least
three hundred years. And yet it could be argued that some of the questions dealt
with are as old as Western thought itself, especially when we consider Plato, in the
Phaedrus, discussing the limitations on mind and meaning imposed by writing.

   Although it might seem appropriate at this juncture to insist that communica-
tions/history research is important and worth pursuing further, such a proclama-
tion is hardly necessary. The field is burgeoning. Some of the most exciting work
in the contemporary human sciences deals with the social implications of communications, and much of it is historically informed. If anything is to be proclaimed
here it is that such preoccupations are not new. Several issues of concern to Rousseau, Condorcet, Tylor, Childe, Innis, and the rest of the pantheon we have surveyed, are today being reexamined in both scholarly and popular writings. What

has changed is of course the context and intellectual equipment used for the task. What persists is an interest in the degree to which communications have influenced culture history. However, since Innis and McLuhan researchers are more likely to confine themselves to given segments of the question, rather than attempt a pan-millennial synthesis.[2]

Despite the fact that most contemporary communications/history research is limited to particular eras and/or technologies, when considered as a whole it covers virtually every facet of the subject. Some researchers are archaeological in orientation, some focus on European history, others on non-Western developments, and a number are concerned with the changing state of contemporary media. What follows is a brief and I trust constructively critical appraisal of the work of several. The list is not exhaustive. I have selected for emphasis studies that I find revealing and representative. It is also my intent to argue that we now have the beginnings of a discipline or subdiscipline, both within communication studies as it is currently defined, and one that crosscuts the traditional social sciences and humanities.

Perhaps the logical place to begin is with research oriented to the earliest periods of history or prehistory. As we have already observed with universal history, social evolution, and the formulations of Childe, Mumford, and Innis, this area has been the subject of much speculative assessment. Recently, through a series of new interpretations of the remains of material culture, the discipline of prehistoric archaeology has directed some of its resources toward questions relating to communications. The results, though still tentative, have shed new light on the nature of the symbol systems through which human knowledge is constituted.

One of the most controversial archaeological interpretations relating to communications is the work of Alexander Marshack.[3] He has made an exhaustive study of art and artifacts that date back fifty thousand years. Traditional scholarship has viewed these finds in a variety of ways: as ritual magic, art for art's sake, or as tools for specific, if unknown, utilitarian purposes. Marshack counters with the hypothesis that many of these remains are prewriting texts, embodying intentionally recorded information about the natural environment. They illustrate a capacity for complex symbolizing, which indicates that paleolithic peoples were far more cognitively aware than had been previously acknowledged. This is especially evident in examples that demonstrate what he calls "time-factored thought." Marshack is referring to the situation whereby what are usually assumed to be decorative embellishments on artifacts and paintings, might be a symbolic, perhaps numerical code for seasonal reckoning. Evidence is presented for the contention that a number of these finds were once lunar calendars. He argues that paleolithic peoples, although governed by a cyclical rather than linear conception of time, could nonetheless deal with it in quite specific ways.

Marshack's project does not derive from a direct awareness of the history of communications as it has been elaborated here. Rather, he was inspired by aspects of modern science as it has influenced the space age—before he wrote about paleolithic lunar calendars he was researching contemporary lunar exploration—and sought to examine its prehistoric beginnings. Nevertheless his work relates to previous communications/history inquiry in significant ways. The notion of "time-factored thought," for example, is an aspect of the cultural orientation of societies that Innis would assess as "time-biased," and can be profitably reexamined in light of this latter concept. It is also complemented by the work of art historian Siegfried Giedion, whose perceptive article, "Space Conception in Prehistoric Art," appears in Carpenter and McLuhan's volume *Explorations in Communication*[4] — though Marshack appears unaware of either this or other writings Giedion has done on prehistory.[5] One final communications/history area that can inform Marshack's perspective is the nature of the oral tradition. Marshack has a tendency to view his prehistoric materials as texts analagous to, or moving toward, writing. But they can also be effectively assessed as mnemonic embellishments to an oral tradition. Fuller understanding of the cognitive dimensions of orality would perhaps have given him an even better sense of how these symbolic artifacts were articulated within the cultural systems of prehistory.

The research Marshack has done on the paleolithic is not the only recent attempt to seek clues to the origins of writing in the prehistoric, preliterate world. Denise Schmandt-Besserat has been independently engaged in the same quest with respect to the neolithic, the period from the tenth millennium B.C. to the rise of the great ancient civilizations of the Middle and Near East.[6] It is her contention that prior to the emergence of writing in the first city states, widely dispersed societies maintained a record of their internal economics and external trade relationships through the use of fired clay tokens. These tokens, one to three centimeters in size, represent objects (although they were conventionalized and did not look like what they represented) and a numerical system. It was, she postulates, this form of communications which led eventually to writing. Evidence is drawn from the fact that the first ideograms in Sumerian script, which were written on clay tablets, resemble the earlier tokens. This shift from three-dimensional to two-dimensional representation paralleled and facilitated the move toward more large-scale settlements and eventually city states. The new medium of writing yielded a more information-rich and centralized way of doing what the tokens had done previously.

The implications of the Schmandt-Besserat hypothesis for the history of communications are far-reaching. This was duly acknowledged by those working in the area when members of what has sometimes been called the "Toronto school of communications," in conjunction with the Harold Innis Foundation, invited her to participate in a symposium titled "Innis, McLuhan and the Frontiers of Communication," in March of 1985. The reciprocity between what her work represented and what others were doing in communications/history was obvious to all present, including this author.

Schmandt-Besserat's research has convinced many that even before writing there were bona fide communications systems, in terms of media intentionally created for organizing and transmitting information. Nevertheless, it is usually believed that the emergence of civilization, and a state form of social organization, necessitates writing. No less an authority than archaeologist Gordon Childe mistakenly assumed this, and Harold Innis and numerous others followed suit. That writing is not the definitive benchmark of civilization has been insightfully demonstrated by Marcia and Robert Ascher in an unheralded book, *Code of the Quipu: A Study in Media Mathematics and Culture*.[7] Their work, it should be noted, like that of Marshack and Schmandt-Besserat, is not based on the discovery of new archaeological remains, but on a reinterpretation of what was already known and explained in conventional accounts.

The view of Ascher and Ascher is that what is necessary for the establishment of civilization is not writing per se, but a "medium" for the keeping of records, which functions in a efficient and comprehensive manner. Among the Incas of pre-Columbian South America, the quipu served this purpose. It was a series of cords of different length, thickness, and colors, which were knotted and braided. Each of these elements constitutes information, the kind used to record crop production, taxation, a census, and a variety of other calculations. The Aschers meticulously decode the quipu and draw important parallels between the information capacity of that medium and what was possible with the writing systems of the ancient Near and Middle Eastern civilizations. Their inquiry builds on a concern with the role of media in the history of civilization pioneered by Edward Tylor, whose account of the quipu is surprisingly uncited. Perhaps even more surprising, and gratifying from the perspective presented here, is their awareness of the work of Innis. The Aschers note how his concept that a light portable medium emphasizes a bias of space over time, consonant with administration over distance, is supported by the Incas' example. The work of McLuhan and Carpenter is also referenced with respect to the relationship between oral and literate modes of communication.

Despite the major achievement of archaic civilizations in the area of culture and communications, it is usually the transition to full-fledged alphabetic literacy that is regarded as the foundation upon which Western civilization has been elaborated. How this occurred in Greece, and its far-reaching consequences, has been the subject of major studies by classicist Eric Havelock.[8] He was once a colleague of Innis, whom he respectfully assesses in a memoir prefaced by McLuhan.[9] Although no longer based in Toronto, Havelock can be seen as part of the "Toronto school of communications." His work has been utilized by McLuhan, and in recent years Havelock has refined further some of the issues that grow out of McLuhan's "probes." Almost every contemporary writer dealing with the question of literacy and civilization has been forced to address aspects of Havelock's perspective.

Havelock contends that the alphabet is the most far-reaching and significant cultural/technological development in Western history. His stance is emphatic, and some see it verging toward, or being, determinist[10]—perhaps because he does not shrink from using the "medium is the message" as a credo and argues that the alphabet is a technology that has exerted a "causative function" to our thought, philosophy, and morality.[11] It is also regarded as a uniquely Greek achievement. Previous scripts representing spoken discourse, such as the Phoenician, are seen as syllabaries lacking the signs for true vowel sounds. They augmented rather than qualitatively transformed the cultural capacity of societies using them. The emergence of a "true" alphabet in Greece is said to have occurred rather suddenly, around the eighth century B.C. It ushered in the shift from a discourse of action to one of reflection by making language a visible artifact. By the time of Plato in the late fifth century B.C., there arose the notion of absolute knowledge and a true science based solely on forms. This way of dealing with the world is, for Havelock, an outgrowth of alphabetic literacy—the characteristics of that medium reflected in a philosophy of nature and culture.

An important element in Havelock's stated goal to produce a social anthropology of Greek culture, is a consideration of its pre-alphabetic oral tradition. He is both astute and respectful in his examination of preliterate Greece. He also scrupulously tries to avoid the romanticism that he feels colored Innis's view of that period. For Havelock a major key to the Greek oral world is the work of Homer. In the most thorough assessment to date, he builds on a tradition of Homeric scholarship that has sought to establish the oral nature of the epics. More recently he has revealed that although the epics are oral compositions, they were influenced by the emerging literacy of the day.[12] Thus he at least partly extricates himself from the trap of thinking solely in terms of a grand dichotomy between orality and literacy, and opens the possibility of considering the nature of transitional states, both in the Greek case and in later epochs in the history of communications.

One of the central questions addressed by Havelock in his examination of the Greek situation, is the nature of literacy. Literacy as a cultural-historical, as opposed to a pedagogical issue, has been the subject of numerous studies over the past twenty years. Indeed, it could be argued that there now exists a discipline or subdiscipline, which could be called literacy studies, just as I am arguing the same status for communications/history. These attempts to deal with the cultural-historical consequences of literacy are of course strongly allied to the main themes of this book, and although they are too numerous to discuss here, several are cited in the bibliography. However, at least two scholars working in this area deserve special mention because of the seminal implications of their work: Walter Ong and Jack Goody.

Ong's research as a historian assessing the transformation of texts and curriculae that occurred after the end of the Middle Ages, particularly as manifest in the pronouncements of Pierre Ramus (1515-1572), has been lauded and incorporated by McLuhan.[13] Ong has in turn picked up and developed further what he feels are some of McLuhan's more insightful observations. In his recent work Ong surveys a vast expanse of the history of communications through an application of the contrast between orality and literacy.[14] This has led to the development of a cultural-cognitive model of what constitutes primary orality, and an assessment of how it is altered by alphabetic literacy (the work of Havelock is extensively utilized), the advent of print, and the emergence of secondary orality accompanying the rise of electronic media.

Rather than describing his approach as a history of media or communications in general, Ong refers to it as a study of the "technologizing" of the world. This entails an ongoing contrast between the dynamic fluid nature of orality, with its numerous formulaic devices to facilitate memorization, and the static, quiescent character of the written word, which endeavors to locate thought in a fixed visual space. These two "ideal types" provide him with a model for the critical examination of a variety of communication genres, particularly in the verbal arts, which range from the Homeric epics to the contemporary detective story. In so doing Ong challenges the traditional linguistic notion that writing is only a complement to speech, which succeeds in preserving it beyond the moment. Instead he cites, as does Havelock, McLuhan's by now immortal "the medium is the message," to argue that writing is a separate system, a code, which at various levels within manuscript and print traditions, profoundly influences and alters the discourse it replicates.

One useful way to view Ong's work is as a fuller explication of some of the suggestive themes announced in the work of Innis and McLuhan, but not fully developed there—though this of course is not his direct intent. Ong's concept of secondary orality, for example, can be seen as providing greater focus to notions McLuhan raised with his sweeping claim that electronic media have a retribalizing effect, returning us to certain modes of perception and thought characteristic of a preliterate world. It is this secondary orality, Ong contends, that eventually sensitized us to the earlier contrast between the spoken and written word: "Our understanding of the differences between orality and literacy developed only in the electronic age, not earlier."[15] However, this observation, while largely true, is not wholly so. It overlooks the insightful struggle to grasp the differences between the spoken and written word that Jean-Jacques Rousseau attempted in the middle of the eighteenth century.

Some of the same concerns examined by Ong have been broached by Jack Goody in the inclusive manner which often characterizes the work of someone coming from that discipline. In a programmatic essay, "The Consequences of Literacy," written with Ian Watt, Goody looks at the passage from orality to literacy in a wide range of societies.[16] The history and implications of various writing systems, differences between myth and history, and further extensions of Havelock's observations of the Greek transformation, are broadly assessed with an eye to the elaboration of future, more thorough studies. Inspiration for the project derives in part from the "Toronto school of communications." The work of Innis and Havelock is cited specifically in this context. Several years later Goody would be invited to the same symposium in Toronto dealing with the history of communications mentioned earlier in conjunction with Schmandt-Besserat.

In a subsequent work, the *Domestication of the Savage Mind*, Goody has developed his position further.[17] Arguing against Levi-Strauss, and an entire tradition in anthropology and philosophy that has postulated a "grand dichotomy" between the thought worlds of the primitive and civilized, Goody proposes a less ethnocentric model, one based on a succession of changes through time grounded in the degree of orality versus literacy. He introduces a concept inspired by Marx's "mode of production": the "mode of communication." Application of this concept entails looking at a culture in terms of its communicative acts and prevailing medium. The intent is to discern the way knowledge is developed and deployed, and to assess the consequences for human relationships. This approach is avowedly nondeterministic. The "mode of communication" is seen as a powerful facilitator rather than a cause. Orality and literacy are not held to be absolutes, but characteristics or directions influencing the culture of given societies.

Goody uses the orality/literacy contrast to assess knowledge and cognition in a wide range of societies, including those that were pre-alphabetic but nonetheless had writing. He holds the view that several aspects of literacy, so apparent in alphabetic scripts, initially developed in other forms of graphic representation. In elaborating this view he inclines toward the position of Innis, who regarded writing per se (not merely the alphabet) as the harbinger of a visual emphasis and other "literate" biases, and away from the position of McLuhan and Havelock, who see literacy in history as virtually synonymous with phonetic literacy. The strength of this approach is perhaps best demonstrated in Goody's perceptive essay, "What's in a List."[18] In it the cultural-cognitive implications of listing are traced through a variety of modes of written communication, from ancient Mesopotamia to the print era. This is a study that enhances our understanding of the taxonomic aspect of written discourse. It also unintentionally complements other approaches to the history of communication, in particular the ambitious project that Foucault referred to as his "Archaeology of Knowledge."

Although Goody's work critiques previous "grand dichotomy" theorizing, it is obvious that his own project is not entirely devoid of dualistic thinking. He has been taken to task in this area by Brian Street.[19] Street's rather strident chastisement of Goody is based on the observation that the latter is guilty of overstating the influence of writing and understating the qualities of oral communication; also that he adheres to a relatively autonomous and technical notion of the "mode of communication," which neglects the analysis of context necessary to a full understanding of literacy in any society. Street suggests that what we should examine is not literacy per se, but literacies, and the wider social and ideological arena in which they function. He illustrates this position with convincing examples from his own field research.

However, in fairness to Goody, his goal was to produce the program within anthropology, not to refine it by examining extensively detailed case studies. It is often easy for those who enter territory using a particular map, to find all manner of detail that the previous cartographer missed because his main concern was in providing a general overview. The key difference between Street's approach and Goody's resides in the level of analysis employed; both after all are in accord regarding the importance of the subject area. Although Street seems uncomfortable with Goody's almost explicit reference to an "ideal" (what sociologists following Max Weber might refer to as an "ideal type") of orality and literacy, he subliminally adheres to this way of thinking himself when he describes situations that are a "mix" of oral and literate modes, rather than a "pure type of either." Does this view not presuppose an "ideal" of what constitutes oral versus literate, against which the "mix" of given societies can be contemplated? Granted, there may be no human group manifesting "pure" orality and "pure" literacy, but an informed concept, or "ideal type" of what that purity entails can be a valuable guide to interpreting what is actually observed in given societies, as Weber well knew. And it is in this area that Goody has made a significant contribution, one which allows for the further refinement that Street seeks.

The previous writers who write about writing would all no doubt be in accord with the view that literacy was dramatically altered by print. McLuhan has belabored this point endlessly in *The Gutenberg Galaxy*. However, only recently, with the publication of Eisenstein's *The Printing Press as an Agent of Change: Communications and Cultural Transformation in Early Modern Europe* has the importance of typography been the subject of a sustained and thoroughly detailed study.[20] Eisenstein has delved into an area often overlooked by traditional historians. In so doing she grudgingly concedes that McLuhan was an inspiration, if not a direct influence. His oracular pronouncements and crass generalizations illuminated an important area and made her aware of the need to develop it further in a more scrupulous manner. Interestingly enough McLuhan's work has also been an impediment. She notes how it has often been counterproductive, discouraging further investigation into the printing revolution on the part of some historians, and casting the stigma of being "McLuhanite" on those so engaged.

Eisenstein's study is concerned with the effects of printing on such interconnected facets of Western history as: the classical revival leading to the Renaissance; the end of the medieval church and establishment of the Protestant Reformation; the dissemination of capitalist enterprise; the Copernican Revolution; and the spread of scientific and technological literature accompanying the rise of the publishing industry. Even the briefest summary of the coverage of any of these topics would fail to do justice to the enormity and importance of her project. Suffice to say it is now widely and favorably cited by researchers in the field of communication studies as well as the traditional social sciences and humanities. It doubtless ranks as one of the finest studies ever done on the introduction and consequences of a new technology, and is even influencing scholars studying the information revolution accompanying the widespread deployment of computer technology.

This is evident in James Burke's recent television series and book, *The Day the Universe Changed*.[21] An entire episode and chapter, informed by Eisenstein, deals with the historical influence of print and its relationship to other information technologies.

Although Eisenstein's project was first published in 1979, a year before McLuhan died, the latter managed to comment on it in a rather disappointing review.[22] Taking a defensive posture he champions the originality of his own book, *The Gutenberg Galaxy*, by accusing Eisenstein of producing a sombre, matter-of-fact, overly detailed narrative. McLuhan fails to see how Eisenstein's work complements his own and describes her approach as "paraphrasing and quantifying." Ironically it is McLuhan's review which is sombre and pedantic, much of it given over to an obscure discussion of the concept of causality. Eisenstein's study, although rich in detail is, despite McLuhan's criticisms, not without flashes of insight steeped in humor, some of it verging close to what could be called "McLuhanisms" or "probes"—though she would probably cringe at this observation. Witness the following gem: "Until the advent of printing, scientific inquiries about 'how the heavens go' were linked with religious concerns about 'how to go to heaven.' "[23]

Major use of Eisenstein's work, as well as that of Havelock, Goody, Ong, Mumford, Innis, and McLuhan, has been made by Neil Postman. In two popular and thought provoking books he has applied the vast resources available from the history of communications to a number of issues relevant to the study of media and society in our own time.[24] In *The Disappearance of Childhood* he argues that contemporary mass media are socializing children into adult patterns of behavior at an early age. The situation is compared to the way socialization occurred in the preprint and print eras. A loose parallel is drawn between our electronic age and the partially literate Middle Ages. In the Middle Ages most of the lifeways and expectations of adulthood were accessed by children as soon as they were old enough to understand and physically deal with them. The coming of print dramatically changed this scenario by giving rise to a new social category, childhood. A communication environment was created where literacy and schooling segregated children from the adult world while they attained reading competence and mastered the intricacies of a more secular and increasingly technological culture. According to Postman, modern electronic media, especially television, are obliterating this nearly five-hundred-year-old phenomenon. To be socialized by the images and into the roles pervaded by contemporary media requires minimal study and reflection. This has created a series of moral dilemmas, which range from twelve-year-old girls attaining notoriety as seductive models, to teenaged boys engaging in adult crimes of violence to a degree that would have been unthinkable a generation or two ago.

Postman's subsequent book, *Amusing Ourselves to Death*, looks at another side of the problems created by contemporary media. Writing in a lively style, with well timed sarcasm and moral indignation, he lashes out at the way our mass media trivialize and render inane, not only entertainment, but what passes for quality or educational programming as well. In fact he deems the latter more nefarious because it is presented to us with the assumption that here at least the model of show biz glitz, which governs conventional fare, is inoperative. Nonsense and hypocrisy, Postman claims, then proceeds to indict "Sesame Street" as well as several highly touted adult programs. A special tirade is levelled at the religious broadcasts of the electronic gospel. Clearly he prefers primetime schlock. At least it is honest. Here the medium is doing what it does best, and doing it with a minimum of pretension.

The major arguments of *Amusing Ourselves to Death*, like those in *The Disappearance of Childhood*, are grounded in historical contrast. This time Postman measures what the electronic media have created by looking at the situation of public discourse in colonial and nineteenth-century America. The Lincoln versus Douglas debate is cited as a prime example of the way things were done then. It was literate, complex, witty, long, and demanding. "Those were the days," Postman seems to suggest: an informed public patiently attended an informed public event where issues were paramount. Today such occurrences are media events, which is to say that they are pseudo events. How did this come to be? It began, he argues, with the telegraph, which initiated a tendency for the medium to become a metaphor for the culture. Further changes in this direction came with radio. Television added the presence of images. No longer can a fat or ugly politician attain high office, no matter how high principled or conscientious he is. Today, Postman might say, "all the world's a stage," but not the Globe theater of this aphorism by Shakespeare; it has been replaced by Caesar's Palace.

In these two books Postman has made judicious use of major resources in the history of communications, taken some of their most insightful features, and utilized them in an accessible format. This deserves admiration, even if a number of his contentions must be questioned. I for one am rather dubious regarding the historical parameters he places on childhood. My feeling is that there may be more universality here than meets the medium. This is a potential criticism he anticipates by citing Piaget's notion of universal stages, and observing that even if there is a basis for such a view, social and technological conditions can suppress or override aspects of it. But to assume this to the degree that Postman does is to verge close to cultural determinism. To assess *how* meanings and categories come into being at different points in history is not necessarily to explain *why*. Postman is convincing when discussing the former, but stays close to McLuhanesque metaphysics when he attempts the latter.

Most who would share Postman's strident criticism of contemporary media would probably dismiss McLuhan as an apologist for its worst features. It is to Postman's credit that he has exhumed and recontextualized some of the "oracle's" more worthwhile "probes." In so doing he has been able to do what McLuhan continually disavowed: develop a critical and moral stance that eschews as illusory notions of media relativism; and here, Postman is more faithful to the spirit of

Innis than McLuhan ever was. Also, intentionally or not, he appears to ally with the position of Lewis Mumford. Both seem to share the view that the best of all possible worlds is the print world.

There are times, however, when Postman is too extreme. His indictment of "Sesame Street" and related programming for succumbing to the attention-getting techniques of media hype and advertising, overlooks aspects of the origin of this discursive style. It is partly a feature of what Ong might call "secondary orality." In other words, it is the recasting, in new technological garb, of certain formulaic devices inherent to primary oral communication, devices that were originally pedagogical in nature, designed to produce "memorable thoughts." This situation is evidenced in much of the mythology of the nonliterate world, where engaging narratives steeped in word play and exaggeration often tell about the adventures of unusual characters; they also transmit facts about geography, ecology, and the social world, and therefore inform as well as entertain. While elements of the "memorable" discursive style of orality have been widely used in modern media for commercial exploitation and propaganda, they have also served less coercive ends. Postman's sweeping criticism of every facet of contemporary media sometimes overlooks the fact that a complete analysis of them often requires a consideration of the uses to which they are put, and content, as well as an assessment of their nature and style. Although Big Bird and Ronald McDonald are both "totems" of the "box," they are not the same phenomenon.

In his consideration of the telegraph in *Amusing Ourselves to Death*, Postman cites Daniel Czitrom's *Media and the American Mind: From Morse to McLuhan*.[25] This is an especially noteworthy study because of the way it elaborates two related projects. The first is a communications/history perspective on the introduction and influence of three major media: the telegraph, motion pictures, and radio. The second part of the book is an intellectual history of communication theory in the twentieth century. This discussion is focussed on a plea for the recovery of a historical perspective. It includes an assessment of Innis and McLuhan consonant with the one presented here, and suggestions for directing the communications/history project toward the analysis of several new media. In attempting at least a partial intellectual history of its subject, Czitrom's book belongs to a small but growing tradition, which includes Hanno Hardt's *Social Theories of the Press*, William Kuhns' *The Post-Industrial Prophets*, and without undue modesty, the present volume.

Communications/history is both a thriving area of contemporary research and a significant tradition in modern (post-Renaissance) social thought and intellectual history. That it is a field of current interest among a variety of interdisciplinary scholars should not be surprising given the proliferation of information technology that saturates today's world and demands critical study. What seems most eye opening is the fact that attempts to reflect on the nature of human knowledge through a historical assessment of the means through which it has been embodied

date back as early as they do. When I first began work on this project I was grati-
fied simply to note the many interesting discussions of communications/history
in the eighteenth and nineteenth centuries. Further research led me to an assessment of what was elaborated in those accounts and I was impressed. Also, the
more familiar I became with the material, the more obvious it seemed to me that
there was a logic of development (often unintended) from one such inquiry to
the next. Here, as with the study of other facets of society, universal history provided a foundation for social evolution, which in turn influenced a variety of
twentieth-century social science perspectives. However, when I started out I assumed communications/history would be an exception, that it was a discontinuous
tradition at best, which would have to be framed through the development of a
fairly discrete chronology. Quite the opposite came to pass.

What I would like to pose in concluding is a twofold division of the communi-
cations/history domain. Prior to the work of Harold Innis, and dating back to the
Enlightenment, we have what I call an "unacknowledged tradition"—though the
adjective *unacknowledged* might be presumptuous and has been used partly as
an attention-getting device. This is to say that there has been development of a
series of approaches relating to the subject but no coherent recognition that it is
a field of study in its own right. Since Innis, and largely because of him, commu-
nications/history has become a discipline or subdiscipline—though one not formally recognized by the academy. (I was tempted to refer to it, almost until this writing, as a *paradigm*, and would have no objections to those who would do so,
despite the contentious nature and overly general applications that often characterize the use of this term.)

My belief that Innis is *the* cartographer of the history of communications should
come as no surprise to those who have followed closely the argument of the last
third of this book. Most, but admittedly not all of the previously assessed contemporary research is in his debt. Even writers who seem completely unaware of
the Innis legacy have produced studies that relate to it. I can think of no finer
example than Stephen Kern's the *Culture of Time and Space: 1880-1918.* [26] Kern
shows how sweeping changes in technology and culture during the period he
assesses gave rise to new and distinctive ways of thinking about time and space.
He considers the implications of the telegraph, telephone, radio, x-ray, photo-
graphy, film, the bicycle, automobile, and airplane—especially how they influenced geographical and personal space, architecture, popular and scientific concepts of time, the use of space in painting, and cultural life in general. Although
McLuhan is briefly and favorably cited, Kern's detailed and historically specific
research seems to fit comfortably within the parameters Innis outlined for assessing the biases of time and space as an aspect of the comparative study of civilization.

To reiterate, it is through the work of Innis and the "Toronto school of communications" that we have a definitive blueprint for the study of communications/

history. Of all recent perspectives on the subject, this is the one that is most inclusive. It frames the field in a way that provides logical space for *all* the contributions we have examined. It yields suggestive leads for assessing the economic, social, and psychological dimensions of media. It transforms the history of communications into an ongoing project for the critical assessment of new technologies. And finally, it does not demand obedience to any theory or interpretation. To extend aspects of the Innis legacy in new directions, which challenge or refute some of his original formulations, is to fulfill that legacy.

Notes

CHAPTER 1

1. Becker 1978.
2. As some of the contributors in Rockwood (1968) point out.
3. Gay 1969, vol. 1, p. 6.
4. Frankel 1948, p. 8.
5. Gay 1969, vol. 1, p. 58.
6. Cassirer 1951, p. 14.
7. Aarsleff 1982, p. 281.
8. Cassirer 1951, p. 43.
9. Leiss 1974.
10. Quoted in Manuel 1954, p. 24.
11. Quoted in Cassirer 1951, p. 94.
12. Yolton 1956.
13. Aarsleff 1982.
14. Locke 1975, p. 116.
15. Leibniz 1981.
16. Saussure notes: "We can therefore imagine *a science which would study the life of signs within society*. . . . We call it *semiology* from the Greek semeion (sign). It would teach us what signs consist of, what laws govern them." (Quoted in Culler 1976, p. 90.)
17. Aarsleff 1982, p. 28.
18. Locke 1975, p. 509.
19. Locke put strong emphasis on the arbitrary nature of language:

   Thus we may conceive how *Words*, which were by nature so well adapted to that purpose, came to be made use of by them, as the *Signs of their Ideas*; not by any natural connection, that there is between particular articulate sounds and certain Ideas, for then there would be but one language amongst all Men; but by a voluntary Imposition, whereby such a word is made arbitrarily the Mark of such an *Idea*; and the Ideas they stand for, are their proper and immediate signification. (Ibid., p. 405.)

20. Aarsleff 1982, p. 155.
21. Knight 1968, p. viii.
22. Ibid., p. 15.
23. Aarsleff 1982, p. 155.
24. Knight 1968, p. 2.
25. Condillac 1971, p. 7.
26. Ibid., p. 117.
27. But not as extreme, for example, as the almost total environmentalism of his contemporary disciple, Claude Helvetius (1715-1771).
28. Aarsleff (1982, p. 69) takes this position.
29. Knight 1968, p. 158.
30. Condillac 1971, p. 8.

CHAPTER 2

1. Marx and Engels 1964, p. 48.
2. Gay 1969, vol. 1, p. 17.
3. Cassirer 1951, p. 207.
4. During the Enlightenment excitement over the accomplishments of Greek civilization increased while interest in Egypt waned. Monboddo was enthusiastic about both and therefore somewhat of an exception. In the early nineteenth century curiosity about Egypt increased as classical archaeology underwent expansion and received increased recognition.
5. Cassirer 1951, pp. 207, 209.
6. Berlin 1976, p. 112.
7. Meek 1973, p. 24.
8. Manuel 1962, p. 17.
9. Turgot, quoted in Meek 1973, p. 44.
10. Ibid., p. 41.
11. Ibid., p. 118.
12. The main change is that today, unlike the eighteenth-century thinkers, we regard agriculture to have preceded pastoralism. The priority of pastoralism in Enlightenment chronologies could be the result of the dominance of this lifestyle in the Old Testament.
13. Manuel 1962, p. 41.
14. Condorcet 1955, p. 3.
15. Ibid., p. 7.
16. Ibid.
17. Today anthropologists have shown that people who live in so-called subsistence economies, especially hunter-gatherers, can often have more leisure time than the inhabitants of more complex agricultural and even industrial societies; for example, see Sahlins in Lee and Devore 1968.

18. Condorcet 1955, p. 99.
19. Ibid., p. 24.
20. Ibid., pp. 73-74.
21. Ibid., p. 97.
22. Foucault 1973a.
23. Condorcet 1955, p. 99.
24. Ibid., p. 101.
25. Lovejoy 1932-1933.
26. This *Encyclopedia*, Edwards 1972, contains only a one-sentence statement on Monboddo, which appears under the heading of "British Philosophy," vol. 1, p. 383.
27. Bryson 1945, p. 66.
28. Stam 1976, p. 62.
29. Cloyd (1972) has done some careful research on the degree of Monboddo's political commitment.
30. Monboddo 1967, vol. 1, p. 25.
31. Monboddo 1779-1799, vol. 4, p. 64.
32. For a contemporary appraisal of the gestural origin theory of language see Hewes 1973; and Hewes in Harnad et al. 1976.
33. Monboddo 1967, vol. 2, p. 431.
34. Monboddo 1779-1799, vol. 5, p. 107.
35. Monboddo 1967, vol. 2, pp. 259-60.

CHAPTER 3

1. Guehenno 1967.
2. Engels 1970, p. 153.
3. Rousseau 1964, p. 103.
4. Masters 1976.
5. Durkheim 1965.
6. Rousseau 1964, p. 102.
7. Montesquieu 1965, p. xvii.
8. Quoted in McLellan 1971, p. 32.
9. Marx 1973; 1967 vol. 1.
10. Rousseau 1964, p. 143.
11. Ibid., p. 118.
12. Rousseau and Herder 1966, p. 38.
13. Ibid., p. 103.
14. Rousseau 1964, p. 126.
15. Rousseau and Herder 1966, p. 10.
16. Ibid., p. 24.
17. Ibid., p. 19.
18. Culler in Sturrock 1979, p. 156.
19. As revealed in the studies conducted by Scribner and Cole (1981).
20. Derrida 1980, p. 98.
21. Ibid., p. 168.
22. Ibid., p. 312.
23. Ibid., p. 270.

24. Ibid., p. 271.

25. Ong 1982, p. 167.

26. Another anthropologist citing the importance of Rousseau for the history of the discipline is Diamond (1974).

27. These contrasts are examined in Goody (1978); also in Darnton (1984) there are intriguing considerations of Rousseau's style in relationship to the nature and expectations of his eighteenth-century readers.

CHAPTER 4

1. Barzun 1961.

2. Aarsleff 1982, p. 299.

3. Barzun (1961) gives a good assessment of these contributions.

4. *Historiographia Linguistica* is the journal.

5. Chomsky 1966.

6. Aarsleff 1982.

7. Robins 1967, p. 134.

8. Ibid., pp. 135-36.

9. Muller 1863, p. 42.

10. In a later work (1887, p. x), he would come to view intellect as an aspect of language.

11. Muller 1863, p. 354.

12. Muller 1887, p. 94.

13. This is discussed in Heyer 1982, p. 109.

14. Muller 1901, p. 75.

15. Muller 1887, p. 40.

16. Muller 1901, p. 114.

17. According to Aarsleff (1982, pp. 294, 320), Whitney was one of the first to make the distinction between philology and the new science of linguistics.

18. Whitney 1867, p. 20.

19. Ibid., p. 50.

20. Ibid.

21. Ibid., p. 364.

22. Ibid., p. 400.

23. Ibid., p. 420.

24. Ibid., p. 447.

25. An excellent recent discussion of the nature and role of the quipu can be found in Ascher and Ascher 1981.

26. Clodd 1920.

27. Taylor 1883, vol. 1, p. 364.

28. Clodd 1920, p. 1.

CHAPTER 5

1. This is the position taken by Burrow (1966) and Harris (1970).

2. Burrow 1966.

3. Hardt 1979, p. 17.

4. Ibid., p. 19.
5. Marx and Engels 1964.
6. Elsewhere (Heyer 1982) I have more thoroughly assessed this question.
7. Marx and Engels 1964, p. 42.
8. Marx 1973, p. 490.
9. Wilden (1980a; 1980b) has critically considered and applied aspects of the Marxian view of language and communications to several contemporary ideological practices.
10. Parker 1981.
11. Ibid., pp. 130-31.
12. Quoted in ibid., p. 137.
13. Leiss, Kline, and Jhally 1986.
14. Morgan 1868.
15. See especially *The Ethnological Notebooks of Karl Marx* edited by Krader 1972; also Engels 1972.
16. Morgan 1964, p. 15.
17. Harris (1970) is certainly justified in his argument against any singular acceptance of Morgan's position(s).
18. Morgan 1964, p. 32.
19. Ibid., pp. 33-34.
20. Ibid., p. 448.
21. Hardt 1979, p. 72.
22. Quoted in ibid., p. 79.
23. Ibid., p. 95.
24. Quoted in ibid., p. 103.
25. Quoted in ibid., p. 106.
26. Park 1967, p. x.
27. Park and Burgess 1969, p. 16.
28. In a famous passage Marx observes:

> Men make their own history, but they do not make it just as they please; they do not make it under circumstances chosen by themselves but under circumstances directly encountered, given and transmitted from the past. The tradition of all the dead generations weigh like a nightmare on the brain of the living. (1969, p. 15.)

Park does not appear to be indebted to Marx in an extensive way. However, although he does not consider social stratification to any great degree, he comes close to a concept of class consciousness (1967, p. xxx).

29. Park 1967, p. xxiii.
30. Introduction to Innis 1973, p. xvi.

CHAPTER 6

1. Quoted in Tylor 1964, pp. vi, ix.
2. Tylor 1970, p. 1.
3. Marett 1936, p. 194.

4. Ibid., p. 14.

5. Tylor 1888.

6. Marett 1936, p. 29.

7. Tylor 1970, p. 208.

8. Ibid., p. 242.

9. Ibid., p. 244.

10. Tylor 1878, p. 373.

11. Tylor 1934, p. 77.

12. As, for example, is done in Harris (1970).

13. As Leslie White notes in his foreword to Tylor 1965.

14. Tylor 1878, p. 204.

15. Tylor 1958, p. 1.

16. A useful and critical appraisal of the concept of culture can be found in Bauman (1973); for my commentary on this study see Heyer 1975; also an assessment of the use of the culture concept by Tylor is contained in Leopold 1980, who at present is completing an extensive biography of Tylor.

17. A similar view is convincingly elaborated by Stocking (1968).

18. Tylor 1958, pp. 1, 2.

19. Ibid., pp. 415-16.

20. Quoted in Tylor 1958a, p. ix.

21. Elsewhere (Heyer 1982) I have considered Tylor's relationship to Darwin more extensively.

22. Stocking (1968) uses this term.

23. This is partly the result of the fact that when Tylor is considered by anthropologists it is usually through an assessment of *Primitive Culture*; *Researches* often receives scanty attention and *Anahuac* has never garnered more than passing mention.

24. Tylor 1878, p. 15.

25. Ibid., p. 44.

26. Ibid., p. 64.

27. Ibid., p. 106.

28. Ibid., p. 98.

29. Tylor 1958, p. 305.

30. Tylor 1878, p. 155.

31. An excellent appraisal of the role of the quipu, and some comparisons between it and various ancient writing systems is contained in Ascher and Ascher (1981).

32. Tylor 1965, p. 35.

33. Ibid., p. 33.

34. Ibid., p. 77.

35. Ibid., p. 78.

36. Ibid.

CHAPTER 7

1. Innis 1951.

2. Trigger 1980, p. 18.

3. Ibid., p. 33.

4. Daniel 1962; 1970.

5. For example, there is an interesting application of Innis's ideas to the situation of the Incas by Ascher and Ascher 1981.

6. Trigger 1980, p. 127.

7. Ibid., pp. 20-21.

8. Childe 1964a, p. 24.

9. Childe 1952, p. 7.

10. *Paleolithic* refers to the old stone age of nomadic big game hunting; *Mesolithic* to the succeeding epoch of diversified small game hunting, fishing, and gathering; and *Neolithic* to the earliest settled agricultural period.

11. Trigger 1980, pp. 44-45.

12. Daniel 1970, pp. 34-35.

13. Particularly the diffusionist view of Egypt as the source for all world civilizations propounded by G. Elliot Smith and W. J. Perry.

14. Childe 1952, p. 7.

15. Childe 1951, p. 148.

16. Mumford 1979, p. 26.

17. A recent bibliography can be found in Newman 1971.

18. Quoted in Conrad 1976, p. 178.

19. These influences are fully traced in Hissey 1986.

20. Hissey provides further commentary on Geddes's influence.

21. Mumford 1963, p. 110.

22. Mumford 1973.

23. Ibid., p. 201.

24. Elsewhere (Heyer 1982) I have argued against the notion of Marx as a determinist.

25. Mumford 1967, p. 24.

26. Ibid., p. 192.

27. Mumford 1952, p. 18.

28. Mumford 1967, p. 101.

29. Ibid., p. 142.

30. Ibid., p. 192.

31. Ibid., p. 201.

32. Mumford 1963, p. 136.

33. Mumford 1952, p. 76.

34. Mumford 1967, p. 285.

CHAPTER 8

1. In particular, most of the articles in Melody et al. 1981.

2. To date, most of our knowledge of this aspect of Innis comes from his biographer Donald Creighton (1978).

3. Havelock 1982, p. 37.

4. For further explication, see the articles by Melody and Watkins in Melody et al. 1981.

5. Innis 1980.

6. As David Crowley elaborates in Melody et al. 1981.

7. Quoted in McLellan 1975, p. 41.

8. Heyer 1982.

9. No recent writer has done a more impressive job in charting and elaborating this dictotomy than Diamond 1974.

10. This aspect of Innis is thoroughly dealt with in Watson 1977.

11. Innis 1973, p. 132.

12. Ibid., p. 137.

13. Sapir 1924.

14. Ascher and Ascher 1981.

15. Childe 1951a.

16. Innis 1951.

17. In Melody et al. 1981, p. 237.

18. Especially in the "Discourse on Language" in Foucault 1976.

19. Mumford 1967.

CHAPTER 9

1. Carey in Rosenthal 1969, p. 281.

2. Kuhns 1971, p. 171.

3. Ibid.

4. Leiss, Kline, and Jhally 1986, p. 150.

5. Summarized in Stearn 1967, p. 87.

6. McLuhan 1967, p. v.

7. Ibid., pp. 62, 70, 126.

8. Ibid., p. 10.

9. Quoted in Stearn 1967, p. 263.

10. Theall 1971, p. 1.

11. Levi-Strauss 1967.

12. McLuhan 1964, p. 90.

13. Marx's approach to history is discussed in Heyer (1982).

CHAPTER 10

1. Reprinted in Barthes 1978, p. 146. Barthes was the only one of the group who could truly laugh at the situation.

2. Especially in Foucault 1973a; 1976.

3. Foucault 1973a, p. xiv.

4. This is the strategy adopted by Sheridan (1980).

5. Such as Foucault 1976a.

6. Foucault 1980a, p. 115.

7. Poster 1984.

8. Foucault 1973a, p. xii.

9. Kuhn 1970.

10. Foucault 1976, p. 224.

11. Lovejoy 1960.

12. Aarsleff 1982.

13. Levi-Strauss 1968.
14. Quoted in Aarsleff 1982, p. 8.
15. Foucault 1973a, p. 133.
16. Eisenstein 1980.
17. Foucault 1980, p. 194.
18. Havelock 1963; 1978.
19. Huppert 1974.
20. Reprinted in Foucault 1976.
21. Poster 1984.
22. Foucault 1978, p. 92.
23. Foucault 1979, p. 137.
24. Ibid., p. 141.
25. Ibid., p. 201.
26. Foucault 1980a, p. 149.

CONCLUSION

1. This is a major theme in Poster (1984).
2. Logan (1986) is one of the few recent communications/history scholars to make such an attempt.
3. Marshack 1982.
4. Carpenter and McLuhan 1966.
5. Giedion 1964; 1967.
6. Schmandt-Besserat 1978; 1982; 1986.
7. Ascher and Ascher 1981.
8. Havelock 1963; 1976; 1978; 1982.
9. Havelock 1982a.
10. As does Street 1984.
11. Havelock 1982, p. 9.
12. Ibid.
13. Ong 1958.
14. Ong 1982.
15. Ibid., p. 3.
16. Goody 1975.
17. Goody 1978.
18. Ibid., pp. 74-111.
19. Street 1984.
20. Eisenstein 1980.
21. Burke 1985; print is also considered in his earlier series and book, *Connections* (1978).
22. McLuhan 1981.
23. Eisenstein 1980, p. 696.
24. Postman 1984; 1986.
25. Czitrom 1982.
26. Kern 1983.

Bibliography

Aarsleff, Hans. *From Locke to Saussure: Essays on the Study of Language and Intellectual History*. Minneapolis: University of Minnesota Press, 1982.

Ascher, Marcia and Robert. *Code of the Quipu*. Ann Arbor: University of Michigan Press, 1981.

Barber, W. H. et al. *The Age of Enlightenment*. Edinburgh: Oliver and Boyd, 1967.

Barthes, Roland. *Roland Barthes*. New York: Hill and Wang, 1978.

Barzun, Jacques. *Classic, Romantic and Modern*. Boston: Little, Brown, 1961.

Bauman, Zygmunt. *Culture as Praxis*. London: Routledge and Kegan Paul, 1973.

Bayle, Pierre. *Dictionaire Historique et Critique*. Rotterdam, 1697.

Becker, Carl L. *The Heavenly City of the Eighteenth Century Philosophers*. New Haven: Yale University Press, 1978.

Berger, M. Philippe. *Histoire de l'Ecriture Dans L'Antiquité*. Paris: Imprimerie Nationale, 1891.

Berlin, Isaiah. *Vico and Herder*. London: Hogarth Press, 1976.

Besterman, Theodore et al., eds. *The Complete Works of Voltaire*. Toronto: University of Toronto Press, 1969.

Bossuet, Jacques Benigne. *Discours sur l'Histoire Universelle*. Paris: Plon, 1875.

Braudel, Fernand. *The Structures of Everyday Life*. Vol. 1. New York: Harper and Row, 1981.

Bryson, Gladys. *Man and Society: The Scottish Inquiry of the Eighteenth Century*. Princeton: Princeton University Press, 1945.

Bucher, Carl. *Industrial Evolution*. New York: Burt Franklin, 1967.

Burke, James. *Connections*. Boston: Little, Brown, 1978.

————. *The Day the Universe Changed*. Boston: Little, Brown, 1985.

Burrow, J. W. *Evolution and Society*. Cambridge: Cambridge University Press, 1966.

Carey, James. "Harold Adams Innis and Marshall McLuhan." In *McLuhan Pro and Con*, edited by Raymond Rosenthal. Baltimore: Penguin Books, 1969.

Carpenter, Edward, and Marshall McLuhan, eds. *Explorations in Communication*. Boston: Beacon Press, 1966.

Carpenter, Edmund. *They Became What They Beheld*. New York: Ballantine Books, 1970.

————. *Oh What A Blow That Phantom Gave Me!* New York: Bantam Books, 1974.

Cassirer, Ernst. *The Philosophy of the Enlightenment*. Princeton: Princeton University Press, 1951.

————. *The Question of Jean-Jacques Rousseau*. Bloomington: University of Indiana Press, 1963.

Childe, V. Gordon. *Man Makes Himself*. New York: Mentor, 1951.

————. *Social Evolution*. London: Watts and Co., 1952.

————. *Society and Knowledge*. London: Allen and Unwin, 1956.

————. *New Light on the Most Ancient East*. London: Routledge and Kegan Paul, 1964.

————. *What Happened in History*. Middlesex, England: Penguin Books, 1964a.

————. *Progress and Archaeology*. Westport, Conn.: Greenwood Press, 1971.

Chomsky, Noam. *Cartesian Linguistics: A Chapter in the History of Rationalist Thought*. New York: Harper and Row, 1966.

Clanchy, M. T. *From Memory to Written Record, England 1066-1307*. Cambridge: Harvard University Press, 1979.

Clodd, Edward. *The Story of the Alphabet*. New York: Appleton, 1920.

Cloyd, E. L. *James Burnett: Lord Monboddo*. London: Oxford University Press, 1972.

Condillac, Etienne Bonnot de. *Oeuvres Philosophiques de Condillac*. Paris: Presses Universitaires de France, 1951.

————. *Treatise on the Sensations*. London: Fauil Press, 1930.

————. *An Essay on the Origins of Human Knowledge*. Gainesville, Fla.: Scholars Facsimilies and Reprints, 1971.

Condorcet, Antoine-Nicholas. *Sketch for a Historical Picture of the Progress of the Human Mind*. Translated by June Barraclough. London: Weidenfeld and Nicolson, 1955.

Condorcet, Marie Jean Antoine. *Esquisse d'un Tableau Historique des Progres de l'Esprit Human*. Paris: Editions Sociales, 1966.

Conrad, David R. *Education for Transformation: Implications in Lewis Mumford's Ecohumanism*. Palm Springs, Calif.: ETC Publications, 1976.

Creighton, Donald. *Harold Adams Innis: Portrait of a Scholar*. Toronto: University of Toronto Press, 1978.

Crowley, David. "Harold Innis and the Modern Perspective of Communications." In *Culture, Communication and Dependency*, edited by Melody et al. Norwood, N.J.: Ablex, 1981.

Culler, Jonathan. *Saussure*. London: Fontana, 1976.

————. "Jacques Derrida." In *Structuralism and Since*, edited by John Sturrock. London: Oxford University Press, 1979.

Czitrom, Daniel. *Media and the American Mind*. Chapel Hill: University of North Carolina Press, 1982.

Daniel, Glyn. *The Idea of Prehistory.* London: Watts and Co., 1962.

————. *The First Civilizations: The Archaeology of Their Origins.* New York: Crowell, 1970.

Darnton, Robert. *The Great Cat Massacre and Other Episodes in French Cultural History.* New York: Basic Books, 1984.

de Kerchove, Derrick. "Alphabetic Literacy and Brain Processes." *Visible Language* 20, no. 3, 1986.

Derrida, Jacques. *Writing and Difference.* Chicago: University of Chicago Press, 1978.

————. *Of Grammatology.* Baltimore: Johns Hopkins University Press, 1980.

Diamond, Stanley. *The Search for the Primitive.* New Brunswick, N.J.: Transaction Books, 1974.

Dobinson, C. H. *Jean-Jacques Rousseau.* London: Methuen, 1969.

D'Holbach, Baron. *The System of Nature on Laws of the Moral and Physical World.* New York: Burt Franklin, 1970.

Diringer, David. *Writing.* London: Thames and Hudson, 1962.

Dreyfus, Hubert L., and Paul Rabinow. *Michel Foucault: Beyond Structuralism and Hermeneutics.* Chicago: University of Chicago Press, 1982.

Durkheim, Emile. *Montesquieu and Rousseau: Forerunners of Sociology.* Ann Arbor: University of Michigan Press, 1965.

Edwards, Paul, ed. *The Encyclopedia of Philosophy.* New York: Macmillan, 1972.

Eisenstein, Elizabeth. *The Printing Press as an Agent of Change: Communications and Cultural Transformations in Early Modern Europe.* New York: Cambridge University Press, 1980.

Engels, Frederick. *Anti-Duhring.* New York: International Publishers, 1970.

————. *The Origin of the Family, Private Property and the State.* New York: International Publishers, 1972.

Febvre, Lucien, and Henri-Jean Martin. *The Coming of the Book.* London: NLB, 1979.

Fontenelle, Bernard Le Bovier de. *De l'Origine des Fables.* Paris, 1932.

————. *Entretiens sur la Pluralité des Mondes.* Paris: M. Didier, 1966.

Foucault, Michel. *Madness and Civilization.* New York: Vintage Books, 1973.

————. *The Order of Things.* New York: Vintage Books, 1973a.

————. *Birth of the Clinic.* New York: Vintage Books, 1975.

————. *The Archaeology of Knowledge.* New York: Harper and Row, 1976.

————. *Mental Illness and Psychology.* New York: Harper and Row, 1976a.

————. *The History of Sexuality.* Vol. 1. New York: Random House, 1978.

————. *Discipline and Punish.* New York: Vintage Books, 1979.

————. *Language, Counter-Memory and Practice.* Ithaca: Cornell University Press, 1980.

————. *Power/Knowledge.* New York: Pantheon, 1980a.

Frankel, Charles. *The Faith of Reason: The Idea of Progress in the French Enlightenment.* New York: King's Crown Press, 1948.

Gay, Peter. *The Enlightenment: An Interpretation.* 2 vols. New York: Knopf, 1969.

Gelb, Ignace. *A Study of Writing.* Chicago: University of Chicago Press, 1963.

Giedion, Siegfried. *Mechanization Takes Command.* New York: Oxford University Press, 1948.

————. *The Eternal Present: The Beginnings of Art and Architecture.* New York: Bollingen Foundation, 1964.

————. *Space, Time and Architecture.* Cambridge: Harvard University Press, 1967.

Goody, Jack. *Literacy in Traditional Societies.* Cambridge: Cambridge University Press, 1975.

————. *The Domestication of the Savage Mind.* Cambridge: Cambridge University Press, 1978.

————. *Cooking, Cuisine and Class.* Cambridge: Cambridge University Press, 1982.

Graff, Harvey J. *The Literacy Myth, Literacy and Social Structure in the Nineteenth Century City.* New York: Academic Press, 1979.

Guehenno, Jean. *Jean-Jacques Rousseau.* London: Routledge and Kegan Paul, 1967.

Harnad, Stevan and Horst Steklis and Jane Lancaster, eds. *Origins and Evolution of Language and Speech.* New York: New York Academy of Sciences, 1976.

Hardt, Hanno. *Social Theories of the Press.* Beverly Hills, Calif.: Sage, 1979.

Harper, Nancy. *Human Communication Theory: The History of a Paradigm.* Rochelle Park, N.J.: Haden, 1979.

Harris, Marvin. *The Rise of Anthropological Theory.* New York: Crowell, 1970.

Havelock, Eric. *Preface to Plato.* Cambridge, Mass.: Belknap Press, 1963.

————. *The Origins of Western Literacy.* Toronto: Ontario Institute for Studies in Education, 1976.

————. *The Greek Concept of Justice: From Its Shadow in Homer to Its Substance in Plato.* Cambridge: Harvard University Press, 1978.

————. *The Literate Revolution in Greece and Its Cultural Consequences.* Princeton: Princeton University Press, 1982.

————. *Harold A. Innis.* Toronto: Harold Innis Foundation, 1982a.

Havelock, Eric, and Jackson P. Herschell. *Communication Arts in the Ancient World.* New York: Hastings House, 1978a.

Helvetius, Claude. *A Treatise on Man.* New York: Burt Franklin, 1969.

Hewes, Gordon. "The Current Status of the Gestural Origin Theory of Language Origins." In Harnad, Steklis, and Lancaster, 1976.

————. "Primate Communication and the Gestuval Origin of Language." *Current Anthropology* vol. 14 nos. 1-2 (1973).

Heyer, Paul. "Review of *Culture as Praxis* by Zygmunt Bauman." *Leonardo,* 8, no. 1, 1975.

————. *Nature, Human Nature and Society: Marx, Darwin, Biology and the Human Sciences.* Westport, Conn.: Greenwood Press, 1982.

————. "Pour une histoire des communications." *Communication Information,* 5, nos. 2 et 3, 1983.

————. "Review of *Foucault, Marxism and History* by Mark Poster." *Labour/Le Travail,* 19, 1987.

Hissey, Lynne. "Each Thought and Thing Allied: Lewis Mumford and Technics and Society." Master's thesis, Simon Fraser University, Burnaby, British Columbia, Canada, 1986.

Humphreys, H. Noel. *A History of the Art of Printing.* London: Bernard Quaritch, 1867.

Huppert, George. "Divinatio et Eruditio: Thoughts on Foucault, History and Theory." *History and Theory,* 13, no. 3, 1974.

Hymes, Dell, ed. *Studies in the History of Linguistics.* Bloomington: University of Indiana Press, 1974.

Innis, Harold. "Communications and Archaeology." *Canadian Journal of Economics and Political Science,* 17, no. 1, 1951.

————. *The Bias of Communication.* Toronto: University of Toronto Press, 1973.

————. *Empire and Communications.* Toronto: University of Toronto Press, 1972.

————. *The Idea File of Harold Adams Innis.* Introduced and edited by William Christian. Toronto: University of Toronto Press, 1980.

————. *Changing Concepts of Time.* Toronto: University of Toronto Press, 1952.

Jaynes, Julian. *The Origins of Consciousness in the Breakdown of the Bicameral Mind.* Boston: Houghton Mifflin, 1977.

Jensen, Hans. *Sign, Symbol and Script.* New York: G. P. Putnam, 1969.

Jhally, Sut. *The Codes of Advertising: Fetishism and the Context of Meaning in Modern Society.* Ph.D. diss., Simon Fraser University, Burnaby, British Columbia, Canada, 1984.

Kardiner, Abraham, and Edward Preble. *They Studied Man.* New York: Mentor, 1963.

Kern, Stephen. *The Culture of Time and Space: 1880-1918.* Cambridge: Harvard University Press, 1983.

Knight, Isabel F. *The Geometric Spirit: The Abbe de Condillac and the French Enlightenment.* New Haven: Yale University Press, 1968.

Krader, Lawrence. *The Ethnological Notebooks of Karl Marx.* The Netherlands: Assen, 1972.

Kroker, Arthur. *Technology and the Canadian Mind.* Montreal: New World Perspectives, 1984.

Kuhn, Thomas. *The Structure of Scientific Revolutions.* Chicago: University of Chicago Press, 1970.

Kuhns, William. *The Post-Industrial Prophets: Interpretations of Technology.* New York: Weybright and Talley, 1971.

La Mettrie, Julien Offrey de. *L'Homme Machine.* Princeton: Princeton University Press, 1960.

Lee, Richard and Irven Devore eds. *Man the Hunter.* Chicago: Aldine, 1968.

Leibniz, G. W. *New Essays on Human Understanding.* Translated and edited by Peter Remnart and Jonathan Bennett. Cambridge: Cambridge University Press, 1981.

Leiss, William. *The Domination of Nature.* Boston: Beacon Press, 1974.

————. *The Limits to Satisfaction.* Toronto: University of Toronto Press, 1976.

Leiss, William, Stephen Kline, and Sut Jhally. *Social Communication in Advertising.* New York: Methuen, 1986.

Leopold, Joan. *Culture in Comparative and Evolutionary Perspective: E. B. Tylor and the Making of Primitive Culture.* Berlin: 1980.
Levi-Strauss, Claude. *The Savage Mind.* Chicago: University of Chicago Press, 1968.
Lively, J. F. *The Enlightenment.* London: Longmans, 1966.
Locke, John. *An Essay Concerning Human Understanding.* London: Oxford University Press, 1975.
Logan, Robert K. *The Alphabet Effect.* New York: William Morrow, 1986.
Lovejoy, Arthur. "The Supposed Primitivism of Rousseau's Discourse on Inequality." *Modern Philology,* 2, 1923.
_____. "Monboddo and Rousseau." *Modern Philology,* 30, no. 3, 1933.
_____. *The Great Chain of Being.* New York: Harper Torch Books, 1960.
McLellan, David. *Karl Marx: Early Texts.* New York: Barnes and Noble, 1971.
_____. *Marx.* London: Fontana, 1975.
McLuhan, Marshall. *Understanding Media.* New York: Signet, 1964.
_____. *The Mechanical Bride.* Boston: Beacon Press, 1967.
_____. *The Gutenberg Galaxy.* New York: Signet, 1969a.
_____. *From Cliché to Archetype.* New York: Pocket Books, 1971.
_____. "Review of *The Printing Press as an Agent of Change* by Elizabeth Eisenstein." *Renaissance and Reformation,* 5, no. 2, 1981.
McLuhan, Marshall, and Harley Parker. *Through the Vanishing Point.* New York: Harper and Row, 1969b.
Maine, Henry Sumner. *Ancient Law.* London: John Murray, 1901.
Manuel, Frank. *The Age of Reason.* Ithaca: Cornell University Press, 1954.
_____. *The Prophets of Paris.* Cambridge: Harvard University Press, 1962.
Marett, R. R. *Tylor.* London: Chapmann and Hall, 1936.
Marshack, Alexander. *The Roots of Civilization.* New York: McGraw-Hill, 1982.
Martin, Henri-Jean. *Le Livre et la Civilization Ecrite.* Paris: Ecole Nationale Superieure de Bibliothecaires, 1968.
Marx, Karl. *The Eighteenth Brumaire of Louis Bonaparte.* New York: International Publishers, 1969.
_____. *Grundrisse: Foundations for a Critique of Political Economy (Rough Draft).* Translated with a Foreword by Martin Nicolaus. Middlesex, England: Penguin Books, 1973.
Marx, Karl, and Frederick Engels. *The German Ideology.* Moscow: Progress Publishers, 1964.
_____. *Capital.* 3 vols. New York: International Publishers, 1967.
Mason, William A. *A History of the Art of Writing.* New York: Macmillan, 1920.
Masters, Roger. *The Political Philosophy of Rousseau.* Princeton: Princeton University Press, 1976.
Meek, Ronald L., ed. *Turgot on Progress and Sociology.* Cambridge: Cambridge University Press, 1973.
Melody, William, Liora Salter, and Paul Heyer, eds. *Culture, Communication and Dependency: The Tradition of H. A. Innis.* Norwood, N.J.: Ablex, 1981.
Monboddo, Lord. *Antient Metaphysics.* 6 vols. Edinburgh: J. Balfour and Co., 1779-1799.

————. *Of The Origin and Progress of Language.* 6 vols. Yorkshire, England: Scholar Press, 1967.

Montesquieu, Baron d. *The Spirit of the Laws.* New York: Hafner, 1965.

Morgan, Lewis H. *The American Beaver and His Works.* Philadelphia: Lippincott, 1868.

————. *Ancient Society.* Cambridge: Harvard University Press, 1964.

Muller, Max. *The Science of Language.* New York: Scribners, 1863.

————. *The Science of Thought.* London: Longmans, 1887.

————. *Last Essays.* London: Longmans, 1901.

Mumford, Lewis. *Art and Technics.* New York: Columbia University Press, 1952.

————. *The Transformations of Man.* London: Allen and Unwin, 1957.

————. *Technics and Civilization.* New York: Harcourt, Brace and World, 1963.

————. *The Myth of the Machine: Technics and Human Development.* New York: Harcourt, Brace and World, 1967.

————. *The Pentagon of Power.* Vol. 2, *The Myth of the Machine.* New York: Harcourt, Brace, Jovanovich, 1970.

————. *Interpretations and Forecasts: 1922-1972.* New York: Harcourt, Brace, Jovanovich, 1973.

————. *Findings and Keepings: Analects for an Autobiography.* New York: Harcourt, Brace, Jovanovich, 1975.

————. *My Works and Days: A Personal Chronicle.* New York: Harcourt, Brace, Jovanovich, 1979.

————. *Sketches from Life: The Autobiography of Lewis Mumford: The Early Years.* Boston: Beacon Press, 1983.

Newman, Elmer S. *Lewis Mumford: A Bibliography 1914-1970.* New York: Harcourt, Brace, Jovanovich, 1971.

Ong, Walter, J. *Ramus, Method, and the Decay of Dialogue.* Cambridge: Harvard University Press, 1958.

————. *Interfaces of the World.* Ithaca: Cornell University Press, 1977.

————. *Orality and Literacy.* London: Methuen, 1982.

Park, Robert Ezra. *Society.* Glencoe, Ill.: Free Press, 1955.

————. *On Social Control and Collective Behavior.* Ed. Ralph Turner. Chicago: University of Chicago Press, 1967.

Park, Robert Ezra, and Ernest W. Burgess. *Introduction to the Science of Sociology.* Chicago: University of Chicago Press, 1969.

Parker, Ian. "Innis, Marx and the Economics of Communication: A Theoretical Aspect of Canadian Political Economy." In *Culture, Communication and Dependency,* edited by William Melody et al. 1981.

Parret, Herman, ed. *History of Linguistic Thought and Contemporary Linguistics.* Berlin: Walter de Gryter, 1976.

Pattison, Robert. *On Literacy.* New York: Oxford University Press, 1982.

Pedersen, Holger. *The Discovery of Language: Linguistic Science in the Nineteenth Century.* Bloomington: University of Indiana Press, 1967.

Poster, Mark. *Foucault, Marxism and History.* Cambridge, England: Polity Press, 1984.

Postman, Neil. *The Disappearance of Childhood.* New York: Dell, 1984.

_____. *Amusing Ourselves to Death.* New York: Dell, 1986.

Powe, B. W. *The Solitary Outlaw.* Toronto: Lester and Orpen Dennys, 1987.

Radin, Paul. *Primitive Man as Philosopher.* New York: Dover, 1957.

Robins, R. H. *A Short History of Linguistics.* London: Longmans, 1967.

Rockwood, Raymond Oxley, ed. *Carl Becker's Heavenly City Revisited.* Hamden, Conn.: Archon Books, 1968.

Rosenthal, Raymond, ed. *McLuhan Pro and Con.* Baltimore: Penguin Books, 1969.

Rousseau, Jean-Jacques. *Emile.* London: J. M. Dent and Sons, 1961.

_____. *The First and Second Discourses.* New York: St. Martins Press, 1964.

Rousseau, Jean-Jacques, and Gottfried Herder. *On the Origin of Language.* New York: Frederick Ungar, 1966.

Sahlins, Marshall. "Notes on the Original Affluent Society." In Lee and Devore, 1968.

Sapir, Edward. "Culture, Genuine and Spurious." *American Journal of Sociology,* 29, no. 4, 1924.

Schmandt-Besserat, Denise. "The Earliest Precursor of Writing." *Scientific American* 238(6), June 1978.

_____. "The Emergence of Recording." *American Anthropologist,* 84, no. 4, 1982.

_____. "Tokens: Facts and Interpretations." *Visible Language,* 20, no. 3, 1986.

Schneider, Louis. *The Scottish Moralists: On Human Nature and Society.* Chicago: University of Chicago Press, 1967.

Scribner, Sylvia, and Michael Cole. *The Psychology of Literacy.* Cambridge: Harvard University Press, 1981.

Sheridan, Alan. *Michel Foucault: The Will to Truth.* London: Tavistock, 1980.

Stam, James H. *Inquiries into the Origin of Language: The Fate of a Question.* New York: Harper and Row, 1976.

Stearn, Gerald Emanuel, ed. *McLuhan Hot & Cool.* New York: Signet, 1967.

Stephens, W. Walker, ed. *The Life and Writings of Turgot.* New York: Burt Franklin, 1971.

Stocking, George W. *Race, Culture and Evolution: Essays in the History of Anthropology.* New York: Free Press, 1968.

Street, Brian V. *Literacy in Theory and Practice.* Cambridge: Cambridge University Press, 1984.

Sturrock, John, ed. *Structuralism and Since.* London: Oxford University Press, 1979.

Taylor, Isaac. *The Alphabet.* 2 vols. London: Kegan Paul, Trench and Co., 1883.

Theall, Donald, F. *The Medium is the Rear View Mirror.* Montreal: McGill-Queen's University Press, 1971.

Trigger, Bruce. *Gordon Childe: Revolutions in Archaeology.* London: Thames and Hudson, 1980.

Turgot, Anne Robert Jacques. *Oeuvres de Turgot.* Paris, 1913.

Tylor, Edward Burnet. *Researches into the Early History of Mankind.* New York: Henry Holt, 1878.

_____. *Researches into the Early History of Mankind.* Chicago: The University of Chicago Press, 1964.

————. "On a Method of Investigating the Development of Institutions; Applied to Laws of Marriage and Descent." *The Journal of the Royal Anthropological Institute of Great Britain and Ireland.* vol. XVIII, 1888.

————. *Anthropology.* New York: Appleton, 1934.

————. *The Origins of Culture. Part 1, Primitive Culture.* New York: Harper Torchbooks, 1958.

————. *Religion in Primitive Culture. Part 2, Primitive Culture.* New York: Harper Torchbooks, 1958a.

————. *Anthropology.* Ann Arbor: The University of Michigan Press, 1965.

————. *Anahuac: Or Mexico and the Mexicans, Ancient and Modern.* New York: Bergman, 1970.

Vico, Giambattista. *The New Science.* Ithaca: Cornell University Press, 1968.

Voltaire. *The Complete Works of Voltaire.* Ed. Theodore Besterman et al. Toronto: University of Toronto Press, 1969.

Warburton, William. *The Divine Legation of Moses.* London: Fletcher Gyles, 1738.

Watson, John. "Innis' Communication Studies and Classical Scholarship." Paper presented to the Canadian Political Science Association Annual Conference, Fredericton, New Brunswick, 1977.

Wood, Robert. *An Essay on the Original Genius and Writings of Homer.* London: H. Hughs, 1775.

Whitney, William Dwight. *Language and the Study of Language.* New York: Scribner, 1867.

Wilden, Anthony. *The Imaginary Canadian.* Vancouver: Pulp Press, 1980.

————. *System and Structure: Essays in Communication and Exchange.* London: Tavistock, 1980a.

Yolton, John W. *John Locke and the Way of Ideas.* London: Oxford University Press, 1956.

Index

Aarsleff, Hans, 10, 12, 53, 148
A Contribution to the Critique of Political Economy (Marx), 67
Adamic Language, 8, 22
Age of Reason. *See* Enlightenment, The
A History of the Art of Printing (Humpheys), 60-61
A History of the Canadian Pacific Railway (Innis), 113
Allen, Woody, 135
Alphabet, 15, 27, 35, 36, 45, 88, 133
Althusser, Louis, 146
America, 128
Amusing Ourselves to Death (Postman), 165, 166-67
Anahuac (Tylor), 77, 78-80, 85
Ancient Law (Maine), 80
Ancient Society (Morgan), 67-69
An Essay on the Original Genius and Writings of Homer (Wood), 36
Annie Hall (Allen), 135
Anshen, Ruth Nanda, 140
Anthropology (Tylor), 78, 81, 84-85, 88-90
Antient Metaphysics (Monboddo), 31-37

"Archeology of Knowledge," 142, 143, 154, 155
Archeology of Knowledge (Foucault), 142, 143
Aristotle, 52
Art and Technics (Mumford), 104, 107, 110
Ascher, Marcia, 121, 160
Ascher, Robert, 121, 160
Aztecs, 79-80, 87, 88

Bachelard, Gaston, 146
Bacon, Francis, 8, 85, 154
Barthes, Roland, 128, 141
Barzun, Jacques, 51
Bau und Leben des Socialen Korpers (Schaffle), 70
Bayle, Pierre, 19, 20
Becker, Carl, 5
Berger, M. Philippe, 58
Bergson, Henri, 103
Berlin, Isaiah, 21
Bias of Communication, The (Innis), 93, 112, 114, 118, 119, 123, 129
Birth of the Clinic (Foucault), 142, 143, 146, 153, 155
Blacking, John S., 128

Block printing, 90
Boas, Franz, 99
Bohannon, Paul, 75
Bopp, Franz, 53
Bossuet, Bishop Jacques, 18-19, 22-23
Brahe, Tycho, 152
Brave New World (Huxley), 128
Bricolage, 132
Bucher, Karl, 71-72
Buffon, Georges, 29
Burgess, Ernest, 72
Burke, James, 165
Burnet, James. *See* Monboddo, Lord
Burrow, J. W., 64
Butler, Samuel, 103

Canguilhem, Georges, 146
Capital (Marx), 66-67
Carey, James, 126
Carpenter, Edmund, 130, 131, 137, 159
Cartesian Linguistics (Chomsky), 53
Cassirer, Ernest, 7
Centre for Culture and Technology, 131
Cervantes, Saavedra de, 134
Changing Concepts of Time (Innis), 112
Chaytor, A. J., 132
Cherokee, the, 87
Childe, Gordon: concept of diffusion, 99; on early writing systems, 100-1; general background, 93-97; Mumford on, 109; in relation to Innis, 93, 95; on social evolution, 97-98, 99
Chomsky, Noam, 53
Christy, Henry, 76-77, 78
Clodd, Edward, 59
Code of the Quipu (Ascher and Ascher), 121
Cod Fisheries, The (Innis), 113
Comte, Auguste, 25, 104
Condillac, Etienne Bonnot de, 11-15, 24, 26, 42, 43, 55
Condorcet, Marquis de, 5, 12, 25-30, 110

Conversations on the Plurality of Worlds (Fontnelle), 20
Confessions (Rousseau), 47
"Connection of Ideas" (Condillac), 12
Copernicus, Nicolas, 8, 152
Crowley, David, 122
Crusoe, Robinson. *See Robinson Crusoe* (Defoe)
Cultural Darwinism, 84
Culture, Concept of, 82, 118-19
Culture of Time and Space, The (Kern), 168
Cuvier, Georges, 145-46
Czitrom, Daniel, 167

d'Alembert, Jean, 6
Daniel, Glyn, 95, 99
Darwin, Charles, 55, 59, 63, 77, 80, 84, 108, 116-17
Dawn of European Civilization, The (Childe), 96
Day the Universe Changed, The (Burke), 165
Derrida, Jacques, 45-48
Descartes, Rene, 7, 134, 154
Descent of Man, The (Darwin), 55
d'Holbach, Baron, 6, 9
Dial, The, 103
Diffusion, Theory of, 79, 80-81, 99
Digressions on the Ancients and Moderns (Fontenelle), 20
Dilthey, Wilhelm, 21
Diringer, David, 52, 59
Disappearance of Childhood, The (Postman), 165
Discipline and Punish (Foucault), 107, 121, 142, 146, 153-55
"Discourse on Language" (Foucault), 153
Discourse on the Arts and Sciences (Rousseau), 39, 40
Discourse on the Origins Inequality (Rousseau), 12, 39-42, 47, 96, 106, 116
Discourse on Universal History (Bossuet), 18

Divine Legation of Moses, The (Warburton), 14, 35
Domestication of the Savage Mind, The (Goody), 163
Don Quixote (Cervantes), 134
Durkeim, Emile, 41, 76, 99, 154
Dutt, R. Palme, 95

Economic and Philosophical Manuscripts of 1844 (Marx), 67
Egyptian hieroglyphics, 15, 90, 101
Egyptians, 87
Eisenstein, Elizabeth, 126, 150, 164-65
Eliot, T. S., 127
Emerson, Ralph Waldo, 103
Emile (Rousseau), 12, 39, 47
Empire and Communications (Innis), 112, 114, 115, 119, 123, 128-29
Encyclopedia, The, 6, 20
Encyclopedia of Philosophy, The (Edwards), 31
Engels, Frederick, 40, 57, 65-66, 67, 98
Enlightenment, The, 3-7, 9
Episteme, 144-45
Erewhon (Buter), 130
Essay on Human Understanding (Locke), 9-11, 150
Essay on the Customs and Spirit of Nations (Voltaire), 19
Essay on the Origins of Human Knowledge (Condillac), 11-15
Essay on the Origin of Languages (Rousseau), 40, 42, 43-45, 47, 58
Evolution. *See* Social evolution
Explorations, project and journal, 130-31, 132, 137
Explorations in Communication (Carpenter and McLuhan), 159

Febvre, Lucien, 132
Ferguson, Adam, 8, 34, 97
Findings and Keepings (Mumford), 107
Fontenelle, Bernard, 19, 20

Foucault, Michel: "Archeology of Knowledge," 141-43, 143-48; "Genealogy of Power," 152-54; general background, 141-43; influence of Nietzsche on, 153-54; parallels with Mumford, 107; on Renaissance discourse, 29
Foucault, Marxism, History (Poster), 144
Frankfort, Henri, 109
Frazer, Sir James, 88
Freud, Sigmund, 83
Fuller, Buckminster, 104
Functionalism, 99
Fur Trade in Canada, The (Innis), 113

Galileo, 8, 152
Gay, Peter, 4, 18
Geddes, Patrick, 103, 105
Gelb, Ignance, 52, 59
"Genealogy of Power," 142, 143, 152, 153, 155
German Ideology, The (Marx and Engels), 57, 65-66
Gibbon, Edward, 4
Giedian, Siegfried, 128, 130, 131, 159
Goody, Jack, 4, 162-63
Grammatology, 52
Great Chain of Being, The (Lovejoy), 147
Grimm, Jacob, 53
Grundrisse, The (Marx), 66
Gusture-language, 85-87
Gutenberg Galaxy, The (McLuhan), 43, 126, 127, 128, 130-34, 136, 147, 165

Hajnal, Istvan, 133
Hall, Edward, 138
Hardt, Hanno, 64, 65, 70, 167
Havelock, Eric, 112, 133, 151, 160-61
Hegel, George Wilhelm Friedrich, 24, 115, 118
Helvetius, Claude, 23
Herder, Johann, 21, 42-43

Herodotus, 35
Hidden Dimension, The (Hall), 138
Hieroglyphics. See Egyptian hieroglyphics
Histoire de l'ecriture dans l'antiquite (Berger), 58
Historical and Critical Dictionary (Bayle), 19-20
History. See Universal history
History of Sexuality, The (Foucault), 143, 153
Hitler, Adolf, 107
Hobbes, Thomas, 33, 41, 56
Home, Henry. See Kames, Lord
Homer, 36-37
Hopkins, Gerard Manley, 127
How Labour Governs (Childe), 95
Hume, David, 4, 5, 7, 8, 9, 32
Humphreys, H. Noel, 60-61
Huppert, George, 152
Hutcheson, Francis, 7
Huxley, Aldous, 128

Immigrant Press and Its Control, The (Park), 73
Incas, 58, 122
Independent invention, theory of, 79, 80-81
Industrial Evolution (Bucher), 71-72
Innis, Harold: general background, 111-14; history of communications, 114-20; major concepts, 120-23; in relation to Childe, 93, 95; in relation to McLuhan, 125, 132; in relation to Mumford, 107, 109; in relation to Park, 67; staples thesis, 113-14
Introduction to the Science of Sociology (Park), 74
Ivins, William, 132

James, William, 73
Jensen, Hans, 59
Jespersen, Otto, 108
Jhally, Sut, 67, 189
Johnson, Samuel, 31
Jones, Sir William, 53

Journal of Economic History, 114
Joyce, James, 127
Jung, Carl, 83

Kames, Lord, 31
Kant, Immanuel, 7, 9
Kepler, Johannes, 8, 152
Kern, Stephen, 168
Kline, Stephen, 67, 128
Knies, Karl, 70-71
Knight, Isabel, 12
Kroeber, Alfred, 21, 115
Kropotkin, Petr, 103
Kuhn, Thomas, 145
Kuhns, William, 167

Lacan, Jacques, 141
Lamarck, Jean Baptise, 145
Lamettrie, Julien Offroy de, 9
Language, (Counter-Memory, Practice) (Foucault), 143, 153
Language and the Study of Language (Whitney), 57-58
Language Origins, 13-14, 24, 33-35, 42-43, 56, 57-58, 85-86, 108
Leibniz, Gottfried Wilhelm, 7, 10
Leiss, William, 8, 67, 128
Levi-Strauss, Claude, 77, 83, 108, 132, 141, 147, 149, 113
Locke, John, 9-11, 12, 32, 54, 55, 150
Lovejoy, Arthur, 31, 147
Luther, Martin, 61
Lyell, Charles, 80, 84

McLuhan, Marshall: comments on Eisenstein, 165; general background, 125-27, 130-31; Gutenberg Galaxy, 131-34; on Innis, 4, 114-15; Mechanical Bride, 127-30; on Park, 74; in relation to Foucault, 147, 150; in relation to Innis, 118, 121, 125; in relation to Mumford, 107; Understanding Media, 135-40
Madness and Civilization (Foucault), 142, 143, 146, 153, 155
Maine, Henry, 52, 64, 80
Malinoswki, Bronislaw, 99

Man Makes Himself (Childe), 94, 95, 96, 97, 100-1
Manuel, Frank, 23
Marett, R. R., 78
Marshack, Alexander, 158-59
Martin, Henri-Jean, 132
Marx, Karl, 40, 41, 57, 65-67, 98, 104, 115, 154
Mason, William, 59
Masters, Roger, 41
Mayas, 87, 98, 122
Mead, George Herbert, 113
Mead, Margaret, 128
Mechanical Bride, The (McLuhan), 127-30
Mechanization Takes Command (Giedion), 128, 130
Media and The American Mind (Czitrom), 167
Megamachine, 107, 109, 154
Melville, Herman, 103
Mendel, Gregor, 145
Mills, C. Wright, 128
Monboddo, Lord, 2, 13, 26, 30-37, 54-55, 83, 86
Monopoly of Knowledge, concept of, 101, 123
Montesquieu, Charles, 6, 9, 41
Morgan, Lewis Henry, 52, 62, 67-69, 84, 98, 118
Muller, Max, 14, 54-56, 57, 108
Mumford, Lewis: on communications, 107-10; general background, 101-3; in relation to Foucault, 154-55; in relation to Innis, 123; in relation to McLuhan, 107, 128; on technics, 103-7
Murray, John, 80
Music, 44
Myth, 87-88
Myth of the Machine, The (Mumford), 103-4, 105, 106, 107, 108, 109, 110

New Light on the Most Ancient East (Childe), 96
New Science, The (Vico), 20-22
Newton, Isaac, 9

Nietzsche, Frederich, 153
Nineteen Eighty Four (Orwell), 128

Of Grammatology (Derrida), 47-48
Of the Origin and Progress of Language (Marboddo), 12, 13, 31-57
Ong, Walter, 48, 132, 101-2
Oral Tradition, 112, 117-18, 132-33, 159, 101, 103
Order of Things, The (Foucault), 141, 142, 143, 144-52
Origin of Fables, The (Fontenelle), 20
Origin of the Family, Private Property and the State, The (Engels), 67, 98
Origins of Species, The (Darwin), 77, 80, 83
Orwell, George, 128

Park, Robert Ezra, 64, 65, 72-74, 113
Parker, Harley, 130, 139-40
Parker, Ian, 66-67
Parkman, Francis, 118
Pentagon of Power, The (Mumford), 104
Phaedrus, The (Plato), 157
Philology, 52, 58
Philosophes, 4-5, 7. *See also* Enlightenment, The
Philosophical Dictionary (Voltaire), 19
Philosophical historiography. *See* Universal history
Philosophical Panorama of the Progress of the Human Mind (Turgot), 22-25
Philosophy of History, The (Voltaire), 19
Physiocrats, 9
Piaget, Jean, 166
Picasso, Pablo, 129
"Place of Thomas Nash in the Learning of His Time, The" (McLuhan), 127
Plan of The Two Discourse on Universal History (Turgot), 22-25
Plato, 32, 157
Poe, Edgar Allen, 129
Polo, Marco, 35
Poster, Mark, 144

Post-Industrial Prophets, The (Kuhns), 107

Postman, Neil, 165-67

Pound, Ezra, 127

Power/Knowledge (Foucault), 143

Preface to Plato (Havelock), 133

Press, the, 73-74

Primitive Culture (Tylor), 78, 79, 82-84, 88

Principles of Geology (Lyell), 80

Printing Press, 24-25, 56, 61, 90, 109, 133-34

Printing Press as an Agent of Change, The (Eisenstein), 126, 164-65

Progress and Archeology (Childe), 97

Psychic unity principle, 80-81

Pyramids, the, 79, 107

Quetzelcohuatl, 88

Quipus, 88

Radcliff-Brown, A. R., 99

Ramus, Pierre, 161

Raymond Roussel (Foucault), 142

Read, Herbert, 102

Reason, 7-9

Rebus Writing, 87

Reflections on the Formation and Distribution of Riches (Turgot), 22

Reid, Thomas, 8

Renaissance, 29

Researches into the Early History of Mankind (Tylor), 75, 77-78, 80-82, 85-90

"Returned Soldier, The," (Innis), 113

Riesman, David, 131

Robinson Crusoe (Defoe), 41

Romanticism, 51-52

Rosetta stone, 15

Rousseau, Jean-Jacques: Derrida on, 45-48; *Discourse on Inequality*, 40-42; general background, 39-40; on language, 42-44; on oral versus written, 27, 40, 44, 47, 48; in relation to Childe, 96; in relation to Mumford, 106, on writing, 44-45

Saint-Simon, Claude, 25

Sanskrit, 53

Sapir, Edward, 119, 137-38

Saussure, Fernand de, 11, 58, 89, 146

Savage Mind, The (Levi-Strauss), 147

Schaffle, William, 70

Schmandt-Besserat, Denise, 159-60

Science, Enlightenment concept of, 7-9

Science of Language, The (Muller), 54-55

Science of Thought, The (Muller), 55-56

"Secondary orality," 107

Semiology. *See* Semiotics

Semiotics, 11, 58, 89

Shakespeare, William, 166

Shaw, George Bernard, 135

Sign language, 85-87

Signs, Condillac on, 13

Silent Language, The (Hall), 138

Simmel, George, 72

Sketch for a Historical Picture of the Progress of Human Mind (Condorcet), 25-30

Small, Albion, 70

Smith, Adam, 8

Social Contract, The (Rousseau), 39

Social Evolution, 63-65, 97, 98-99, 100

Social Theories of the Press (Hardt), 70, 107

Society and Knowledge (Childe), 97

Space, concept of, 120-22

Space, Time and Architecture (Giedion), 131

Spencer, Herbert, 52, 64, 76, 84

Spengler, Oswald, 21, 74, 115

Spinoza, Benedict, 7

Spirit of the Laws, The (Mantesquieu), 41

Stalin, Joseph, 107

Staples thesis, 113-14

Stewart, Duglad, 8, 34

Story of Utopias, The (Mumford), 103

Street, Brian, 163

Structuralism, 141-42
Suy-jin, 88

Taylor, Issac, 58-60
Technics and Civilization (Mumford),
   102, 103, 104, 106, 107, 110, 128
Technics and Human Development
   (Mumford), 104
Telegraph, 139
Television, 139
Theall, Donald, 131
Theoretical History. *See* Universal his-
   tory
Thoreau, Henry David, 103
Through the Vanishing Point (McLuhan
   and Parker), 139-40
Time, concept of, 120-21
Tonnies, Ferdinand, 72
"Toronto School of Communications,"
   160, 168
Toynbe, Arnold, 21, 115
Transformations of Man, The (Mum-
   ford), 140
Treatise of the Sensations (Condillac),
   12
Trigger, Bruce, 95, 96, 99
Tristes Tropiques (Levi-Strauss), 77
Tylor, Edward Burnett: on diffusion,
   79-80, 81-82; general background,
   75-78; on gesture, 85-86, 88-89; on
   independent invention, 79-80, 81-
   82; on language, 89; major works,
   78-85; on myth, 87-88; social evolutionism, 52, 64, 98
Turgot, A. R. J., 6, 22-25

Understanding Media (McLuhan), 110,
   127, 128, 130, 133, 135-40

Universal history: basic precepts, 17-
   18; Condorcet's scheme, 25-30;
   Monboddo's legacy, 30-37; precursors, 18-20; Turgot's scheme, 22-25;
   Vico's approach, 20-22

Veblen, Thorstein, 103, 113
Vei, the, 87
Verstehen, 21
Vico, Giambattista, 20-22, 104, 108
Voltaire, 5, 9, 10, 19, 40
von Humboldt, Alexander, 53, 76, 80,
   87
von Humboldt, Whilhelm, 53
Voyage of the Beagle, The (Darwin),
   77

Wallas, Graham, 103
Warburton, William, 14, 35
Watt, Ian, 162
Weber, Max, 72, 164
What Happened in History (Childe),
   95, 96
"What's in a List" (Goody), 163
White Collar (Mills), 128
Whitehead, Alfred North, 103
Whitman, Walt, 103
Whitney, William Dwight, 54, 57-58
Whorf, Benjamin, 137-38
Wilde, Oscar, 135
Wood, Robert, 36-37
Wordsworth, William, 88
Writing: Childe on, 100-1; Condillac
   on, 14-15; Condorcet on, 26-27;
   Innis on, 117, 120-23; Morgan on,
   69; Muller on, 56; Taylor on, 58-
   60; Tylor on, 86-88; Whitney on,
   58. *See also*, the alphabet

PAUL HEYER is Associate Professor of Communication at Simon Fraser University, Burnaby, British Columbia, Canada. His earlier works include *Culture, Communication and Dependency: The Tradition of H. A. Innis*, (with William Melody and Liora Salter), *Nature, Human Nature and Society: Marx, Darwin, Biology and the Human Sciences* (Greenwood Press, 1982) and articles appearing in *The Structurist, Leonardo, Communication/Information*, and *Philosophy of the Social Sciences*.